A NEW GODLY PERSPECTIVE

GREAT HOPE
PUBLISHING
Coconut Creek, FL

BLINDERS NO MORE:
A GODLY PERSPECTIVE WORTH CONSIDERING

By Jack Alan Levine

Published by Great Hope Publishing LLC, Coconut Creek, Florida
For bulk book orders email: GreatHopePub@gmail.com

Cover Design & Layout By Scott Wolf

www.JackAlanLevine.com

E-mail: Jack@JackAlanLevine.com

Copyright© 2022 Jack Alan Levine. All rights reserved. Printed in the United States of America. Excerpt as permitted under United States copyright act of 1976, no part of this publication may be reproduced or distributed in any form, or by any means, or stored in a database retrieval system, without the prior written permission of the copyright holder, except by a reviewer, who may quote brief passages in review.

Neither the publisher nor the authors is engaged in rendering advice or services to the individual reader. Neither the authors nor the publisher shall be liable or responsible for any loss, injury, or damage allegedly arising from any information or suggestion in this book. The opinions expressed in this book represent the personal views of the authors and not of the publisher, and are for informational purposes only.

The information in this book, print and/or e book version, whether provided in hardcopy or digitally (together 'Material') is for general information purposes and nothing contained in it is, or is intended to be construed as advice. It does not take into account your individual health, medical, physical or emotional situation or needs.

Many of the various stories of people in this book draw from real life experience, at certain points involving a composite of stories. In some instances, people's names have been changed in the stories to protect privacy.

ISBN – 978-0-9825526-9-8   Paperback
ISBN – 978-1-7356075-2-8   E-Pub
Library of Congress Control Number: 2021950666

BLINDERS NO MORE
A GODLY PERSPECTIVE WORTH CONSIDERING

By Jack Alan Levine

TABLE OF CONTENTS

viii	WHAT PEOPLE ARE SAYING
11	INTRODUCTION: REQUESTING YOUR ATTENTION TO SOME WORDS WORTH CONSIDERING
13	CHAPTER 1: RESETTING AN ATTITUDE IN ORDER TO CONNECT WITH PURPOSE
35	CHAPTER 2: SHAPING OUR FOCUS TO EXPERIENCE CLARITY AND UNDERSTANDING
51	CHAPTER 3: REALIZING THAT THE PRESENT PLAN MAY NOT BE THE BEST PLAN
69	CHAPTER 4: QUESTIONING OUR DESTINY AND THE "WHO KNOWS"
85	CHAPTER 5: EXAMINING PURPOSE AND PLAN PERSPECTIVES AND THEIR SHIFTS
103	CHAPTER 6: DIFFERENTIATING THE DESIRES AND REALITIES OF WANTS AND NEEDS

117	**CHAPTER 7:** FOCUSING ON COURAGE AND STRENGTH WITH SPIRITUAL ENDURANCE
139	**CHAPTER 8:** CHECKING AND ALIGNING YOURSELF WITH YOU, GOD OR BOTH?
157	**CHAPTER 9:** ASKING BY SEEKING, CALLING AND TRUSTING SIMULTANEOUSLY
167	**CHAPTER 10:** REMOVING THE DOUBT BLINDERS TO CLEARLY REVEAL OUR CHOICES
191	**CHAPTER 11:** CONSIDERING A GODLY DIRECTION WITH NO MORE HESITATION
210	**SPECIAL THANKS:**
212	**DEDICATION:**

WHAT PEOPLE ARE SAYING!

Blinders No More is an eye-opening book. A great book that will truly impact the lives of men and women. A call to action, with a clear-cut focus on the truth of God on how to take the blinders off satan tries to put on you. I believe the book will be a tremendous blessing to your life. A godly perspective you want to have and one that will enrich your life and help you grow and walk closer with God. Jack's book will help make sure you benefit from all of the blessings and Promises of God both on Earth and in Heaven. Take your blinders off now... The truth is waiting!" See the light... Because the view is amazing.

REX TIGNOR
Founder of MAN UP Ministries, Author

Jack Levine has a heart for people. Everything you read in the pages of *Blinders No More* is fueled by his love for people, undergirded by stories of battles that everyone faces in life. Jack's personal victories in life are solely because of his steadfast connection to Jesus. Through these pages, you'll find that kind of victory too. All it takes is a little change in perspective, and *Blinders No More* will shift your focus to what really matters. If you're looking to change things up and do life a little differently, this book is a game changer.

DAVID DUSEK
Speaker/Author/Executive Director-
Rough Cut Men Ministries

Jack Levine is the real deal. I love his books. Jack brings an enthusiastic attitude to everything in his life. He has been a valued partner in ministry for many years and is always ready, willing, and able to stand side-by-side when called upon. Jack truly lives life with the blinders off and in this book shares how important a true Godly perspective is for all. Don't miss it! I'm honored to call him a friend.

JOHN DELANEY
President & Co-Founder, Wesley Brotherhood
President, Florida Conference United Methodist Men

Right up front Jack lets us know, what I think, is key to taking our blinders off; changing our focus. Since I work with mostly men, I'd have to say many, if not most, Christian men have allowed their focus to drift to the cares of the world. People (men especially) have become ignorant of the Scriptures, as Jack points out when he uses the very words of Christ to reinforce this; "You are in error because you do not know the scriptures or the power of God." Matthew 22:29. I recommend *Blinders No More* because it is a useful tool to get us on a right path with God. On most every page Jack has brought us back to God's Word and challenges us to cooperate with God in the blinder removal process- as we ask, "God what do you want me to know"?

DAVE ENSLOW
Director, Next Steps for Men

As some days are long, with our years too short, there's no time like now to reflect on your life with our 'Blinders Off.' Do you feel weighed down by circumstances? Are you struggling to experience joy? Wrestling with purpose? Then this is a must-read book. Jack Alan Levine's handling of Scripture intertwined with real-life illustrations uplifts God's perspective for our lives - captured in large measure by this: 'The Word of God is alive. If you're not reading the Word of God, then you're missing God speaking to your heart.' Learn how better to run life's race unfettered, aligning your life to God through the power of His Holy Spirit. Renew your heart in remembrance of his love and forgiveness, and all of the good that he desires for you. This day, seek first God in His Word, running this race with *Blinders No More.*

GREG STOUGHTON
CRU Partnership and Projects Coordinator Office President

Introduction

REQUESTING YOUR ATTENTION TO SOME WORDS WORTH CONSIDERING

The last thing I really wanted to do was write another book. I've written many and each one has been a blessing. Six of them have been God-related and that is, of course, my passion. One is a business book, two about overcoming addiction, one on motivation, and I have a couple of workbooks, as well. And yet God in His wondrous and amazing ways continues to throw ideas and perspectives at me, and I continue to write them down… which I've been doing all my life and has served me well; thus, giving me the opportunity to capture those thoughts, not missing them or forgetting them, and, most importantly, to share them with you.

I am so excited about this book. Perhaps because, like an unplanned baby, it came as a surprise. But like that child, once you see it, you love it so much. I really thought I had covered my insights and input about God in a bottom-line way in my previous books, but yet there was more. Thank you God for that.

I hope and pray that this book is a new perspective for you. That it gives you a new view and outlook on God that impacts your life, brings you to a closer walk with Him throughout this life and for all eternity.

I pray it marries your perspective with God's perspective, so that you will come to the truth and see things differently, regarding God, your life, Heaven, religion, and happiness.

I pray that after you read it, that your life view and world view will be different. Your prospects will be different. Your life will be different as you go forward, refocused, with a new understanding of God's reality and your reality. So, in essence, this is a reality check. An important one that I pray will ensure the outcome for your life that you deserve and desire!

Thank you for investing time in my work. I hope it is a blessing to you. Remember, we put blinders on a horse so they can only see what is in front of them and so that they are not distracted by things going on around them and lose focus and interest in the race in front of them.

But God didn't put blinders on you. He gave you an open heart and open eyes to see everything and choose for yourself. So, we want to make sure that the world, Satan, others' influence, and even our own flesh/hearts have not, in essence, put blinders on our lives and caused us to miss out on what is all around us... and that is the abundant blessings that God has for us on Earth and in Heaven.

So, I echo for you the prayers of the Apostle Paul... that God may give you the spirit of wisdom and revelation "so that the eyes of your heart may be enlightened," so that you will live with blinders no more! So that you would know the hope to which God has called you and the riches of His glorious inheritance and His incomparably great power for you and your life!

You're already a winner in Christ. But there are more races to run and more victories to be had on earth for the Kingdom of God. Yes, Jesus has won the ultimate victory for us and our victory is assured, and yet we are called to be warriors, representatives, ambassadors, and sons and daughters of God here on earth with a mission and a purpose as God declared in Ephesians 2:10, John 15:16, and 1Peter 2:1. So I pray that your life would be to God's glory as I truly believe that is the greatest blessing any believer can have – that is to know your life matters for the Kingdom. If you know that, I believe you will never have a regret for all eternity both here on earth and in Heaven.

God bless you. To God be the glory!
Jack

Chapter One
RESET YOUR ATTITUDE IN ORDER TO CONNECT WITH PURPOSE

You know, life can be difficult sometimes. It can be tough. Yet with every assurance God has given us, I think it comes down to one question: Do we believe it?

Do we believe God's Word is the truth?

You know, a lot of people have an affection for God, but they don't believe God. They don't believe in God. I think it's a tragedy to know God but not believe Him or live a life that glorifies Him.

If you are a Christian, you probably know what the Word of God says – but sometimes we need to be reminded of it. In Psalm 119 Gods word says, "I rejoice in following your statutes as one rejoices in great riches. I meditate on your precepts and consider your ways" (v. 14-15 NIV).

Look at what the psalmist is saying. He's rejoicing in the statutes of God as one would rejoice in great riches. As if you'd won the lottery, as if you hit the Powerball – the Mega Millions. You'd go, "Whoa! I can't believe it was me! The odds were 1:302,000,000, but it was me – it was me! How lucky I am. This was amazing!" That's the exact attitude we should have when we know God Himself and the Word of God and the truth of God as the Holy Spirit exposes it in our heart.

He goes on to say, "I meditate on your precepts and consider your ways." This needs to be my attitude and your attitude.

In Isaiah 44:22, God reminds us of His promises: "I have swept away your offenses like a cloud, your sins like the morning mist. Return to me, for I have redeemed you."

That is God's desire: that you return to Him. God has swept away your offenses and sins like a mist – they are gone. So, here's my question: If you are saved, if you are redeemed, shouldn't you be living like it? I believe that you should.

Let's consider what's important. My son Jackson, when he was in high school, had done something wrong at school and I was looking forward to getting home that day and hammering him. Not physically; I haven't spanked him since he was a little kid and

I've only done it twice – I hope it worked! But I was looking forward to making him accountable for what he had done. I was going to disciple him. I was not happy about what he had done. I was upset and I couldn't wait to get home and let him have it. That's a nice way to say it.

Then I got a call that morning about a wonderful couple at our church in Orlando saying their son committed suicide. It was horrible. He had shot himself. He had been suffering with anxiety and depression but had been managing it for quite some time. They had experienced a great family day with him the day before this tragedy happened.

I hope you never have had to experience it, and I couldn't even imagine what it was like for this family. All I know is that my perspective immediately changed. When I got home that afternoon, after Jackson got home from school, I just hugged him and told him how much I loved him – because what he had done wrong at school just wasn't important anymore. I never brought up what had happened. My perspective just changed on what was important. That was a prime example for me of resetting an attitude in order to connect with purpose.

You might have heard about the singer Michael Bublé. He's a famous pop singer. He said recently that he's retiring from singing. He's giving up on his career because his four-year-old son has cancer. He said the cancer his son is going through has given him a new perspective on life.

He was discussing the struggle of balancing his career with being a caretaker to his son. He remarked that he had been worried about sweating things like concert ticket sales and it made him rethink his priorities when his son got sick. He said, "The diagnosis made me realize how stupid I'd been to worry about these unimportant things. I was embarrassed by my ego that had allowed this insecurity." He, too, had a recognition of what's important.

There was a tragedy in upstate New York. A limousine on the way to celebrate a birthday crashed. It was carrying 20 people – all of them died in the crash. Apparently, the limo had not been maintained properly.

The question everybody was asking, at the heart of that small upstate New York town, was, "Why did this happen? Why did 20 individuals have to be taken from us so quickly, so unexpectedly? We want to know why!"

The reverend at the funeral referred to a quote from Mother Theresa in which she said she never asks "Why?" Because there may not be an answer until we get to Heaven. Instead, she asks, "Who? Who do we put our faith in? Who do we trust?" And, of course, her answer was "God." I hope and pray that your answer would be the same.

Interestingly enough, another famous person died, Stephen Hawking the famous physicist, scientist, and a man who seemed to have the secrets to all kinds of science on Earth. He was considered one of the most brilliant minds of this generation – he died at age 76. He left behind this message on October 17th of this year: "There is no God. No one directs the universe." That is the message he wrote in his book *Brief Answers to the Big Questions*.

Well, guess what? He knows now. Either he's right or he's wrong. But he isn't guessing about it anymore. He knows now. And we know, of course, that there is a God. I feel sorry for this brilliant man who lived 76 years and will not spend a day in Heaven. Yes, he will live in eternity; except he'll spend it in Hell. He will not spend it in Heaven, in the glory that God intended for all people.

I pray that you and I would not make that same mistake. It's all about perspective, and as believers, we need to take on a mindset of gratitude toward God.

You can think of a caterpillar trudging along and grumbling, saying, "Ugh, I'm a caterpillar. It's a very hard life. It's hard being a caterpillar. I move so slowly. I have to inch everywhere – and it's hard." If he only knew that in a very short while he was going to be the most beautiful butterfly, his whole mindset would change. If he knew he would have these amazing patterns on his wings and the world would be looking at him and going, "Oh my gosh, you're beautiful!" He wouldn't be complaining. If he knew that pretty soon he would be able to soar anywhere he wanted to, free as could be, he wouldn't be complaining about being a caterpillar. He'd be jumping up and down rejoicing! Because he would know what's to come.

That's how you and I should be looking at our lives here on earth. Listen to what God says in 1 John 3:2: "Dear friends, now we are children of God, and what we will be has not yet been made known. But we know that when Christ appears, we shall be like him, for we shall see him as he is."

This is God's promise to you and me. Right now, we feel like that caterpillar and we're saying, "Oh, man. I'm slugging along and life's tough and I can't believe this and that…"

No! We're going to be even better off than these butterflies. We should have this assurance. We should know for sure that we're going to be in Heaven – that our place in Heaven is reserved – that God is with us. We should be rejoicing. That's why God says all throughout the Bible – all throughout the Old Testament and the New Testament – "Rejoice! Be happy. Be glad. Sing! Be glad."

Sometimes we say, "God, how can I rejoice with all these problems?" Oh man, I don't know. I guess we don't have any examples to look to… but wait, yes we do, we have some great examples. Think of the Apostle Paul. The Apostle Paul was in prison; he was in chains, yet he was singing. He was looking at his chains as an opportunity for the gospel. He was considering his sufferings to be joy because he was suffering as an opportunity to promote the gospel. He knew his purpose and mission and he was happy about it.

How is it that we look at our sufferings differently? Why do we look at our problems and issues as if they're not for the purpose and glory of God, as if God were lying when He said, "All things work together for the good of those who act according to His will," in Romans 8:28? No, we need to have that same attitude.

So, as I examined my own life, I realized that I occasionally have regret. I was looking at it and I said, "Whoa!" – Regret is just a failure to acknowledge the providence of God. It's a lack of faith in the providence of God. Regret is thinking my life should have been different. But that just means I don't trust God, that I don't have faith in God's plan, in God's way. Personally, I've decided that I'm not thinking like that anymore. I'm going to trust God. For me another example of resetting an attitude in order to connect with purpose.

I only fear because of a lack of faith or trust in God delivering me. I only fear because I can't see a way out. But when I succumb to fear, I'm like the murmuring Israelites – I'm thinking that going back to slavery would be better than going ahead because I can't see how God is going to unblock the perceived roadblocks in my life; I can't see how God is going to accomplish the miracle or bring me out or deliver me or do what I think God should do instead of being satisfied with what God is doing.

The issues, problems, and circumstances that I see in front of me seem impossible in my eye's limited view. In my power, in my limited understanding, it seems impossible for them to be changed or rectified for the better; but that is a lack of faith on my part because God says that all things are possible through God. I just need to keep my eyes on Jesus. God says, "I will keep you in perfect peace whose mind is focused on me" (Isaiah 26:3).

Think about when Peter got out of the boat, and Jesus said, "Come." Peter was able to walk on water until he took his eyes off God; then he began to sink. Of course, Jesus, in all His love, rescued him, and said, "Ye of little faith. Why did you doubt?" I believe God says the same thing to you and me.

Here's a bit of back story to that story. It's in Luke, chapter 5. The fishermen were out fishing, and they came back; they had caught nothing all night long and Jesus told them, "Put the nets back again."

They said to him, and I'm paraphrasing, "Are you crazy? You must be nuts. We are experienced fishermen. We have been out all night. We know how to fish. It was a bad night at sea, man. We got nothing and we'd be crazy to go back for more of the same." But then Peter said, "However, because you asked, we're going to do what you say." So, they put the nets out again; the story tells us in Luke chapter 5 that the nets overflowed with the catch – on both sides of the boat – so many fish that the boat was weighed down. Unbelievable. It's a miracle of God.

You may know what Peter said at that point: "Depart from me, Lord! I am a sinful man." At that point, Peter recognized that he was in the holy presence of God. Right then and there, Peter saw the holiness of God.

There's no question that God is holy. Even Satan knows that God is holy. Even Satan knows who God is.

Peter would have another experience with Jesus where he would learn another side of Jesus. Before Jesus was crucified, Peter denied Him three times, as Jesus predicted.

Jesus had said, "Before the rooster crows twice you will deny me three times," and sure enough, Peter denied Him three times before the rooster crowed.

Peter's response was probably something like this: "Oh my gosh! I said I was never going to deny you. I said I was going to be with you always, but I failed! I can't believe this." Regret. Despair. Peter was destroyed. The Bible tells us Peter wept bitterly. As he looked into Jesus' eyes, he knew what he'd done. He probably thought, "I've failed you. I've let you down. I sold you down the river. I ratted you out. I said I was your guy, but I'm not!"

So, Peter lived with his failure and all his humanness; he was down and out. But the Word of God tells us in Luke 24:34: "It is true! The Lord has risen and has appeared to Simon."

One of the first things Jesus did after He rose was He came back to Peter (Simon) because there was a little more Peter needed. What did Jesus tell Peter? I don't know and neither do you. It's not in the Bible. You can ask Peter in Heaven. But we can speculate – and most theologians would agree – that Jesus came to Peter and forgave him! We can assume that Jesus told him He loved him, and He was going to build his church on Peter. Of course, you know the end of the story, He did build the church on Peter. Peter became the rock. Peter became the man. Peter was awesome. Why? Because when Jesus came back and visited him after the resurrection, Peter experienced the love of God. Oh, he first experienced the holiness and power of God, but now he experienced the love of God.

I want to tell you that it is not enough to know the holiness and power of God. You need to know, personally, the love of God. That's the love which is available to each one of us.

We saw God's holiness in the Old Testament. We see God's grace and love in the New Testament. God loves you. That's the truth. So, here's the key to avoiding pain and suffering. Now that would be a pretty good deal – if you read this book and found the key to avoid pain and suffering, that wouldn't be bad! What is the key? It's simply this, which I've trained myself to do and I would encourage you to do the same. We always, always, always need to default to the truth of God – the sooner, the better.

We need to train ourselves to have spiritual muscle memory. I have a default setting on my phone. You have a default setting on your computer. You have a default station on your TV; it's automatic. It returns there every single time you turn on the TV. Likewise, we need to train our minds to default to the truth of God instantly – so we don't have to struggle for days and weeks and months.

Let me tell you what happens in my life. I get bummed out about something. I get frustrated, angry, and depressed – and I find myself moving away from God a little bit. And 100% of the time, always, the answer is always, I come back to God and His truth and His love and His sovereignty. Sometimes it takes me a day, sometimes a week, sometimes even a month – and I struggle. I'm in pain; I'm suffering, yet I keep on struggling for a week or a month. Then finally I come back to the Word and truth of God. God fills me with His Word and truth, and I'm restored.

So, after following that cycle time and again, I've begun to ask myself, "What kind of idiot am I? Why do I need to spend a week or a month suffering? Why don't I just eliminate that part and come right back to where I'm going to return to anyway?" I need to simply return to the Word and the truth of God. To the promise of God that, "I am with you always. I'll never leave you or forsake you. All things work together for your good. God's loving kindness is better than life. No weapon formed against you will prosper. There's no condemnation for those in Jesus Christ."

God has so many promises. "I know the plans I have for you," says the Lord, "plans to prosper you, to give you a hope and a future – not to hurt you" (Jeremiah 29:11). There are so many wonderful truths of God and that is our position in Christ. We simply need to accept it and embrace these truths.

If you are a football fan, you probably won't mind a football analogy. How do you win in football? Well, let's see. You're on the team. You study the playbook. You learn the plays. You execute the plays and you win the game; you win a lot of games and now you're a champion. Now, let's see how it works in Christianity. You're on the team. You study the playbook – that's the Bible. You learn the plays. You execute the plays. You win the game; you win a lot of games and you're a champion. It's the same theory. What's the catch? You must do it. You must execute and learn and play and be part of the game.

Last month, I thought to ask God, "Lord, what are You thinking in regard to every issue and request I'm praying about?" I don't always do that. I usually ask God for what I want. My prayer usually lies on the lines of, "Well, here's what I want, and can you give it to me as quick as possible? And God, if You're on the same page as me, You will give it to me right away."

But I thought I would ask God this time, "God, what are You really thinking?" Proverbs 3:5-6 says this in regard to how our relationship with God should look: "Trust in the Lord God with all your heart. Lean not on your own understanding. In all your ways acknowledge Him and He will direct your path."

So, I'm going to not lean on my own understanding. I'm going to trust in Him and ask Him to direct my paths. I have to acknowledge Him in order to do that – so I thought that would be a good idea.

I was up in New York one time, driving from Upstate New York to New York City, and MapQuest got me lost. Instead of being on the highway, I was off on all these back roads. I kind of knew I was going in the right direction, but it was taking a little longer than I planned, and I wanted to be on the highway.

I was in the Catskill Mountains of New York and it was 10 o'clock in the morning on a weekday, and there was a one-lane road in each direction. There was nobody on the road and I was in the middle of nowhere. All around me were these beautiful mountains. I mean, I was driving for a half an hour and all around me was lush mountains and trees and green – and I was overwhelmed. I was smothered by the glory of creation. I was just blown away! I was thinking, Oh my gosh! God, you're so awesome! This is so beautiful. I can't even believe this!

It was a very spiritual moment and I thought perhaps this is a little bit like what Paul felt when he was called up to the third

Heaven. I don't know what he saw, man, but this is as close as I'm getting to it until I get to the real Heaven. This is amazing.

God spoke to my heart – not audibly, but very clearly the Spirit spoke to my heart and He said, "Jack, let me ask you a question."

I said, "You have my full attention. I'm overwhelmed by your creation. What's the question?"

He asked, "How would life be different if all of this was yours? If everything you saw, as far as your eye could see, was yours?"

So, I was pondering the question, and I was thinking about how God owns the cattle on a thousand hills, and everything is the Lord's. I was pondering and thinking about it and after about five minutes, finally, I came up with the answer. God had asked me how life would be different if all of this were mine, and I said, "Nothing would be different. Really, nothing in my life would be different. I'd have more stuff, but nothing would be different."

God said to me, "Exactly." He said, "You see, it's not about how much land a man has that matters – it's about what he does with the land he has." Which is, of course, the parable of the talents, but God gave it to me in a very specific and personal way that day.

So, what is God saying to you and me? I believe it's the same thing God said to the Galatians when He used Paul to say it. I believe God wants to remind us we're all parts of Christ – we're all parts of the body. We all have a purpose and a plan – and part of that is for us to suffer for the sake of the gospel. When we do suffer for the sake of the gospel, when the world is against us, when our own flesh is against us, when Satan is against us, when our hearts are deceitful among all things – we must find strength and comfort in the memory that we are among a great fellowship. We are part of a community in which, through every age and every generation and every land, members have suffered for Christ rather than deny their faith.

Paul had a question for the Galatians, and I believe God has that same question for you and me. I want to remind you that the Galatians were believers. Paul was speaking to a church full of believers and he said this: "You foolish Galatians! Who has bewitched you? Before your very eyes Jesus Christ was clearly portrayed as crucified" (Galatians 3:1).

Paraphrased, he said, "Here's what I want to know: Are you so foolish, having begun in the Spirit, that you're now being made perfect by the flesh?"

He was saying, "Listen, what's the matter with you guys? You know the truth. Has anything changed? You know you were born again for the Spirit of God – you're now to live for the Spirit – you're transformed by the renewing of your mind. The old man is dead, the new man is here. You're meant to live in freedom; it is for freedom that you've been set free. Who fooled you to where you're back living again under the law – looking at other gods and thinking that other things in life are more important than God and the Kingdom and your purpose here on Earth? Who fooled you?"

They knew the truth, but they couldn't follow it. The question for us is this: do we trust God and His timing? Psalm 75:2 promises us there's an appointed time. If you're a football fan, you know when your team is kicking off. If you have a doctor's appointment next week, you know what time it is for. If you're taking an airplane trip soon, you know the day and time the flight leaves. Would you go to the airport two days early? Would you go to church a day early and wait a day and a night for the service? Of course, you wouldn't!

Why wouldn't you do that? "Well, Jack. Don't be stupid. That's ridiculous. Why would I come two days or a day before something was going to happen? I come on time – when it's time to be there."

"Why?"

"Because I know the time! I'm certain of the time – I have no doubt – and that's when I get there."

Look at what Psalm 130 says: "I wait for the Lord, my whole being waits, and in his word I put my hope. I wait for the Lord more than watchmen wait for the morning, more than watchmen wait for the morning" (V. 5-6).

He's saying, "Look, I'm waiting for the Lord. My whole being, every part about me, waits in His Word. I'm waiting like a watchman on the watchtower." Why? That's the watchman's job. It's the watchman's job to be waiting in the watchtower or in the lighthouse waiting for the morning – waiting to see if there's a boat. Like an airplane traffic controller waiting to see when the planes come in because that's his job.

And you and I have a job, too.

What do you do when you can't feel, see, or believe God has answered your prayers? You keep living in faith and in gratitude. You keep trusting and glorifying God in all that you do. You love God. You believe His timing. You don't get discouraged; you don't get depressed. You remain in the joy of the Lord, remembering God has done great things for you. You're focusing on what He has done, not focusing on the things you perceive He hasn't done. You trust God.

Last month, I was thinking about the wasted time in my life, and I was thinking, you know, the clock's ticking. I'm not getting younger; I'm getting older. Sometimes I think, Maybe I missed my purpose. There's more I wanted to do – there's more I wanted to accomplish. As if what God accomplished through me wasn't enough. So now I'm being God. But I always come to the same conclusion: I need to trust God – I need to trust God's timing in my life. I need to trust the truth of God and not my emotions and feelings. I need to default back to the truth of God, and so do you.

There are some examples of God's appointed timing in the Bible. How about Moses? Acts 7:30 says, "After 40 years had passed, an angel appeared to Moses in the flames of a burning bush in the desert near Mount Sinai." Forty years in the wilderness! How about Job? How about God's appointed timing for Job after he had lost everything? What about Joseph in prison? How do you think Joseph felt? What about the Israelites wandering around 40 years? But there was an appointed time. We clearly see God had a plan and a purpose.

God is sovereign. He is loving. He has a plan. We know about that great cloud of witnesses in Hebrews 11: Noah, Moses, Job, Daniel, and others. They waited and waited, and they couldn't see how circumstances were going to change. Many didn't see it before they died, but you know what they didn't do? They didn't quit. They didn't kill themselves – even though things seemed impossible and there seemed to be no way out. They didn't quit; they kept going in faith and we see how God used them. Rest assured now that they are in Heaven with God they see how God used them mightily and they are also reaping the benefits of their faithfulness and will for all eternity.

Here is the key and the reason why I believe you're reading this today. To answer this question: "What should we do?" There is an appointed time and I can prove it by the Word of God. It's found in Habakkuk chapter 2, and I don't know how it could be any clearer: "For the revelation awaits an appointed time; it speaks of the end and will not prove false. Though it linger, wait for it; it will certainly come and will not delay. See, the enemy is puffed up; his desires are not upright— the righteous person will live by his faithfulness" (v. 3-4)

Another version says this: "… the just shall live by faith."

That is your assignment. That is my assignment. That is the key to everything and anything – to any question, any thought you have. Here is what I believe God is saying, "Your faith is the currency I use to evaluate. Not money, not power, not prestige, not looks, not your house, not who loves you and who doesn't – no! I use your faith. And God tells us, "the just shall live by faith." Righteous and just are other words for believers. We're justified and made righteous not by our own actions, but by what Christ did for us on the cross. We're clothed in His righteousness – holy, blameless, and above reproach as the Word of God tells us – clothed in the righteousness of Jesus Christ.

The bottom line is God tells us to have faith in Christ.

If you're wondering, "How could I do it, Lord? How could I live a life that glorifies You? How do I bear fruit that lasts? How do I live out the perfect work that You've planned in advance for me to do? How am I to be a light to a generation of darkness – a salt to a tasteless generation?" Just believe in this simple answer.

You live by faith! "The just shall live by faith" (Romans 1:17). That is your assignment. You are not responsible for the outcome of your life. You are only responsible for your obedience to God and your actions. God will use you how He sees fit. Your job is to continue to live by faith – as all these guys did in Hebrews chapter 11, as Paul did, and as we are supposed to do.

Listen to God's warning through the prophet Zephaniah: "'I will sweep away everything from the face of the earth,' declares the Lord. 'I will destroy every remnant of Baal worship in this place… those who turn back from following the Lord and neither seek the Lord nor inquire of him.'" (Zephaniah 1:2, 3, 6)

Well, I guess you shouldn't have turned back from following God. I guess you should have inquired of Him and sought Him. I pray you're not in the group today who hasn't done that. If we are, we need to switch gears immediately.

It's like being lost in traffic. If you're going somewhere and you realize you're lost, what do you do?

Do you say, "Oh, I'm lost! Let me keep being lost."

No! The minute you realize you're lost, you seek directions to get back to where you were going. Now, you might have wished you didn't get lost – as getting lost was unfortunate – but you still want to get to where you're going. You might get there a little late, but far better to get there late than not to get there at all and to remain lost. You would be an idiot to realize you were lost and keep wanting to be lost. God says He is going to have a major problem with those who turn back from following the Lord, and those who don't seek Him or inquire of Him.

I did a spiritual U-turn a couple weeks ago. Perhaps you need to do the same today. Here's what happened to me: I was going to speak at a men's conference in Port Charlotte. I've never had this happen to me in 25 years of preaching and evangelism – but I didn't want to go. That was the strangest thing, because I always want to pursue these opportunities! I'm always excited to talk about the Lord, whether it's to one person or many. There's nothing I'd rather do than talk about God and share how God impacted my life and share the Word of God. But I did not want to go to this conference.

I felt Satan was attacking me. It was the night before the conference and I said, "Okay, I'm going to fight through it." I went to bed and I got up at three in the morning because I needed to drive to Port Charlotte, which was three hours from Orlando. And I still didn't want to go. I was miserable and I thought to myself, Maybe I'll just call and cancel. There are other speakers there – I'll just call and tell them I'm not coming.

Yet I knew that was the wrong thing to do, and I knew Satan was after me, so I just plowed through. I figured I'd feel better when I got in the car. Nope. After three hours in the car, I was still miserable. I've never experienced anything like this in my life! I've never experienced not wanting to go, not wanting to be there. It was the weirdest feeling.

I got to the conference; I spoke; I did my part. It was an "overcoming addiction" seminar – and God let me see the impact on a few people's lives. I was very grateful for that. I could see that it really did matter that I went. One guy came up to me after I spoke. His name was Sam and his mother had abandoned him at nine years old and sent him to military school. He was basically blaming her for ruining the start of his life and believed she was the reason he was an addict and the reason why everything had gone wrong.

So, I asked him this question: "Have you ever forgiven her?" Without missing a beat, he said, "Oh no, no, no. I could never do that. I could never forgive her."

I reminded him, gently of course, that Jesus demands that we forgive others as He has forgiven us. This is what the Apostle Paul said, and Jesus said it too. Basically, Jesus said, "If you have a charge against anybody, put it on my account. You forgive as you've been forgiven and more – so keep forgiving."

The guy looked at me and, as we continued to talk, I said to him, "Listen, your mother burned you. I agree that she did the wrong thing." Maybe there were circumstances I'm not aware of – but I was making a judgment at that point. I said, "What mother would abandon a nine-year-old kid? I mean, clearly, she did the wrong thing by you." I said, "But, if not for her, you would not be alive. If not for her, you wouldn't have your kids and grandkids who mean the world to you. If not for her, you'd have nothing. So even though she did something that was clearly not in your best interest, you need to forgive her. You benefitted greatly from her being alive. You're looking at this thing wrong. Your perspective is all off."

I went home and, a day or two later, God started speaking to my heart. He said, "That message was for you."

"What are you talking about?" I asked.

The Lord said, "That's for you, Jack. You see, you say that you've forgiven everybody – but there are still a couple people in your life that you haven't forgiven. Oh, you say you forgive them, and maybe you think you've forgiven them, but no. You think they did the wrong thing."

And they did do the wrong thing by me; they burned me; they did do the wrong thing. But I started to think and meditate on these people and what had happened in my life because of them – who I met, the opportunities I had, and what had come. I realized that the blessings so far outweighed the wrong that they had committed against me and that, indeed, I was so blessed to have them in my life (even though I was still mad at them for what they did).

God showed me that Romans 8:28 is true. All things are working together for my good and I need to perceive it that way. So, there was unforgiveness in my heart and God used that opportunity to let me know that I needed to make a change. The bottom line is that it was all about perspective.

Do I look at life from a perspective of joy and God's perspective, or from a perspective of fear and a fleshly perspective? That's a choice I need to make, and I believe you need to make this choice also. It comes from within. Circumstances and events don't change; it's how I view them that determines my happiness.

I was thankful to God for that revelation, for showing me that His joy is always there and that I just need to focus on God, and I believe you do too.

We need to know the Word of God so that Satan can't use it against us out of context. I love in Matthew 22:29, where Jesus says to the people, "You are in error because you do not know the scriptures or the power of God." You're in error. You're not understanding. You don't get it. Why? Because you don't know the scriptures of God or the power of God.

In order to know the power of God, you need to know the Word of God. That's how you know the power of God. God says His Word is alive. The Holy Spirit is inside of you, and God's Word is alive – you need to know both.

If I said to you, "Let's repeat the pledge of allegiance: I pledge allegiance to the wall and the foundation on which it stands," you would say, "Wait, stop."

"What do you mean, stop?"

"Well, that's not the pledge of allegiance."

"Well, how do you know?"

"Because I know the pledge of allegiance."

That's right. You would know. And you should know the same things about God.

There's an old movie called *The Godfather*. It's a movie about mafia guys, but if I told you: "Hey, that was a movie about an old baker. He used to bake loaves of bread for people, and his grandchildren called him papi, grandfather," you'd laugh at me. You may not remember every line in that movie. You may not remember every actor who played every part. But you know the story. It's enough to know that if I told you the wrong thing, you'd tell me that's not the story.

Shouldn't we know the same about God?

Here's the great news. God's not mad at you.

It's like me with my kids. If you are a parent, you know this, too. I love my kids. I just want them to get it right for their blessing. Second Corinthians 7:10 says this: "Godly sorrow brings repentance that leads to salvation and leaves no regret, but worldly sorrow brings death."

We need to turn to God and repent, believing all our sins are forgiven. God's not upset with you; God just wants you to get it right. He wants you to turn around and come back to the right spot. This is God's message to you and me today

Jesus said to Peter, "Get behind me, Satan! You are a stumbling block to me." Why did Jesus say that to Peter? Because Jesus had just revealed to Peter that He would be crucified and He would be raised up on the third day and Peter said, "Absolutely not! Out of the question! You're God. That's no way happening. You're wrong, Jesus. You're wrong, God."

Have you ever said that to God? "God, you must have gotten this wrong. I put in my paperwork request. You must have mixed it up with somebody else because I'm not getting what I want." He said to Peter, "Get behind me, Satan" He didn't mean Peter was Satan. He meant he was acting like Satan; he was not acting like God. The next line is the killer, and this is the line for you and me to be aware of. He says, "Get behind me, Satan. You're a stumbling block to me."

Why was Peter a stumbling block? Here's why: God says, "You do not have in mind the concerns of God, but merely human concerns. That's why you're a stumbling block, Peter, Jack, and anybody else who's listening – because you don't have in mind the things of God. You're worried about your flesh and earthly concerns, and that's not what's important. I've told you to work for the things that won't rust, moth, and decay – for your spiritual treasures in Heaven. I've told you because I love you and I want you to have that blessing. I told you, 'Live by faith'. That's what's important. Why are you focused so intently on all these things of the world as if they matter?"

We must focus on spiritual things.

So, let's remember God's wonderful promise for His children. "I know the plans I have for you. Plans to prosper you, to give you a hope and a future, not to harm you" (Jeremiah 29:11).

"Okay, God. I get it. I get that I'm your guy, God. I get that these are plans to prosper me, not to harm me – I get that everything is going to happen according to Your will, that You're going to take care of me, that everyone will get what they deserve in the end, but one question, God. I hope this isn't too much to ask, but could You tell me when this will happen? When will those who disobeyed you pay the price? Could You just tell me when is the appointed time? I'm curious, I'd like to know."

God does tell us. Here it is. It's found in 2 Thessalonians 1; this answers the question of when will God avenge. When will justice be served? This is the key to everything. You can believe it or not. The choice is yours, but this is the bottom line: "God is just. He will pay back trouble to those who trouble you and give relief to you who are troubled and to us as well. This will happen when the Lord Jesus is revealed from Heaven in blazing fire with His powerful angels" (v. 6-7).

He will punish those who do not know the Gospel and who do not obey the Lord Jesus Christ. They will be punished with everlasting destruction and shut out from the presence of the Lord and from the glory of His might. Sorry, Stephen Hawking, you may have followed a scientific belief... But this is reality!

It goes on to say this: "He will punish those who do not know God and do not obey the gospel of our Lord Jesus. They will be punished with everlasting destruction and shut out from the presence of the Lord and from the glory of his might on the day he comes to be glorified in his holy people and to be marveled at among all those who have believed. This includes you, because you believed our testimony to you." (2 Thessalonians 1:8-10)

That is God's promise to you; it includes you and every believer. A day is like a thousand years, and a thousand years like a day to the Lord.

So, how are we to live, knowing this? We are to live just like those in the Hall of Fame of faith; Hebrews 11:16 tells us how they lived, "They were longing for a better country and a Heavenly one. Therefore, God is not ashamed to be called their God for He has prepared a city for them."

That's how they lived on Earth – longing, knowing God is real, that Heaven is real, that they had a plan and a purpose, and that their job was just to continue in faith no matter what their eyes saw or didn't see.

So, here's the big question: Are you tired?

Are you tired of waiting for the appointed time? Are you tired of waiting for God's plan for your life to play out? Here's God's advice to the coach and players of the triple-overtime Super bowl game... Here's God's advice to the Navy Seals on the 180th day of their mission in a foreign country in the desert and swamps... Here's God's advice to the doctor in the 16th hour of life-saving surgery... And here's God's advice to every child of God living this life on Earth.

You will not be able to say that the Word of God doesn't speak or that His Word isn't loud and clear. Here's His advice from 2 Thessalonians 3:13, "And as for you, brothers and sisters – never tire of doing what is good."

It's the greatest motivational, inspirational speech you'll ever hear. Knute Rockne, Tony Robbins, I don't care who your motivator is – God says, "Never tire of doing what is good."

So, what if I do tire? What if I have failed? What if I haven't been faithful? Here's some great news: it's not too late for you!

I'm going to share with you the greatest comeback story of all time. It's talked about in Philemon. Paul was old and he made this appeal to another brother. He said, "Therefore I could be bold and order you to do what I need you to do." What he was saying was, "Look, I have position and power. I'm Paul. I could simply tell you to do this for me and you'd really have to do it, but I'm not going

RESET YOUR ATTITUDE IN ORDER TO CONNECT WITH PURPOSE

to do that – I'm just going to ask you. Here's what I'm going to ask you for."

He said, "I prefer to appeal to you based on love. It is none other than Paul. I, an old man now, and a prisoner of Jesus Christ, appeal to you for my son Onesimus."

Onesimus was not his physical son by birth; Onesimus was a spiritual son to Paul. He had come and served with Paul in ministry. Paul has a plea on behalf of Onesimus. He wrote, "Onesimus became my son while I was in chains – while I was in prison. Formerly, he was useless to you, but now he has become useful both to you and to me."

Formerly, he was useless! Hey, that could be you and me. Maybe we felt that we were formerly useless to God. "But now he has become useful to you and me."

I want you to take that as encouragement. God is not done with you. Whether you're ten years old or 100 years old, God has more to do with you if you're breathing on this Earth. God has a plan. God is not done. You are not useless. There's a purpose for your life and I want to share with you what it is: "I consider my life worth nothing to me. My only aim is to finish the race and complete the task the Lord Jesus has given me. The task of testifying to the good news of God's grace" (Acts 20:24).

That's it. That's the purpose. That's all Paul cares about. "Look, I don't care about anything. I just want to testify to God's grace in my life." That's your purpose too!

It doesn't have to be from the pulpit; it's just the way you live your life. People should see Christ coming through you. They should see the love and mercy and grace and kindness and fruits of the spirit coming through you in the life you live. That's how you glorify Christ. And if God has given you a position of power, of wealth – you're to use that for the glory of God as well.

That's your mission. It wasn't just for Paul; it is to be the mission of all believers to finish the race and complete the task.

If you have been in the military service, there's something about the military that amazes me. Guys enlist in the military in any branch and they subject themselves to people they have never met before in their entire lives: commanding officers, sergeants, lieutenants, colonels – whatever the rank may be. Here comes this guy who enlisted and, immediately, they do everything the commanding officer says. They obey everything and do anything they say.

They don't say, "Wait a minute, you didn't even know me."

Why would they do that; why would they obey strangers? Because they believe. They are taught, trained, and believe 100% that they have a purpose and a mission that is greater than their life! They are willing to fight and lay down their life and die for their country.

This is a very noble thing; I applaud that and admire that. They really believe that this mission and purpose belongs to them and they are part of it; they have a passion for this mission and purpose.

How is it that we don't do the same thing for Jesus Christ? How is that possible? We would do it for a stranger – I mean that in a good way for the country. I'm not down playing it. It's wonderful. But how is it we wouldn't do that much for our God, our Creator, our Father – the one who loves us so much? Why do our lives not reflect that?

2nd Corinthians chapter 4 is the key to everything and what every believer must do in order to have the best life possible.

> It is written: 'I believed; therefore I have spoken.' Since we have that same spirit of faith, we also believe and therefore speak, because we know that the one who raised the Lord Jesus from the dead will also raise us with Jesus and present us with you to himself...
>
> Therefore, we do not lose heart. Though outwardly we are wasting away, yet inwardly we are being renewed day by day. For our light and momentary troubles are achieving for us an eternal glory that far outweighs them all. So we fix our eyes not on what is seen, but on what is unseen, since what is seen is temporary, but what is unseen is eternal. (v. 13-14, 16-18)

That's why we do it! And that should be our motivation each day; that's our purpose and we should never forget the mission.

I have a theory. I share this when I'm motivating sales, management, or businesspeople when they're not performing up to speed. I'm a business guy at heart, so I often get called upon to do that. I get them in a room, and I say, "Listen, you're complaining about your boss, your job, everything else you have to do – I get it. You should be the boss – I get it. Well, here's my question: If I gave you two million dollars a year, would you do your job according to the boss's instructions and the company's procedures and do it enthusiastically?"

"Oh, yeah! You know, I'm only making $50,000 or $150,000 – but for two million dollars?! Jack, for $2 million dollars, you would have the greatest employee in the history of mankind!"

Okay, so let me get this right: you could do it now – you just don't want to. It's not worth it to you. You don't think the value of what you're getting is enough to make you do it. So, let me ask you a question in the spiritual sense: If I gave you two million dollars a year, could you wait patiently on God and His timing and live a godly life of faith? Could you trust His timing?

If I gave you two million dollars a year, could you love others unconditionally? Hey, I could. For two million dollars, I could be the most loving guy you've ever seen. I mean it. I'll love the snot out of you for that much.

The question for me and for you is, what's the Kingdom of Heaven worth to us? What value do we place on immortality and eternity and our place in Heaven with God? I would do it if I believed that what I was getting in return was worth it. I think we need to focus on the value of Heaven.

I have a buddy in Orlando whose named is Bobby. Bobby's a great Christian guy. He's got a young son and he shared this story with me. He said he was at Walmart, waiting in the checkout line; and if you shop at Walmart, you know it's a long line.

He was waiting patiently as there were ten or so people in front of him. Finally, he gets up to his turn and the cashier says, "I have to go on a break."

Bobby was furious. I mean, he was raging mad. He was ready to give them the what-for of all time and say, "This is ridiculous! I was standing here. How could you? This is crazy! No way is this happening – you're not going on a break – get back here!"

But then he thought about it and he said, "I can't say this." He couldn't say it because he works for the City of Orlando. On his shirt, he had an emblem with "The City of Orlando". It was very evident who he worked for.

He said, "If I express my feelings, if I yell at this girl, I'm going to get into trouble because I represent the City of Orlando and the City will not like that. Even though I was right, they would not like that."

He told me that God spoke to him on the spot. Instantly, the Holy Spirit spoke to him and said, "Bobby, let me get this right. That's why you wouldn't yell at her – because you represent the City of Orlando? Not because you represent Me?"

The Holy Spirit said, "Bobby, your life needs to be representing Me and what I would do. You need to be thinking about that all the time."

The promises of God are real ... and they are better than winning the lottery. Do you believe it?

Clearly Bobby saw in this instance that resetting his attitude was critical to connecting with his purpose. Perhaps you can look at your own life and see many examples were resetting an attitude to connect with purpose is not only an obvious choice but also a good idea. One last thought on resetting your attitude. I believe the promises of God are real... And they are better than winning the lottery... What do you believe?

Chapter Two
SHAPING OUR FOCUS TO EXPERIENCE CLARITY AND UNDERSTANDING

What does it mean when you're driving your vehicle and you hear somebody honking at you? Why do they honk? They want to get your attention. I hope this chapter will give you a heavenly honk from God.

It might help if you start with a prayer, asking, "God what do you want me to know? What do you want me to hear? Why are you honking at me, God?"

What if God says, "You can't follow me with your feet in one direction and your faith in another." That's the first honk from God that we have today.

I recently read an article that gives an example of a guy who got a honk from God. Bret Archerwald was accidentally left behind in the ocean. He spent 20 hours in the water at sea; experts said he should have drowned in 10 to 14 hours, but he didn't. He said, "This experience gave me a new outlook on life because it made me realize how fragile our existence is."

As he was out in the sea, and getting stung by jellyfish and passing out and waking up and trying not to drown, here's what he came to conclude: "The things I thought about when I was missing were the things you should focus on: faith, family, and friends. Not the other garbage." When it all came down to it, when his life was on the line, all he could think about was God, his family, and friends. I hope it won't take a life-altering experience for you and me to focus on what's important – God, family, and friends.

Now here's a honk from God for you. I want to ask you a tough question. Are you possessed? A Christian songwriter once put it this way, "You got to serve somebody. It may be the devil, or it may be the Lord, but you got to serve somebody." So, who are you possessed by? Obviously, if you are possessed by Satan, we would expect that you manifest the things of the devil. But if you were possessed by God, we would expect you to manifest the things of God. Scripture tells us that a tree is known by its fruit.

You've probably heard the old stories of Robert Johnson, the old blues guitar player who said he sold his soul to the devil at a highway crossroads. At the time he met the devil at the crossroads he was not a very good guitar player. When he came back from that meeting with the devil, he was one of the best guitar players ever. It's interesting how some rock stars, businessmen, and, unfortunately, regular people too, sell their soul to the devil. They make this deal with the devil for the riches of the world, but they don't realize that he owns title to their soul for all of eternity. You see, when they get a glimpse of eternity, they have a new perspective on time, and then they realize it was a very bad deal. Earthly riches are but for a fleeting moment, but eternity separated from God is forever. I believe that is a realization that is truly shaping our focus to experience clarity and understanding

Eternity with God is also forever. May that be what we are aiming for!

I was thinking of the Stoneman Douglas High School shooting tragedy in Parkland, Florida. Seventeen innocent lives were gunned down by a deranged madman. The world's response to this tragedy was very interesting – wow! Talk about change and revolution. "We're going to march on Tallahassee (the state capitol), and we're going to get something done because this is unacceptable!" It was unacceptable, and they did a very good job of demonstrating that; it's good that there was change because of that. But millions of people are going to Hell every year; millions are dying and going to Hell – separated from God for all eternity – and I don't see anybody marching on Tallahassee about that. I don't see revival happening in our church and in our streets. We're just letting this happen. We're just letting life go by.

I want to share something with you. This is what I've been taught and what I believe is the truth, I believe that revival starts by one individual on their knees in prayer. That individual can be you and me, on our knees praying to God that revival would start in our hearts, in our church, in our city, and that we wouldn't take this lying down – that we'd be out there, telling people about Jesus Christ and speaking about what's important.

So, what's holding you back? That's the question I have for you.

We also know Jesus Christ was crucified on the cross. How could we possibly think any different or act any different? Paul reminds us in Galatians of our position in Christ: "Because you are his sons, God sent the Spirit of his Son into our hearts, the Spirit who calls out, 'Abba,Father.' So you are no longer a slave, but God's child; and since you are his child, God has made you also an heir" (Galatians 4:6-7).

We're heirs to the throne of Heaven. We've inherited it already. We have it already.

My uncle died recently. He left some money to my mother and my brother and me as well as to my cousin. It wasn't a great deal of money, but it amazed me. My Uncle Herb lived in Washington, D.C. He was a professor and a writer, and he remained single all his life; he was a great guy, a wonderful guy. But here's what amazed me, I thought, "Let me get this right. Uncle Herb worked all his life and everything he did came to us."

But wait a minute... we did nothing to deserve it. Nothing. I didn't write any of Uncle Herb's books. I didn't teach any of his classes. I saw him on holidays. I loved him very much. He was a great guy, but everything he did ended up being for our benefit.

I want you to understand this, everything God did was for your benefit. You and I are the beneficiaries of God, both now on Earth and in Heaven for eternity; but, sometimes we don't live like that. When God talks in the Bible about an heir, Scripture says, "Look, the heir may be under rules and regulations because he may be underage." Maybe he's under 21 and he inherited something at six years old; we're not going to give a six-year-old boy all the money and the keys to the Kingdom. No, but it's his. He is the heir to it. Yes, there may be teachers and parents and people to guide him until he comes to the appointed age.

It's the same with us. Until you and I reach the appointed age at the appointed time, there may be things we haven't inherited the fullness of yet. But we will one day have full access to it. It's all for our benefit and, at the appointed time, we will see it all.

Now if you could imagine the heir to the throne being a six-year-old boy. Could you imagine that kid finding out he's the heir and he goes, "Well, can you get me toys? Can I go to McDonald's?"

He probably doesn't really know the full scope of what his inheritance means yet and what it entitles him to have. Yet by the time he's 12, 14, 16 – he gets it. And he's thinking, "Holy cow! This is all mine, baby." He's not scared. He's not worried. He knows that he's under the authority of those who are governing him until he's of age, but he's excited. Why? Because he knows he possesses it; he doesn't have a question in his mind that it's his.

There shouldn't be a question in your mind that the Kingdom of Heaven is yours, that the love of God is yours, that the mercy and joy and peace and sacrifice of the Lord is yours because God has already given all these things to you. It's yours now, and for all eternity.

Paul asked the Galatians a question, and I believe God is asking us this same question today: "But now that you know God, or rather, that you are known by God, how is it that you are turning back to these weak and miserable forces? Do you wish to be enslaved by them all over again?" (Galatians 4:9)

It's not just about working to earn God's love, which is ridiculous. After all, it's a gift of grace that we have. It's a free gift; but it's also important for us to consider the way that we live our lives. Are we getting entangled in the things of the world or are we getting entangled in the things of God? What are we looking at? What are we living for? Are we getting caught up in the stuff of this world?

That doesn't mean you're not part of the world. Of course, you're part of the world. Of course, you're functioning in it; God has a purpose and a plan for your life, which is why He created you. That first plan is to have a relationship with Him. That second plan is that He would use you to impact the Kingdom of God for His glory. So, "… how is it that you are turning back to these weak and miserable forces?" God reminds us through Paul of the importance of staying focused on Kingdom work. He confirms it. Paul repeats this in Galatians 5:1: "It is for freedom that Christ has set us free. Stand firm then, and do not let yourself be burdened again by a yoke of slavery."

What is burdening you today? What has you in slavery? Is it an addiction? Is it a sin – confessed or unconfessed? Is it anger, rage, jealousy, malice, or covetousness? Is it pride? Is it something that's very individual for you? What is it that has you engulfed again in a yoke of slavery? God has called you to be free and in Galatians 6:4 God gives us some instruction along these lines. "Each one should test their own actions. Then they can take pride in themselves alone, without comparing themselves to someone else."

Each one should look at themselves. Don't go around looking at everybody else, worried about what they're doing. Look at yourself and say, "What about me? How am I doing? I have to test my own actions."

God's saying, "Look, if you look at your actions and you're doing good – you should be happy about that." You know you're loving God, you're serving God, and you're living a godly life. That's great. If not, you should fix what's wrong. You shouldn't just leave it be; you should look at and examine your life. It shouldn't have to take somebody calling you up and telling you that you are backsliding, or you winding up in jail, or you winding up in some sinful behavior that you didn't expect to happen because you were going down that road and you weren't even looking in the mirror at yourself and where you were headed.

Here's the question God's asking me: "Am I going to act like Jack or Jesus?" I believe He's asking you that same question today. That's the bottom line. God has been getting very personal with me lately. But the bottom line is – who am I going to act like? Because Jack does not act like Jesus. On occasion he does; but for the most part, no. God's really called me out to my face – or my heart, or my spirit, or my soul, "Are you going to act like Jack or Jesus?" I want to ask you that same question.

He also asked me another question, "Are you going to live like a son or a slave? Are you going to live like a slave to your flesh, to your desires, and to the world – or are you going to live like a son who I have set free, who I have given my inherence to? You are free; you have everything! Why aren't you dancing? Why aren't you joyful? Why aren't you singing? You have everything; you have been set free from death, from bondage; you have been set free from everything!"

Well, you could say, "Well, Jack, you don't know my circumstances. You know, it must be good for you since you're in a place where you can write a book like this one. But you don't know my circumstances; you don't know how tough things are for me: my finances, my health, my marriage, my kids, the spiritual path I'm on."

I'm sure you might be going through some tough times. I have too, from time to time, in my life. And here's what I've been taught to do, what I believe I'm supposed to do. I'm to ask the Holy Spirit, "What is the Father's will for me in this situation?"

The Holy Spirit lives within you and me upon salvation, and we're meant to ask Him, "What is your will for me in this situation? What do you want me to learn? What do you want me to do? How will you grow me?" We're supposed to ask, "Are these the trials and tribulations you're using to mold me and shape me so that my joy will be complete and so that I lack nothing? What do you want to do through this situation?"

But there's more. Then I need to wait and listen for the Spirit of God to reveal His will. We're not meant to just ask God, and then jump in and do what we want. I'm to wait for the Holy Spirit to reveal His Will. God says, "Be still, and know that I am God" (Psalm 46:10).

Then there's one more thing, I'm to examine myself and ask myself this tough question: "What is going on in my spirit that is not allowing God's will to happen in my life? Is there something going on in me spiritually?"

Remember, we're supposed to examine ourselves. Make it a habit to ask this same question yourself: "Is there something going on in me spiritually that is not allowing God's will to happen in my life?" 1st Thessalonians 5:21 tells us to test ourselves and hold on to what is good. Now that is an eye-opening truth that I believe is truly shaping our focus to experience clarity and understanding.

God plants thoughts in my head. I've been saved over 25 years. I know that God speaks very clearly through His Spirit to my spirit. It is not an audible speech, but it is no doubt the voice of God in my spirit. I know I heard the Spirit of God telling me and my family to move to Orlando years ago. Thank God that I responded to His Spirit.

How did that look at the time? Well, first God planted a thought in my head. Orlando. And I responded with a thought that sounded like, "Leave me alone. Orlando? We live in south Florida."

But it kept coming; it was not relenting. It was clear to me that I wasn't insane – yet – and that this clearly was God speaking to me through circumstances, people, places, events, and the Holy Spirit and His Word confirming everything. I've learned to follow the promptings of God upon my spirit in these things, but sometimes it's a process.

The other day, I was driving along, minding my own business, when out of the blue and into my head, something new popped in there. By the way, if a thought comes into my head, I don't automatically assume that it's a thought from God. You definitely want to check it out and be sure. Sometimes it's just my thoughts. Perhaps it's a dart of the enemy in my head. We need to be careful in this. But I was driving along the other day, and all of a sudden music from *The Sound of Music* popped into my mind. You know, Julie Andrews singing, "The hills are alive with the sound of music."

I was thinking, "Ha-ha, *The Sound of Music*." I haven't thought about, seen, or heard it in about 40 years. But it was very blatant that these words from *The Sound of Music* were blaring in my head.

I've learned a little about how God speaks to me and this is just one way that God might speak to me and you. He certainly speaks most authoritatively and clearly when I'm in His Word, reading His Word and listening to the Holy Spirit of God in my heart, but I believe He uses circumstances, people, and places to speak with us, as well. And we need to confirm that with the Word of God. That's how you know for sure.

So, I thought to myself, Okay God, we'll see. That's a good one. The next day, Jackson and I were in the movie theatre seeing a movie and there were some trailers before the movie. You know how trailers go in the movies; it's quick, it's a little glimpse. So, there was a scene in the kid's bedroom and on the wall was a poster that said it's for *The Sound of Music*.

I thought, "Okay, God. That's two. That's pretty good. I was driving yesterday, thinking about *The Sound of Music*, and now there's a poster in the movie trailer for *The Sound of Music*. All right, let's see what else you have in store."

The next day, I was in my quiet time in the morning and God told me to open up to a particular verse. This does not happen every day – where God specifically tells me to go to a verse or a page. Sometimes it happens though; when I'm listening, I can hear.

By the way, is God always talking? I believe God is always speaking, but I'm not always listening. See, I'm talking to my kids and telling them what to do, but they are not always listening. God said to me specifically, "Open up Isaiah 44:22." So, I went to Isaiah 44:22 and here's what it says: "I have swept away your offenses like a cloud, your sins like the morning mist. Return to me, I have redeemed you."

I kept reading and the next verse states: "Sing for joy, you heavens, for the Lord has done this; shout aloud, you earth beneath. Burst into song, you mountains, you forests and all your trees, for the Lord has redeemed Jacob, displays his glory in Israel."

Burst into song. Sing! *The Sound of Music*. I'm like, "Okay, God. That's how you want me to live. You want me to live this way. You want me to remember that I've been redeemed. You want me to remember that. You want me to shout for joy, and sing – literally!"

And I believe that's how God wants you and me to live. Yet we fail and we sin. I can never make myself right with God by my works or my actions and neither can you. Only Christ can make me right with God and He already has. So, we must decide: Are we going to live by grace or by rules?

As God said, if you're going to live by the law, you must fulfill all the law or you're falling short of it. It's a decision we must make.

I was at Iron Sharpens Iron, a men's conference in Jacksonville, and Jeff Kemp, a retired quarterback, was one of the speakers. He was talking about God being our foundation and our rock. He said, "Just imagine you're standing on something, and it's God's below you. You've got a solid rock you're standing on. God is your foundation and you can't be shaken. God is your foundation and your rock."

I said to myself, "Okay, that's a reminder for me that as I live my life in this world, God is my foundation. God is my rock. He is solid. I don't have to worry about me. I just have to focus on Him. I can stand on Him and my position will be firm. The only reason that my foundation would ever be shaken is if it were created and built on something not solid, but rather something unsure and shaky like sand."

If I created my foundation of my own things, it would be sand and it would be washed away, God tells us. But when it's a solid rock, and Jesus is my Rock, I have nothing to worry about. I thought to myself, "That is great. That's a good reminder. I appreciate that."

Then the next Tuesday morning I was in a Bible study, and the pastor was speaking, and he says these exact words: "Remember this. God is your solid rock. Imagine if you're standing here and Jesus is standing underneath you."

I thought to myself, that's pretty good, God – the same exact thing out of the mouth of two different people – I guess I'm supposed to heed that.

God is trying to talk in a lot of different ways. I encourage you to pick up your Bible and read it. I've written books. But my books shouldn't matter and none of the books should matter compared to the Word of God. If we just read the Bible and did what God said, we wouldn't need any other books to do anything. But remember that God will speak to you in other ways – through worship, through prayer, through other people. Always confirm what you hear against the truth of God's Word to confirm it is of and from God.

But you've got to be listening. Here's a great example and I hope this encourages you. When Billy Graham the great evangelist died , here's what his grandson said about him: "I don't think people ever saw the extent of his humility. He didn't go around thinking he was a big deal. He was genuine. He didn't walk around with some big posse and want special treatment everywhere. He bought his suits at Sears and usually drove a Ford. He was just a normal guy. And I think another thing people don't always see was that he could be pessimistic sometimes. In other words, if there was a big meeting he was holding, and it was an outdoor meeting, and he woke up that morning and looked out the window and saw a cloud on the horizon, he was convinced that within a few minutes the cloud was going to develop into a storm and ruin the meeting and no one was going to come that night. Or if he had a headache, he was convinced it was a brain tumor and that he was going to die. So it was that side of him that people didn't see, because they always saw him as a great, strong, powerful preacher but he never moved away from a deep understanding of 'I'm a sinner just like everyone else.'"

I hope that encourages you. Billy Graham, by the world's standards, would have been one of the all-time great Christians. But he was just like you and me. He was worried and frustrated from time to time. He got anxious, upset, and concerned. He was no better than anyone else.

Many major Bible characters – David, Noah, Jacob, Isaac, the list goes on – everybody had flaws and faults. Their great redeeming value was that they kept the faith. When they got knocked down, they got back up. They believed that Jesus was the solid rock and that's where they were standing no matter what. They might not have liked what was happening, they might not have understood it, but they didn't waver in their faith. That was what made them great heroes.

So, you might ask, "Well, what do I do?" Well, it's interesting. I was complaining about money a while back and somebody told me I need to give away more. Okay, that was good advice. I was complaining about the things I had to do and was focusing solely on myself. Somebody told me I need to be about serving others and I shouldn't worry so much about myself or be so focused on myself. I need to be worrying about others, focused on serving others, because that's what Jesus did.

You know the story of Jesus' life, but do you realize that, as He was dying on the cross, He still served others? He did three things as he was dying on the cross. First, he introduced John to His mother. He said, "Woman, this is your son and son, this is your mother." Even in the midst of agony, He was thinking, Who's going to take care of my mom now if I'm not around to take care of her? He basically said, "You guys are going to take care of each other. You're now mother and son," on the cross as He was dying. He was not thinking about Himself; He was thinking about making sure his mom was taken care of.

Secondly, he brought the thief on the cross to Heaven. The minute the thief on the cross acknowledged Him as God, He guaranteed his place in Heaven. Jesus was always about saving the sinner. He was always about the welfare of the other guy.

Thirdly, as you know, He forgave those who were killing Him. He said, "Father forgive them; they do not know what they do." As He was dying, Jesus performed these three acts of service for other people. Do you think we could, as we're living, at least do one or two sacrificial acts for somebody else? The answer is to take the focus off yourself and put it on other people.

I want to share with you a secret weapon that I've begun to use for myself. This is practical; I hope it helps you. If it doesn't, find something else that works for you. I've learned to separate my thoughts into three categories: emotion, fact, and truth. Those are my three categories. When I have a thought, I try to recognize, "Which category does it fit into?"

For instance, let's say I had the thought of anger. Let's say I'm mad at someone or something that has happened; I do get those thoughts. I say, "Well, Jack, that's an emotion. You're having an emotion."

Then I ask myself, "Well, what is the fact?" Perhaps the fact is that someone has done something wrong to me. Perhaps they have cheated me. Perhaps they have not treated me right. That is a fact.

Finally, what is the truth? The truth is, I'm supposed to forgive them no matter what they've done. See, the truth is the Word of God. I may have emotions; those are legitimate. I'm human. I'm going to have emotions. I may have an emotional fear. There may be fact in a situation that happened. The fact may be that I lost my job and I don't have income. The truth would be that God says He's going to be with me always; He'll never leave me nor for-sake me. The truth would be that all things work together for my good; that when He created me, He had a perfect plan for my life and His plan is to give me a hope and a future, to prosper me, not to cause me harm. That is the truth.

So, the question is: What am I going to focus on? My emotions; and let them run wild? "Oh, I'm angry and fearful!" I could let them run wild if I just focus on them. What about the facts? "I've been wronged! This isn't right!" Yeah, I could focus only on those. No, I need to focus on the truth of God. Stand on the rock – the foundation of the truth. That is the bottom line. I believe it is a matter of life or death. It's just that simple. "Man cannot live on bread alone but on every word that comes out of the mouth of God" (Matthew 4:4).

You've probably heard that verse before, but you need to get into the verse. That is the truest verse ever. I think that the older I get, the more I realize the truth of this statement. And it is not that you need 25 years of walking with the Lord to get to this point; you should be at this point the first day that you're saved with Jesus because it's the truth. "Man cannot live on bread alone." That's how you live through everything: good, bad, or indifferent.

You live on every word that comes out of the mouth of God and then you will have the joyful Christian life. You may have hardship on earth. Think of Paul. Do you think he had no hardship on earth? Paul went through a shipwreck, prison, everything – multiple times – yet he was singing joyfully at midnight in prison. Why? Because he knew his purpose; he knew who his God was. The minute Paul got saved, it was no longer about Paul. It was about fulfilling his purpose and it was about other people. That should be our attitude. That should be our exact attitude the minute we get saved.

I was at another Iron Sharpens Iron men's conference not long ago. Brian Doyle is the founder of Iron Sharpens Iron. He previously worked at Promise Keepers for years, and about 15 years ago he started Iron Sharpens Iron. I met him three or four months ago at a breakfast, we got to talking, and he invited me to this conference to speak. I was excited about it.

I got there at 7 o'clock in the morning and we were setting up. I was excited about seeing Brian, and I asked one of the guys, "Is Brian here?"

The guy looks at me without missing a beat and he asked, "You didn't hear?" As if I was the only guy in the world who didn't know some news.

I said, "No, no. What?"

He said, "His wife died at 4 o'clock this morning. (His wife, Barbara, was battling cancer) He won't be here today. You didn't hear?"

"No, I didn't hear." But when I heard, my whole perspective changed.

Is it possible there are some things you haven't heard about God? Is it possible you haven't heard this message? In Psalm 4:6-8: "Many, Lord, are asking, 'Who will bring us prosperity?' Let the light of your face shine on us. Fill my heart with joy when their grain and new wine abound. In peace I will lie down and sleep, for you alone, Lord, make me dwell in safety."

That's how God wants you to feel. His Word says, "You have put gladness in my heart more than in the season that their grain and wine increased." In other words, "More than anything the world could give me, Lord, you put gladness in my heart."

That's the good news. Didn't you hear that? Maybe you didn't hear. That's how God wants you to feel and live. If that's true and you believe it, you will have the joy and peace of God. How do you get that? By understanding, appreciating, and receiving what God has done for you and by walking and living in the truth of God. That's how you come to that conclusion.

Did you hear the message in Psalm 46? "God is our refuge and strength, an ever-present help in trouble. Therefore we will not fear, though the earth give way and the mountains fall into the heart of the sea, though its waters roar and foam and the mountains quake with their surging. There is a river whose streams make glad the city of God, the holy place where the Most High dwells. God is within her, she will not fall; God will help her at break of day. Nations are in uproar, kingdoms fall; he lifts his voice, the earth melts. The Lord Almighty is with us; the God of Jacob is our fortress. Come and see what the Lord has done." (v. 1-8)

Didn't you hear? I want to make sure you've heard some of this stuff, because sometimes in our Christian walk, we live like we don't know of these great and precious promises. God says this in Psalm 37: "Do not fret because of those who are evil or be envious of those who do wrong; for like the grass they will soon wither, like green plants they will soon die away. Trust in the Lord and do good; dwell in the land and enjoy safe pasture. Take delight in the Lord, and he will give you the desires of your heart." (v. 1-4)

Don't fret because of the evildoers. Oh, it looks like they're ahead; it seems that they've gotten everything. Their day of judgment will come.

God is our refuge and strength. We should not fear. Perhaps the most important "you didn't hear" is found in John 8. You know the story: there was a woman caught in adultery. Jesus was teaching when the people came up to Him carrying rocks and asked Him what they should do. He began to write in the ground. We don't know what He wrote but one thought is that He possibly wrote down the sins of the other people standing in the circle and, one by one, they dropped their stones.

They were going to stone this woman caught in adultery because that was the punishment according to the law in those days. They walked away, dropping their stones, and Jesus was the only one there with the woman and He said, "I do not condemn you." Then he said one more thing, "Go and sin no more."

He said the same thing to the invalid man he healed in the pool at Bethesda. When Jesus healed the former invalid man, he came running back to Jesus and John thanking him and Jesus said, "Go and sin no more."

His words both extended mercy and demanded holiness at the same time. "You've been given a second chance," was what He said to the woman caught in adultery. She didn't deserve a second chance, and she knew it. That was what He also said to the invalid. He'd been given a second chance and so, "Go and sin no more." Obviously, Jesus knew that their condition was caused by sin. No doubt about it. But Jesus said, "I've forgiven your sin. You're forgiven. I don't condemn you."

He says the same thing to you and me today. "You're free. I don't condemn you." Jesus has paid the price of your sin on the cross. But He does say, "Go and sin no more."

Remember the man he healed with leprosy; the man said in the book of Luke, "Lord, if you're willing, you can make me clean."

Jesus reached out his hand and touched the man and said, "I am willing. Be clean."

Jesus says the same thing to you today: "I am willing. Be clean."

If you will reach out to Jesus, He will reach back to you. Like the prodigal son, God doesn't condemn anybody who comes running back toward Him. He only forgives with love.

Didn't you hear?

Didn't you hear that Jesus said we need to be dressed and ready for service and keep our lamps burning? He didn't say it would be easy. He said to keep at it incessantly; to finish the race; to win the prize. He equated it to servants waiting for their master to return from a wedding banquet so that when the master comes back and knocks, they can immediately open the door for him.

Didn't you hear it when Jesus said that it would be good for those servants who the master finds watching when He comes? Truly, God tells us in Luke Chapter 12. He'll dress and serve those servants; He'll have them recline at the table with Him and He will come wait on them.

> It will be good for those servants whose master finds them watching when he comes. Truly I tell you, he will dress himself to serve, will have them recline at the table and will come and wait on them. It will be good for those servants whose master finds them ready, even if he comes in the middle of the night or toward daybreak. But understand this: If the owner of the house had known at what hour the thief was coming, he would not have let his house be broken into. You also must be ready, because the Son of Man will come at an hour when you do not expect him. (Luke 12:37-40)

Didn't you hear that God is asking you to be faithful? It's not because He needs your faithfulness, but because He wants to bless you abundantly and exceedingly – more than you could ask or imagine.

How do you get these blessings of God? Well, God told you. Just be faithful. Love Him with all your heart; put Him first; seek Him. God says, "You'll find me when you seek me with all of your heart" (Jeremiah 29:13).

I pray that we are asking ourselves this question daily: "Are we possessed?" And if so, by whom? I pray that we remember we are the beneficiaries of Jesus Christ. He already died and has given us everything; we have the promise of eternal life forever. I pray that we remember to take our thoughts and emotions and stack them up and remember to ask, "Are they emotions or fact or truth?" I pray that we would always default to the truth of God –in everything.

Like Brett Archibald who was lost at sea, I pray that we would remember what's important. We don't need to be lost sea to remember it is God, family, and friends. I pray that you have heard the honk from Heaven and that it gets your attention.

What should we do? The Bible tells us to turn our hearts to God with fasting, with weeping, with mourning – to give our hearts to Him; not our garments, not our actions, but our hearts. The Word of God says that we should return to God, for He is gracious and merciful, slow to anger, and of great kindness.

It's not too late! It's not too late to have victory; it's not too late to turn to God and be like the prodigal son right at His feet. May the Holy Spirit speak to you about what you need to do, how you need to act, and what you need to give up so that you may live in freedom, regardless of the circumstances of the world.

May the Holy Spirit truly engage and change our hearts in such a way that truly is shaping our focus to experience clarity and understanding not just to impact our life here on earth but the impact of rewards and blessings in heaven for all eternity.

Chapter Three

REALIZING THAT THE PRESENT PLAN MAY NOT BE THE BEST PLAN

The Flying Wallendas are a long-time circus family who have a high-wire act. Their history and generations have been beset by tragedy – by deaths. They never perform with nets. They say, "Absolutely not," and so many of them died because of this.

The Wallendas who are performing today have said, "The show must go on!" They also said, "We've had our fair share of tragedy. But life is all about perspective. How can I be an inspiration to someone if I allow that stuff to overtake me? No matter what tragedies occur in life, you go on. Situations happen in life for a reason. We can turn that into motivation." What commitment, dedication, and perseverance!

So, we need to look at our own lives, our own attitudes, and ask how we can turn what's happening right now into motivation. Do we believe God in Romans 8:28 that all things work together for our good?

When my father passed away we had the task/privilege of clearing out my dad's files. I was in his closet and saw a four-drawer file cabinet. It took me about 30 minutes to take out all the files and throw nearly all of them into the trash. We kept what was important. There were some important documents, but we had gone through all of them years ago when the early stages of dementia were upon my father.

I looked at the files of his life and thought, Man, this is kind of tragic. His whole life, 85 years, and I ended up throwing away these files in 30 minutes. I realized the same thing was going to happen in my life. It will happen in yours too, we will all die at the time God has appointed for each one of us. I wondered for a moment, Wait a minute. Did his files matter? Did his life matter? I thought about it and concluded, those files mattered to him a lot.

I can tell you, my files matter to me. And I'm sure yours matter to you. But they also mattered to my family because everything he did, he did for us. That's why those files mattered. Even though they were in the trash later, they mattered to him, and they mattered to us. What you do matters to you, and it matters to your family and to those you impact with your life.

I had the privilege of telling my dad, as he lay in a hospice bed, that I loved him. I think I've told him that for most of my life. I said, "Dad, I love you." He looked up, very weakly, and he said, "I love you, too." I thought that was great to hear, but more importantly, he showed me all his life that he loved me. He didn't need to say it. He showed me.

I hope and pray that the same would be said of you: By your family, your friends, and your loved ones. I hope it will one day be said of me. That I loved people and they knew it.

My family is Jewish. To my knowledge, up to the point of my dad's sickness, he hadn't accepted Jesus Christ as his Lord and Savior. On a couple of my trips back and forth down to Boynton Beach, while he was going through the last few weeks of his life in hospice, I thought and prayed, Lord, do I need to tell him again? I'm sure you understand the thoughts going through my mind... I need to tell him. I need to make sure that he goes to Heaven. This is by far the most important thing in the world. I mean, this is my dad. I love him so much. He's got to go to Heaven, and I got to tell him.

But, he was in a state where he was clearly not coherent. He could moan or groan, but not really respond. But God spoke to my heart as I was wrestling with this. He said, "You did tell him. You told him many times in his life. In conversations, in preaching, in books, and with the actions of your life." He's read many of my books. God gave me peace and comfort that it wasn't about that last second. I didn't need to tell him about the gospel one more time and say, "Dad, Dad, you need to make sure you're saved!" He had already had the opportunity. Of course, I hope and pray that he did accept the work of Christ on the cross. I pray this for my dad, for everyone in my family, and for everyone in your family.

It's my belief and my prayer that Jesus in His mercy would come to that dying individual, not audibly, but in their spirit and speak to them and give them one more chance before they pass on to accept Jesus and His Kingdom.

I hope and I pray my dad responded accordingly. But the point is, I did tell him. I don't mention this from a prideful standpoint; I mention it because I want you to have that same peace and comfort. It's not our job to make people respond, it is our job to tell them – in our own style and way.

It's also about perspective. I have a friend whose son died when he was young – four years old. That changed the lives of my buddy and his wife as they now considered every moment precious. The question is how we are going to respond to circumstances: Are we going to be bitter, or better? Are we going to run to God, or away from God? I'm happy to say that my friend used that tragedy in his life to glorify God and bring him closer to God.

John Walsh whose son, Adam, was tragically kidnapped and murdered at six years old, turned that tragedy into America's Most Wanted television show. That show put away thousands of criminals so they wouldn't have the chance to hurt other people. He had a generational and historical impact because he responded to God and to the call of God to do something good with what had happened. It's all about perspective.

Over the last few months, I've found God's Word washing over me in the most wonderful of ways. I realized God's Word was always there, willing to wash over me in the most wonderful of ways. I think my heart is becoming more sensitive. I think I am becoming less satisfied with the world and wanting more of the Spirit of God. And, in the process, God's words come alive more. It's not because God is more alive, but rather because I'm more responsive.

I want to share with you what God has been teaching me. First, a little math lesson: if $a=b$, $b=c$, then $a=c$. Now, for all your math teachers, how could that possibly be? How could $a=b$ and $b=c$, so $a=c$? One thing would have to happen for this to be true. They would have to be the same. Keep that in your head as we go forward.

We're going to talk about similarities today between Abraham, Paul, and us (a, b, and c). I want to start with Abraham. Before God changed his name to Abraham, he was known as Abram. In Genesis, here's what God said to Abram: "Do not be afraid, Abram. I am your shield, your very great reward." But Abram said, "Sovereign Lord, what can you give me since I remain childless and the one who will inherit my estate is Eliezer of Damascus?" And

Abram said, "You have given me no children; so a servant in my household will be my heir" (Genesis 15:1-3).

Here, God had come and said, "Don't be afraid, I am your shield and your exceedingly great reward. I have these great things in store for you;" but immediately Abram has a question: "Well, what are you going to give me?" Abram says to God, "Look. Right now, the heir to my throne is somebody in my house named Eliezer, but he's not my son. That's not my son. Technically, he'd be the heir, but only because I don't have a son." This bothered him. He was upset. And he said to God, "What can you do to fix this for me?"

God responds in Genesis 15:4-5: Then the word of the Lord came to him: "This man will not be your heir, but a son who is your own flesh and blood will be your heir." He took him outside and said, "Look up at the sky and count the stars—if indeed you can count them." Then he said to him, "So shall your offspring be."

Holy cow! I mean, God just came and made the most ridiculous, outstanding, unbelievable promise in the history of mankind to Abram. He says, "Listen, don't worry. I'm going to give you a son," which was a little bit of a mystery to Abram because he was a very old man. By the time Isaac was born, Abraham was a hundred years old. His wife was ninety years old.

"How are we going to have a son? We're past the age. God, you told me to look up at the stars and this will be the number of all my descendants from a son that I'm going to have, which is impossible for me to have?" Yet that's exactly what God said.

God has promised us Heaven and eternity. That's something that looks impossible from an earthly perspective to have. What is our response to God? Let's look at Abram's response. In verse 6 of Genesis 15, it says: "Abram believed the Lord and it was accounted to him for righteousness."

Abram, soon to have God change his name to Abraham, believed God for this ridiculous promise. It's the same as us believing God for eternity. Abraham asked God for a sign, and God provided him a sign that day. I understand the skepticism of a non-believer. I get it. I get how non-believers ask, "Yeah, let me get this right, you're going to Heaven and you're going to be with God for all eternity?"

We look at the ISIS terrorists and their many terrorist activities. Many of them are told in their religion that if they die as a martyr, they're going to get 72 virgins in Paradise (Heaven). They believe it and they say, "Hey, this is great. I'm going to get 72 virgins."

What's the difference between what we believe and what they believe? Well, we look at them and we say, "Well, it's crazy to believe that." That's how the rest of the world looks at us. They say, "It's crazy to believe that you're going to go to Heaven for all eternity." Right, but there's one difference. We have the Holy Spirit of God who is alive in us. God Himself confirms His Word in our hearts. That's how we know.

Abraham believed God. Let's look at God's Word to see what happened next. You would think, "Okay, now he believes Him." But in Genesis 16 the story takes an interesting turn. His wife says to Abraham, "Hey, listen. I have a great idea. God promised you that you were going to have a kid, but it doesn't seem to be happening so quickly."

Does that ever happen to you? You're standing on the promise of God and it doesn't seem to be happening so quickly, so you say, "All right, maybe I better help you, God." Hey God maybe you got this wrong, maybe you need to be realizing that the present plan may not be the best plan.

Sarai (Abram's wife) comes up with an idea. She says, "Look, here's what we're going to do, Abram. We need to have a son, and I can't bear children. I'm nearly ninety years old; why don't you go and lay with the maid, have her kid, and we'll call it ours; that's how we'll inherit the kingdom and that's how we'll move our lineage forward." The Bible tells us in Genesis 16 that Abram heeded the voice of Sarai. Sarai came up with this idea to help God along, because you know, God needs help and He can't accomplish what He wants to without our help. (Yes, this is sarcasm.) They came up with this idea to help God, and Abram agreed.

Now, Abram is 99 years old and the Lord appears to him in Genesis 17. God had a message for him: "As for me, this is my covenant with you: You will be the father of many nations. No longer will you be called Abram; your name will be Abraham, for I have made you a father of many nations. I will make you very fruitful; I will make nations of you, and kings will come from you. I will establish my covenant as an everlasting covenant between me and you and your descendants after you for the generations to come, to be your God and the God of your descendants after you … God also said to Abraham, "As for Sarai your wife, you are no longer to call her Sarai; her name will be Sarah. I will bless her and will surely give you a son by her. I will bless her so that she will be the mother of nations; kings of peoples will come from her" (Genesis 17:4-7, 15-16).

Genesis 17:17 gives us Abraham's reaction, it says, "Abraham fell on his face and laughed." He's like, "God, that's so funny! You're going to give me a child with Sarah – Sarah's going to have a kid?! God, you are hilarious. Can we get down to business?" He didn't believe God. Again, God said that He's going to do something, so why didn't he believe Him? Because, in Abraham's mind, it was inconceivable that this could happen.

Do we sometimes do the same? Do we limit God? Sometimes we put Him in a box and say, "God, because I can't understand how you could do this, then it can't happen." The problem is, when we do this, we're basically making ourselves into God. That's not a good place to be.

Abraham was saying, "God, thanks for the offer. You know, I appreciate you offering that you're going to help me have a kid, but obviously there's been a mistake and you got the paperwork messed up. That's not going to work out, so I'm going to help You accomplish Your plan. I believe Your plan, God, but You were clearly mistaken."

But God said to him, "No. Sarah your wife shall bear you a son. You shall call him Isaac. I will establish my covenant with him, an everlasting covenant, with his descendants after him."

Abraham was still arguing here. He said to God, "Well, listen. What about Ishmael? Take Ishmael and make him the 'it.'" Ishmael was Abraham's son by his handmaiden, not Sarah.

God answers, "Look, I know about Ishmael, but it's not Ishmael through whom I'm going to fulfill my promises. It's going to be through Isaac."

Gods word says this: "And as for Ishmael, I have heard you: I will surely bless him; I will make him fruitful and will greatly increase his numbers. He will be the father of twelve rulers, and I will make him into a great nation. But my covenant I will establish with Isaac, whom Sarah will bear to you by this time next year" (Genesis 17:20-21).

Why do I share this with you? Abraham had a plan, saying, "Look, let's use Ishmael, the son I had with the maidservant, and we can go that way."

But God said, "That's not going to be the plan, but I heard your prayer! I'm going to take care of Ishmael. It's in accordance with my will. I'm going to bless you accordingly."

Remember that. God hears your prayer.

In a later chapter, Sarah overheard the Lord telling Abraham that a child will be born to Abraham and Sarah, and she started laughing, too. She started cracking up. Again, it's the same response: "This can't happen; it's impossible." Then Sarah denied laughing. Sarah laughed to herself as she thought, "After I am worn out and my lord is old, will I now have this pleasure?" Then the Lord said to Abraham, "Why did Sarah laugh and say, 'Will I really have a child, now that I am old?' Is anything too hard for the Lord? I will return to you at the appointed time next year, and Sarah will have a son." Sarah was afraid, so she lied and said, "I did not laugh." But he said, "Yes, you did laugh" (Genesis 18:12-15).

When I read that verse, I thought of Adam and Eve. A similar thing happened with them, right? The truth is, we also do the same thing. We don't trust God to do what He says. They didn't believe. I believe God would have said, "Ye of little faith. According to your faith, it shall be done to you."

Personally, I've seen the miracles of God in my life, even in this last year. Two other times, Abraham didn't trust God's provision. Two other times – in Genesis 12 and Genesis 20 – he lied about being married to Sarah. Sarah was beautiful, and he was worried that when he went before the local king, that they would kill him (Abraham) and take Sarah because she was so pretty. So, he said to Sarah, "Look, here's what we're going to do. Tell them you're my sister. We'll be like brother and sister and that way they won't kill me. I'll live, so we'll be good, right?"

Sarah went along with this and, both times, the kings found out that Abraham had deceived them. They responded by asking, "What are you doing by lying to me? Why would you do this?"

Why did he do it? Because he didn't trust God's provision. He didn't believe that God would protect him. God had made him His promise: "I'll give you so many descendants that they will be like the stars. I'm with you. I'm blessing you." Still, Abraham had a hard time trusting God in some areas.

God has made the same promise to you and me: "I'll never leave you or forsake you. I'm with you always. All things work together for your good. As far as from the East is from the West, I'll remember your sins no more. As high as the heavens are above the earth, that's how much I love you." All these and more are the great promises of God. Sometimes, we don't step into the promises that we have been given. Sometimes we don't believe them.

How does this apply to our lives today? Abraham couldn't comprehend the power of God, just like you and me. Sometimes he didn't believe God could do what He said He would. Abraham and Sarah laughed – they didn't believe God would do what He said in giving them their own child. They didn't trust God, both for the child and to protect them from kings. They didn't trust God to do what He said, so they took control and did what they thought needed to be done.

The Word of God tells us there is a way that seems right to a man, but in the end, it leads to death. Proverbs 3 tells us this: "Trust in the Lord with all your heart and lean not on your own understanding; in all your ways submit to him, and he will make your paths straight" (v. 5-6).

We need to believe God.

Something interesting happened not that long ago right in our church. A guy came into church one Sunday morning looking for deliverance. I hadn't seen him before. He was a stranger, and he said, "I need deliverance."

Another pastor and I went back with him to pray. The guy poured his heart out and said, "I been to six churches looking for deliverance." He added, "After you guys give me deliverance, I'm still going to need more!"

I lovingly told him, "Listen, that's fine. But, that's not what God says. God says, 'who the Son sets free is free indeed'. And God says if he delivers you – you're delivered! You don't need to be re-delivered, and re-delivered, and re-delivered, and re-delivered!"

The other Pastor and I lovingly took the guy through prayer and offered him deliverance and performed a prayer of deliverance on him. The guy didn't need other churches or more deliverance; he needed to believe in the power of God.

That's what you and I need to believe. I believe that message was for me. God wanted to use that guy to remind me of that very same thing: that I need to step into the promises and truth of God. There's no condemnation for those who are in Christ. Perfect love casts out fear and I can accomplish all things through God, who stands with me. I need to step into the truth of God.

What does Christ's death on the cross mean for you? How should we view life, death, and eternity? Romans chapter 8 is complex, but I am telling you, understanding it is having a key to life. I believe it's the difference between freedom in Christ and slavery to the flesh.

We looked at Abraham. Now let's look at Paul.

You know the story of the Apostle Paul. In Romans 7, he makes this point: "For we know that the law is spiritual, but I am carnal, sold under sin. For what I am doing, I do not understand. For what I will to do, that I do not practice; but what I hate, that I do. If, then, I do what I will not to do, I agree with the law that it is good. But now, it is no longer I who do it, but sin that dwells in me. For I know that in me (that is, in my flesh) nothing good dwells; for to will is present with me, but how to perform what is good I do not find. For the good that I will to do, I do not do; but the evil I will not to do, that I practice. Now if I do what I will not to do, it is no longer I who do it, but sin that dwells in me" (v. 14-20).

Yikes! Ever felt like that? Every believer knows in your heart what to do and yet there's this fight, this struggle. "Hey, I know what to do, but my flesh is different. There's this war going on between my flesh and my spirit." You're not alone!

A = Abraham
B = Paul
C = You and me

We're all the same. The same as Abraham – the earthly father of faith. The same as Paul, the unbelievable apostle. So, here's what Paul concludes:

> I delight in the law of God according to the inward man. But I see another law in my members, warring against the law of my mind, and bringing me into captivity to the law of sin which is in my members. O wretched man that I am! Who will deliver me from this body of death? I thank God—through Jesus Christ our Lord! (Romans 7:22-25)

Wouldn't you say that, as a believer, you delight in the law of God? But each of us also faces this "other law" – the law of the flesh. But we can thank God, through Jesus Christ our Lord, that we are rescued.

Abraham and Paul both struggled intensely in spite of knowing God personally! Abraham, in spite of walking with God hand in hand – he still struggled in his flesh. Paul, in spite of having an unbelievable conversion experience on the road to Damascus, was still struggling with his flesh till the day he died – as will you and I. But God has given us victory, and in this chapter, we're going to talk about how to step into the truth of that victory.

Romans chapter 7 ends with this observation: "So then, with the mind I myself serve the law of God, but with the flesh I serve the law of sin" (v. 25).

Romans 8 goes on to say, in verse 1: "There is therefore now no condemnation to those who are in Christ Jesus, who do not walk according to the flesh, but according to the Spirit."

Let me get this right, there's no condemnation for those who are in Jesus? Even though I'm struggling with my flesh, even during the times it seems I'm losing the battle with my flesh, even though I'm fighting with my spirit, Even when I'm realizing that the way I feel things should be, the way I was choosing to live life is not getting me the best results. Even when I'm realizing that the present plan may not be the best plan. I do not need to be condemned? That's right! It might seem like I'm losing because I know what I'm supposed to do, or because I'm not doing it all the time – but God rescued me. God rescued you. Therefore, there's no condemnation for me or you, who are in Christ Jesus, if we don't walk according to the flesh, but according to the Spirit.

This is one of the toughest lines in the Bible! Man, if I could just do that, I'd have no problems. All I have to do is walk according to the Spirit, not according to the flesh, and there's no condemnation. Well, yeah, but there's more. Why? Because if you think like that, you'll be like the guy in the back room looking for deliverance six times and never being satisfied. Satan will kick the crap out of you every day of your life. Oh, you might be a good Christian, you know you'll go to Heaven if you die, but you'll waste the abundant life God has in store for you – the life of victory, the life of no condemnation.

Here's how it works. Here's how you get there. This is the key, and it's this simple:

> For the law of the Spirit of life in Christ Jesus has made me free from the law of sin and death. ...
>
> For those who live according to the flesh set their minds on the things of the flesh, but those who live according to the Spirit, the things of the Spirit." (Romans 8:2, 5)

Here it is again. Here's this thing that seems like an impossible task. Well, in order to get it, we must set out minds on the things of the Spirit. Why? He gives the reason why in the next verses:

> To be carnally minded is death, but to be spiritually minded is life and peace. The carnal mind is enmity against God; for it is not subject to the law of God, nor can it be. So then, those who are in the flesh cannot please God. (v. 6-8)

Aw, man. I've got a problem. See, I'm in the flesh. You're in the flesh. Does that mean I can never please God? No, that's not what it means. This can be hard to understand.

I don't have to do everything right all the time to please God. I'm not under the Old Testament law or rules, regulations, and requirements. I'm under the New Testament freedom of the shed blood of Jesus Christ that He has paid for my sins. Here is the verse, and this could easily be the most powerful verse in the Bible. You get this, and you get it all; you miss this, and you miss everything.

Here's positive proof with 100% certainty, the only litmus test; it's Romans 8:9: "But you are not in the flesh, but in the Spirit, if indeed the Spirit of God dwells in you."

This is how we know if you live in the flesh or the Spirit; you're not in the flesh if the Spirit of God dwells in you. That is the requirement for being in the Spirit - that God dwells in you. The requirement is not that you live a perfect life. The requirement is not that you never fail or that you always do everything that you think God wants you to do. Of course, we're going to strive for that.

This is not an excuse to sin; quite the opposite. We always want to do our best to strive for God, but Satan is a deceiver and a liar and he's tricking you into thinking there's this bar you can never hit. "Well, look at you, Jack. You're in the flesh. You had an evil thought; you're bad." Oh, you mean like Abraham, Paul, David, Noah, everybody? Every person who ever lived – you mean I'm just like them? "Right, Jack. That makes you no good. You stink." But God says no, I am good. I'm wholly blameless and clothed in the righteousness of Christ by His death. So, if Christ dwells in me, that means I'm living in the Spirit and not in the flesh. Look at Gods word in Romans 8:12-14: "Therefore, brethren, we are debtors—not to the flesh, to live according to the flesh. For if you live according to the flesh you will die; but if by the Spirit you put to death the deeds of the body, you will live. For as many as are led by the Spirit of God, these are sons of God."

We expect to see evidence of Christ in your life. We expect you to live a life that glorifies God. Clearly, we should see that. As many as are led by the Spirit of God, these are sons of God. Are you led by the Spirit of God? If I'm led by somebody, that means I follow them. Yes, I am a follower of Jesus Christ. Yes, that means I am in the Spirit and not in the flesh. Of course, I'm living in the flesh for as long as I'm living this earthly life – as did Abraham and Paul, and as do all the rest of you; but I'm not bound by its rules and regulations. I'm not condemned by it. I'm free from it because I live by the Spirit, because Christ dwells in my heart and through His Spirit I am led by Him.

Why am I not condemned? It's not because I'm perfect. It's not because I did this or that. It is only because of what Christ did and by my stepping into the truth of God and accepting His Word and not letting Satan trick me or fool me or condemn me. That is the proof.

Does Christ dwell in your heart? Are you led by the Spirit of God? If you know that's true, then you should have 100% certainty. If I said to you, "Listen, I decided to make a new set of rules. Here's the deal, you can only eat what I tell you, you can only drive 30 miles per hour, you can only go where I tell you, work where I tell you, and do what I say," you would laugh at me.

You'd say, "Jack, pretty funny but we're not doing that."

"Why?"

"Because you don't control us."

Well, how come you're not laughing at Satan? He doesn't control you. He's got no control over you. Paul goes on to make a powerful statement: "For you did not receive the spirit of bondage again to fear, but you received the Spirit of adoption by whom we cry out, 'Abba, Father.' The Spirit Himself bears witness with our spirit that we are children of God" (Romans 8:15-16).

The only way I know God is real is by the Holy Spirit in my heart. That's what separates us from ISIS and their idea of heaven with the 72 virgins and everything else. God Himself confirms His truth in our hearts. If you don't have that confirmation, you don't know God yet. You can know God anytime you decide to know God. Simply call on Him, accept Him as Lord and believe in Him. He is there as a loving Father, wanting to love you and bless you in everything you do.

Of course, if we're children of God, then we're heirs of God, joint heirs with Christ. Christ is our brother; if we suffer with Him, we will also be glorified together. This is the point expressed in the next verse. The Apostle Paul goes on to say: "For I consider that the sufferings of this present time are not worthy to be compared to the glory which shall be revealed in us" (Romans 8:18).

Wait a minute, God. Now we just went through all this stuff. I get that Abraham and Paul equals you and me, and that we're all the same; I'm convinced by your Word, Lord, that I am dwelling in the Spirit; I get that there's a battle going on against the flesh, I get that there is spiritual warfare; I get you've given me the tools of victory (Ephesians chapter 6: "put on the full armor of God"); I get that if I resist the devil, he'll flee from me; I get that if I come closer to you, you'll come closer to me. I get it; I understand… but now you're telling me that there's this suffering. That I must suffer with you to be glorified with you?

At this point, there's a choice in front of you. Don't be like Abraham, doubting that God could do what He said. God says, "This is nothing that you're going through. It's like a little headache. Oh, I know it seems like tragedy and life and everything to you, but it's nothing compared to the glory of all eternity. A small price to pay compared to what you will receive in return."

Do we believe God or not? "Well, God. I don't understand how that could be!" That's right. You don't understand because you're not God. God says, "My ways are higher than yours. Now you only know in part what you'll one day know in full." So, the sufferings of this present time: the Las Vegas school shooting, the Puerto Rico hurricane, sex trafficking, sickness, economic collapse, drug addiction, rape, abuse, degradation of human life – man, there's so much suffering. Anything that you go through in this life, that you do for the Kingdom of God, could count as you suffering.

How could you be surprised at what's happening in the world today? God has told you everything that's going to happen, past and present and future. I would think, as you see events unfold, you would rejoice in the fact that God has authored our ending and our eternity. I don't think you'd be surprised. But I want to prove it with from the Word of God. Keep this in context with your life and what's going on in the world:

> *To everything there is a season, a time for every purpose under Heaven.* (Ecclesiastes 3:1)

There's a time for every purpose under Heaven. There's a season for everything. So why are you surprised at these seasons? In the following Bible verses from Ecclesiastes chapter 3:2-8, He breaks that down so we're sure to know what it means.

> *There is a time to be born and a time to die.*

A baby was recently born in our church ministry while my father just got buried. Isn't there a time for everyone to be born? And there is a time for everyone to die.

There is a time to plant and a time to pluck what is planted.

Every farmer knows that. Every person in the farming business knows, "I put the seed in, and then I wait, and then I harvest it." There's a time to plant and a time to harvest, no doubt.

There is a time to kill, and a time to heal.

What's that? There's a time to kill? Well, sure. If somebody walked through the door of our church shooting at us, I'd hope somebody would kill him quickly. There's a time. But He also says that there's a time to heal.

There's a time to break down, and there's a time to build up.

A time to build the set for the show, and a time to tear it down after the show is over. There's a time for each of these things.

There's a time to weep, and a time to laugh.

There are times when you should be crying, and there are times when you should be hysterically laughing your butt off. There's both. There will be darkness and light. There will be sunshine and rain. There's both in this world. It's all here.

There's a time to mourn, and a time to dance.

Personally, I was dancing when my dad died in celebration of his life, because I had the greatest dad in the world. He lived the greatest life; that's the difference between saved people versus unsaved people; between people who see it from God's eyes and people who don't. Seeing through God's eyes, I'm like, "Thank you, God. You gave me the greatest father ever and he lived on earth for 85 years. You must love me so much! Thank you for the time I had and the time he had. My dad enjoyed his life. He loved people and people loved him."

The one who doesn't have God is thinking, "Well, I needed more time! Why did he go?!" Why? Because there's a time to be born and a time to die. Who are we to question God's timing? As Christians, we should be giving gratitude and thanks for everything that we have.

> *There's a time to cast away stones, and a time to gather stones.*

A time to throw them away, and a time to get them.

> *There's a time to embrace, and a time to refrain from embracing.*

There's a time I should be hugging you and a time I shouldn't be, depending on the circumstance.

> *There's a time to gain, and a time to lose.*

It often depends on your perspective. It depends on how you look at it. But God has ordained all these things; there's no surprise.

> *There's a time to keep, and a time to throw away.*

There's a time you should be saving stuff and a time you should toss certain crap in the garbage.

> *There's a time to tear, and a time to sew. There's a time to keep silent, and a time to speak. There's a time to love, and a time to hate.*

And lastly, it says,

> *There's a time for war, and a time for peace.*

Hasn't God covered it all? Hasn't He covered every purpose? So why would you be surprised? Here's what Solomon lays out in that chapter of Ecclesiastes, the last thing he says is:

> God has made everything beautiful in its time. He has put eternity in our hearts. Except that no one can find out the work that God does from beginning to end.

Only God knows what He is doing from beginning to end. But He has put eternity in our hearts. Thank you, Jesus. Solomon goes on to say:

> I know that nothing is better for them to rejoice and to do good in their lives. That every man should eat, drink, and enjoy the good of his labor. It is the gift of God. I know that whatever God does it shall be forever, nothing can be added to it.

REALIZING THAT THE PRESENT PLAN MAY NOT BE THE BEST PLAN   67

Nothing is better than to rejoice. Isaiah, Joel, Thessalonians, all through the Bible, God tells you how He wants you to live. Be thankful, joyful, happy, rejoicing, singing, excited about this moment in life; it's your turn at bat. This is your life. Don't be scared it's going to end. Don't be frustrated about what's happening.

You don't wake up on a stormy day and say, "I can't live today because it's raining." No. You'd rather it be sunny, but you embrace the circumstance. Even when I'm realizing that the present plan may not be the best plan. I embrace the circumstance. I trust God. I pray continually

Psalm 1:18 has a great line. It's a famous line: "This is the day the Lord has made – we will rejoice and be glad in it."

I've heard that verse thousands of times. I read it the last couple of months and God brought it out to me in a different way. It made me realize, "This is the day the Lord has made" is a fact. No believer would tell me differently; no Christian would argue that God has made this day. "This is the day the Lord has made." That's a fact.

"I will rejoice and be glad in it." That's a choice. I need to make that choice every morning. God has been washing over me with His Word over the past couple of months. He's been reminding me of this every day; I'm getting up every day and I'm saying, "This is the day the Lord has made. I am choosing to rejoice and be glad in it."

That is my choice, and it is affecting the way I live and think in the most positive of ways. So, I want to remind you that it is a choice.

I know the Lord is real. I've known it since March 10th, 1991, the day the Lord came into my life – that wonderful, glorious day. The truth is, the Lord was always in my life. That's was simply the day I responded to His work and accepted Him as my Lord and Savior. On that day, I said, "Lord, I'm giving you my life. I've tried to run my own life and I just made a mess of it. I was never satisfied by the things of the world and I had all of them: money, power, jobs, relationships, yet I was empty inside. God, you showed me that you were the way to peace, happiness, and joy."

I invited Christ into my life that day, and everything He said has been true. Day after day, it's gotten better and better – for the last 26 years – and it will keep getting better. My prayer is that it is getting better for you every day as well.

Reflect on the points that came up in this chapter. Ask the Holy Spirit what His message is for you. Was it the lessons of Abraham? Is it that you have a hard time believing in the power of God? Is it that you don't trust Him? Are you trying to make your own plans to help God along? If that's the case, I pray that you would trust God today.

Was it the message of Paul? The reminder that the Spirit of God dwells in us; therefore, we are not of the flesh. We have all of God that we need, and we simply need to step into it and walk into the truth of God.

Was it the truth from Ecclesiastes, from Solomon? The realization that the Lord oversees everything. He has ordained all of time – past, present, and that which is to come for everyone. He has ordained eternity. That's why He has instructed us in His Word to leap and rejoice. That's why we're to be so happy; the Holy Spirit is with us every step of the way, and our eternity in Heaven is guaranteed. What a great deal!

I hope and pray that you look into your heart and ask the Holy Spirit what you and He need to resolve and settle. I pray that we would settle on the fact that God is God. Even though your flesh is fighting against you, you can decide that you're just going to believe God, go His way, and live a godly life.

May we walk through our lives with the safety net of knowing that God is with us every step of the way. We need not fear falling.

You can be sure that your Redeemer lives. He lives and His Word is true. I pray you would be excited to walk that journey and have that reward for all eternity.

Chapter Four

QUESTIONING OUR DESTINY AND THE "WHO KNOWS"

A friend of mine believes that God might have given him the gift of healing. I'm not sure if he has that gift or not, and I'm not sure that he knows for sure at this point, but we were having lunch recently and he made a comment that blew me away.

He said, "Listen, if I had this gift of healing, then everything would change."

"How so?" I asked.

He answered, "If I knew it was real, I'd have to spend my whole life helping people. How could I not?"

God pierced my heart, and I began thinking about it. I thought, wait a minute. We already have the gift of the Holy Spirit. We already have the gift of God in our lives and we know it's real. How could we not spend our whole lives living sacrificially on earth for the Kingdom of God? This is exactly what God calls us to do. How can we not do that? I'm asking myself that and, in this chapter, I'm asking you, too.

Another friend, Marsha, serves the elder community as a Guardian ad Litem, where she protects the rights and dignity of elderly people who have no one to look out for them. She is in a Tuesday morning Bible study group with me. I've known her for three years. During that whole time her daughter, Stephanie, had terminal cancer. I watched Marsha deal with this until Stephanie passed away. Everyone in the Bible study group watched, her family watched, her neighbors, the community, the medical professionals who were all treating Stephanie, and others watched her deal with her daughter slowly dying from cancer. She exhibited the grace of God, the mercy and love of God, every minute of every day throughout this ordeal.

God used her in her trial and tribulation as a shining light for the Kingdom of God. She had the peace of joy, the joy of God in her life through this difficult time, and so did her husband as they went through this trial. They celebrated when Stephanie died, knowing she was in the Kingdom of God for all eternity and knowing for sure that they would see her again.

It's unbelievable how God used her trial and tribulation. I was thinking about this as I was reading about the Apostle Paul in Colossians, Philippians, and all through Corinthians. If I had to summarize Paul's whole ministry during his whole life, it was simply this: Be the message!

There's a big difference between knowing the message and being the message. I believe Marsha was being the message. I believe Paul was being the message. Being the message is singing in jail at midnight. Being the message is praising God through all your trials and tribulations, no matter what they are. That is how you be the message. That's what we are called to be – living sacrifices, as Jesus was – for the Kingdom of God. Our lives are to be the messages and people should see us living out this message no matter what we go through.

My kids, whom I love very much, never tell me how great I am when their needs are met. In other words, when they have what they want, they never just come up voluntarily and tell me how great I am arbitrarily. However, when they need something, oh man!

I hear, "Daddy, you're great."

It's wonderful. I mean, I really must be this amazing dad, because they tell me so whenever they need something. It's comical with our kids, but I thought, oh my goodness; am I doing that with God? I was at God's feet recently and I thought, I'm truly at the feet of God, but am I here because I'm desperate and I'm helpless and I'm in despair? Is that what has driven me to the feet of God? And why am I not here all of the time?

God spoke to my heart – just as I hope He speaks to your heart – and I repented. I said, "God if that truly was my motive and I'm only here because I need something, then please forgive me. I repent and see the error of my ways. Change my heart." So, what should you do?

I love the message in this word from God:

> 'Even now,' declares the Lord, 'return to me
> with all your heart, with fasting and weeping
> and mourning.'

> Rend your heart and not your garments.
> Return to the Lord your God, for he is gracious
> and compassionate, slow to anger, abounding in
> love, and he relents from sending calamity. Who
> knows? He may turn and relent and leave behind
> a blessing. (Joel 2:12)

Understand the context here: God had shut off blessings from the people of Israel because they had been disobedient, and nothing was flowing their way. You think they were questioning their destiny and the "who knows"?

I love the question, "Who knows?"

You've got to understand the context of the "who knows." It's not a context of, "Well, I wonder who really knows."

No, it's a context of "who knows, so you should be paying close attention to this because this is probably going to happen."

For instance, if we were having a hurricane in Florida and it was probably coming our way and I said, "Who knows! We could get a direct hit," that means I had better be prepared. I better be at Home Depot or Lowe's getting my stuff together and making sure I'm prepared because who knows? It could hit us.

Here is Joel saying, "If you do the right thing, if you turn back to God, who knows! Maybe God will turn and relent and leave a blessing." Of course, God being God, He does.

In Job 34:33, a friend of Job was speaking to him and he said this great line. You don't need to know the whole context of the Job story, but here's the line: "Should God then reward you on your terms, when you refuse to repent?"

This is a great philosophical question. He was asking it almost sarcastically when he was talking to Job about stuff. He basically said, "Let me get this right. I hear your argument, so let me ask you this question: If you're giving God an argument that's not in line with God's Word, should God reward you on your terms when you refuse to repent and get in line with the Word of God?"

And do we often do this with God? Do we put God in a box limiting His power and position to our own understanding? Do we negotiate with God? Do we justify our own wants and desires that are not in context with the Word of God? Do we tell God our terms of surrender, but refuse to listen to His?

Should God reward you on your own terms when you refuse to repent? Can you imagine a kid just saying, "Hey, give me everything I want when I don't listen to what you say!"? We understand, as a parent, that's not quite the way it works.

Here's what God said to Job, and I love this. God broke my heart with this because I had to ask myself if I could make the same statement. I pray you would ask yourself this same question today. Job said, "Let God weigh me in honest scales, and He will know that I am blameless" (Job 31:6).

Of course, you probably know the story of Job. Job was persecuted, had everything taken away, and yet God rewarded Job's righteousness at the end of the book and blessed him for his faithfulness. This is the lesson for us: we are to stay faithful. But as Job was being accused, here was his response to his friends and to God. It was, "Hey, wait a minute. Let God weigh me in honest scales," which means let God look at my heart and my actions and my life. When He sees all of me, He will know the truth about me… and then He'll know that I am blameless," because Job really was genuinely blameless before the Lord.

Can you and I say the same thing? Remember, this is not about perfection in your life. This is not about Old Testament – 600 plus laws and commandments that you must abide by to get into the Kingdom of Heaven. No, this is about the grace and love and mercy of Jesus Christ being showered onto your heart and life. Do you have gratitude and joy reflecting that back into the world at large? That would make you righteous in God's eyes.

I have a story to tell you in this chapter. You may or may not know the story, so I want to describe the main characters first.

We have a hero in today's story, and that's Esther. This story comes out of the book of Esther. We also have a king – King Xerxes – who was king of Persia at that time. He was a son of Darius. He had taken over and the Persian Empire was looking to expand and grow and take over more of Greece. They were on an acquisition spree highlighted by killing, war, and death. We have his queen, Vashti. That was King Xerxes' wife. We have a villain, Haman. You need a good villain in a story, right? Haman is our villain. He's the Joker, the Riddler; he's the evil guy. We also have Esther's uncle, whose name was Mordecai, and he was Jewish. Mordecai took

Esther in as a little girl, because Esther had no mother and father; he was Esther's uncle, but literally raised her as her father.

So those are the characters. Let's look at how the story begins. "King Xerxes was in high spirits," says Esther chapter 1. He was having a seven-day party. Seven days straight – that's a good party. I mean, Thanksgiving is only one day, so seven days sounds like a major party. As they were partying during those days, they would eat and drink, and make merry. Pretty much, they were drinking for seven days straight.

The king was with all his buddies, and to put it mildly he was very buzzed and having a great time. I'm paraphrasing this story. The king was with all his buddies and he wanted to show off, so he said, "I have the most beautiful wife and I'm going to bring her out so you can see how beautiful she is."

The king sent his man to go get his wife and Vashti says, "I'm not coming." Now that is not a good move on the queen's part. In those days, you did not disobey the king, no matter who you were. I have no clue why she did that, except that God's hand was probably at work so we would have an amazing story.

It says in Esther chapter 1, verse 12, "Queen Vashti refused to come; then the king became furious and burned with anger." He was not happy with his wife's behavior. We go on to chapter 2, and Xerxes' fury has calmed down. The party is over, but he remembered what his wife had done.

His advisors said, "Listen, King, why don't we scour among the beautiful young virgins for the king? We need to get you a new wife."

The king said, "Absolutely. This is a great idea. I would love a wife who would actually listen to me." They went through the town and they started to look at all the young women. They narrowed them down into a group that would be appropriate for the king. I don't know if they're down to 20 or 30 or 50, but they narrowed it down further and further and wouldn't you know it, Esther, our hero, was one of the girls. She was beautiful; she was one of the ones who was chosen to be among the finalist for the king.

The king's servants took care of all the girls for at least a month. They made them beautiful and got them ready and told them how to act and behave before the king. You need to understand that

Esther did not reveal her nationality – that she was Jewish because Mordecai had forbidden her to do so. Esther chapter 2, verse 10 says, "Every day, Mordecai would walk back and forth to the courtyard, to the harem, to find out how Esther was doing and what was happening to her."

As a Jew, he was not allowed to go inside the king's castle and headquarters. But he stood outside the gate every day as people were coming and going. He would say, "Hey, what's going on inside there?"

"Well, we're down to ten finalists, Esther's one of them."

"How's Esther doing?"

"Well, she's doing pretty good so far."

"Sounds good." His ear was to the ground, because she was the daughter whom he loved. Esther's turn came, and wouldn't you know it, the king picked Esther. Esther was the chosen one. He was attracted to Esther more than any of the others and he set a royal crown on her head and he made her the queen instead of Vashti. Esther is in; Vashti is out.

Mordecai, who was hanging around the gate, heard that two of the king's servants were very upset with the king. The king's servants, Bigthana and Teresh, guarded the door to the kingdom. They became angry with the king and they had a plot to assassinate him. You know, it's hard to find good help these days. Really, when your own guys are going to kill you, that's not a good thing.

Mordecai heard this and sent a message to Esther and told her what was going on. Esther told the king. The king, in turn, killed these two guys and was happy with Esther; it was a great thing. When Esther reported it to the king, she gave credit to Mordecai.

Now we get to chapter 3, and King Xerxes was honoring Haman – the villain! Haman was an officer in the king's court. He was not a soldier, but a nobleman; he was a man of high honor. He was an advisor to the king, and the king was taking the time to elevate Haman even further. He was saying, "You are my number one man. I've given you the highest seat, the seat of honor, higher than all of the other nobles."

Well, all the royal officials at the king's gate bowed down and knelt to pay honor to Haman, but Mordecai would not kneel or pay him honor. By the way, if that sounds familiar, yes, it's the same thing Daniel wouldn't do. He wouldn't submit to another god. Haman found out that Mordecai was not bowing down, and Haman was furious. It tells us this in Esther 3:

> When Haman saw Mordecai would not kneel down or pay him honor, he was enraged. Yet having learned who Mordecai's people were, he scorned the idea of killing only one of them. Instead, Haman looked for a way to destroy all of Mordecai's people, the Jews, throughout the whole kingdom. (v. 5-6)

Haman went up to the king; remember, Haman was in a great spot. He was literally the number one guy under the king, and he said this:

> There is a certain people dispersed among the peoples in all the provinces of your kingdom who keep themselves separate. Their customs are different from those of all other people, and they do not obey the king's laws; it is not in the king's best interest to tolerate them. If it pleases the king, let a decree be issued to destroy them, and I will give ten thousand talents of silver to the king's administrators for the royal treasury.
> (v. 8-9)

Basically, Haman said, "So, let's get rid of this nuisance and, by the way, I'm going to give you all this money." So, the king took his signet ring, which was a king's seal and signature of authority. When kings stamped something with the signet ring, it meant that it had come from the king, that it was an order from the king. That's how you knew. If it didn't have the stamp, you didn't know if it was an order from the king."

The king took his ring, gave it to Haman, and said, "Do with the people as you please. Do whatever you want." So, Haman was very excited. He wrote up a decree, a decree from the king himself, signed it with the signet ring, and sent couriers throughout the towns and provinces with this message: "On this day of this month, we're going to kill all the Jews. We're going to annihilate them and take everything they have as plunder." He sent this to all the people in all the provinces so they could all act accordingly on this particular day.

Chapter 4 tells us Mordecai learned of what is going to happen to the Jews. He heard, as other people heard too, and it says, "He tore his clothes, put on sackcloth and ashes, and went out into the city crying loudly and bitterly. But he only went out as far as the king's gate because no one clothed in sack cloth was able to enter" (v. 1-2).

So, Mordecai said, "Look, my people are going to get wiped out." He was crying, he was distraught, he was praying – what was he going to do? Esther's representatives came and told her about Mordecai. They had seen what was happening; they had seen Mordecai's response. Esther heard this, and remember she was now the queen, and she was in great distress. She sent clothes to Mordecai to put on instead of the sackcloth he was wearing, but he didn't accept them. He turned away the clothes. So, Esther summoned one of her trusted servants and ordered him to find out what was troubling Mordecai and why.

Here's where the story gets good. The servant went out to Mordecai and Mordecai told him everything that had happened, including the amount of money Haman had promised to pay to the treasury. He gave him a copy of the text of the edict for the annihilation of the Jews which had been published so all could see. He said, "Show to it Esther and explain what's happening."

He also told the servant, "Instruct her to go into the king's presence to beg for mercy and plead with him for her people." (v. 8) Now, this was not a simple thing to ask. No, no, no. Why? Because, unless you were invited into the king's presence by the king – if you came into the king's room and he looked at you and he didn't hold up the gold scepter – you were killed, immediately. The gold scepter meant, "Hey, it's cool, you can come in." There was a lot of instant justice back in that day. You died immediately. So, this was not, "Oh, by the way, go talk to your husband and see if he'll do this for us." No, this was, "Your life is on the line."

Esther responded, "Look, I haven't seen the king in 30 days. I'm scared that if I go and talk to him and he doesn't extend the gold scepter, I'm going to die." Esther said that to Mordecai and the servant responded to Mordecai with what Esther said.

Mordecai responded and he said, "Don't think that because you're in the king's house you alone will be saved. For if you remain silent at this time, relief and deliverance for the Jews will arise from another place but you and your father's family will perish" (v. 13-14).

Don't take that line lightly. Mordecai says, "Get this right: if you remain silent, relief and deliverance will come for the Jews, but it will come from another place." What does that mean? That means, regardless of what you do or what you don't do, God's will is going to be accomplished.

The same is true in your life and my life. Hey, we can miss the blessing. Esther could have missed the blessing, but Mordecai was reminding her, "Look, regardless of what you do or don't do, God's going to take care of what God needs to take care of because God's Will is going to be accomplished no matter what."

The only question we should be asking ourselves is, "Do we want to be along for part of the ride and get the blessing and be a part of the Kingdom?" I would think that the answer is yes. So, this is the great line; see if it rings a bell with you.

Mordecai added "And who knows! Who knows, but that you have come to your royal position for such a time as this." (v. 14)

Who knows!

Perhaps all this has happened, you've come to this spot, this point in time, for such a time as this – to act on behalf of the Kingdom of God. One time – one place. This time – this place – your time.

Who knows? How about you in your life? How about me in my life? Have we been in those spots? Will we be in those spots where we have an opportunity to respond for or against the Kingdom of God? And, oh, by the way, if you don't respond for, you're responding against. There is no neutral ground.

There will be times in your life where God calls you and uses you for such a time as this. Hey, maybe it's just giving a comforting word to somebody. Maybe it's to offer mercy, peace, and hope.

Maybe you, like Marsha, had to deal with your child's death and it's for such a time as this – so the world could see.

That doesn't mean that's the only purpose of your life, but it certainly means it's a key one. It's a key purpose of your life… for such a time as this.

Esther said to Mordecai, "Okay, listen. Go get all the Jews who are in the city and provinces and have them fast for me – don't eat or drink for three days – and my attendants and I will fast also. When this is done, I will go to the king."

Esther was smart. She knew, "I better pray." Jesus knew when things got tough, "I better pray."

I hope you and I remember that we had better pray. Oh, but then, we had better act. Esther prayed and then she acted. We should pray and then act, and move forward and act on behalf of the Kingdom of God. She made the choice to follow God and do the right thing.

Whatever trials and tribulations you're going through in your life, could it be you're born for such a time as this? Could it be that, as God says, "I have created you to do good works which I have prepared in advance for you to do?" (Ephesians 2:10) Could it be that your whole life hinges on that verse?

God is not a liar; He's telling the truth. "I created you to do good works which I have prepared in advance for you to do … for such a time as this." Yes, but you must do them. You must do that, and you do that by making the right choice each day. By walking with God each and every day, you don't have to think about what His right wishes are because you're so close to God, you're so sensitive to the Spirit of God that – like Marsha and I hope like all of us – God is oozing out of you as you go through the trials and tribulations of this world.

So, what happened to our hero and our story? Esther did go before the king. The king gave her the gold scepter. In other words, he said, "Come on in." She was spared; she didn't die. And then the king said, "What is your request? Even up until half the kingdom, it will be given to you."

Now, that's just a formality line the King used to show satisfaction in a situation. We also heard it in the days of Herod when the wife's daughter came and danced before him and he said, "What do you want? I'll give you up to half my kingdom." It's a formality; they really did not mean the person could have up to half the kingdom (I think if you took it they'd probably kill you so they could get it back). It was the phrase of the day. "Take half my kingdom. What do you want? What's your request, up to half the kingdom?"

So, Esther said, in chapter 5, verse 4, "If it pleases the king, let the king together with Haman, come to a banquet that I have prepared for him."

"Bring Haman at once," the king says, "so we may do what Esther asks" (v. 5).

So, the king and Haman went to the banquet that Esther had prepared. They were drinking wine, and the king again asked Esther, "Now what is your petition? It will be given to you – even up unto half the kingdom – it will be granted" (v. 6).

Esther replied, "My request is this: If the king regards me with favor, and it pleases the king to grant my petition and fulfill my request, let the king and Haman come tomorrow to the banquet I have prepared for them. Then I will answer the king's question" (v. 7-8).

Haman left that day and he was happy – he was like the happiest man in the world. He saw Mordecai at the gate, and he observed again that Mordecai neither rose nor showed fear in his presence. The Bible tells us he was filled with rage against Mordecai. Nevertheless, Haman restrained himself and went home. Haman called together his friends and he said, "Look, I can't believe this," boasting to his friends about his great wealth, and his many sons, and all the ways the king had honored him and had elevated him above all the other nobles and officials.

He went on to say, in Esther 5, verse 12, "And that's not all, I'm the only person Queen Esther invited to accompany the king to the banquet she gave." Me. Me alone. I am the man. I go with the king. How cool was that? "But all this…" Haman said to his friends, "… gives me no satisfaction as I see that Jew Mordecai sitting at the king's gate."

So, his wife and his friends said to him, "Listen, we have an idea. Let's set up a pole, a long pole, 75 feet high, so we can impale Mordecai on it. That's a good way to get revenge on him" (v. 14). Haman was delighted just thinking about it. Oh, this is going to be so great. I get to go to the banquet tomorrow. I'm going to impale Mordechai on this pole. This is like the greatest day ever. And Haman ordered the pole set up.

We go into Esther chapter 6, which is very interesting:

> That night the king could not sleep; so he ordered the book of the chronicles, the record of his reign, to be brought in and read to him. It was found recorded there that Mordecai had exposed Bigthan and Teresh, two of the king's officers who guarded the doorway, who had conspired to assassinate King Xerxes. "What honor and recognition has Mordecai received for this?" The king asked. "Nothing has been done for him," his attendants answered. (v. 1-3)

Now before we go further, let's get this right. The king could not sleep. Why do you think that happened? Then he said, "Bring me my records, I want to read them just at random," and he opened the page because he couldn't sleep. No, it wasn't random. God was at work in his life. In Mordecai's life, in Esther's life, God was at work even when they couldn't see it. God is at work even when you are questioning your destiny and the who knows.

God is at work in your life, 24/7, night and day, for all of eternity, if you can imagine – even when you can't see it. God woke up the king. God had the king turn to that page. God had the king say, "Hey, what have we done to honor Mordecai?" This is God at work when you can't see it. Therefore, you need to have faith. Therefore, you need to keep going, no matter what you see. No matter what your circumstances look like, you need to trust God and have faith stated in Romans 8:28, "that all things are working together for the good of those that love God."

So, when the king said, "What honor and recognition has Mordecai received for this?" He was told "Nothing has been done for him." The king said, "Who is in the court?" Now Haman had just entered the outer court of the palace to speak to the king about impaling Mordecai on the pole he had set up for him. (v. 4)

This was his priority. He said, "I can't wait to come see the king to tell him I'm going to impale Mordecai." But then the king was up and can't sleep and says, "Bring Haman in."

> When Haman entered, the king asked him, "What should be done for the man the king delights to honor?" Now Haman thought to himself, "Who is there that the king would rather honor than me?" So he answered the king, "For the man the king delights to honor, have them bring a royal robe the king has worn and a horse the king has ridden, one with a royal crest placed on its head. Then let the robe and horse be entrusted to one of the king's most noble princes. Let them robe the man the king delights to honor, and lead him on the horse through the city streets, proclaiming before him, 'This is what is done for the man the king delights to honor!'" (v. 6-9)

In other words, parade him through the streets and let everybody see how much you want to honor him, because Haman thought, you're going to be doing this for me.

Of course, the king was looking to honor Mordecai when he realized that Mordecai had saved his life from an assassination. God woke him up and helped him realize it.

"So, go at once," the king commanded, and Haman is the one chosen to be leading Mordecai out through the streets. He is furious that he's got to do this, but he also knows, "I'm going to impale this guy soon so I guess I can stand it for five more minutes."

The parade is over, Mordecai is honored, it's time for the banquet. Chapter 7:2-10 tells us the king and Haman went to Esther's banquet:

> As they were drinking wine on the second day, the king again asked, "Queen Esther, what is your petition? It will be given you. What is your request? Even up to half the kingdom, it will be granted."

Then Queen Esther answered, "If I have found favor with you, Your Majesty, and if it pleases you, grant me my life—this is my petition. And spare my people—this is my request. For I and my people have been sold to be destroyed, killed and annihilated. If we had merely been sold as male and female slaves, I would have kept quiet, because no such distress would justify disturbing the king."

King Xerxes asked Queen Esther, "Who is he? Where is he—the man who has dared to do such a thing?" Esther said, "An adversary and enemy! This vile Haman!"

Then Haman was terrified before the king and queen. The king got up in a rage, left his wine and went out into the palace garden. But Haman, realizing that the king had already decided his fate, stayed behind to beg Queen Esther for his life.

Just as the king returned from the palace garden to the banquet hall, Haman was falling on the couch where Esther was reclining. The king exclaimed, "Will he even molest the queen while she is with me in the house?"

As soon as the word left the king's mouth, they covered Haman's face. Then Harbona, one of the eunuchs attending the king, said, "A pole reaching to a height of fifty cubits stands by Haman's house. He had it set up for Mordecai, who spoke up to help the king."

The king said, "Impale him on it!" So they impaled Haman on the pole he had set up for Mordecai. Then the king's fury subsided.

What Haman had meant for evil, God had used for good. The last chapter tells us there was a happy ending to the story. Mordecai became second in rank to King Xerxes. He was prominent among the Jews. He was held in high esteem by his fellow Jews. Why? The

Word of God tells us it was because he worked for the good of his people and spoke up for the welfare of all the Jews. It's a happy ending.

Your story also has a happy ending. Who knows, but you were born for such a time as this – maybe it's an act of kindness, maybe it's sharing the love of Christ, maybe it's forgiveness or mercy, maybe it's keeping the faith, maybe it's fighting a furious battle – but your job and your mission is to do the right thing and God will take care of the rest. He has taken care of the rest both here and in Heaven and in eternity.

So, what do we make of this? What do we make of Mordecai's faith and Esther – "for such a time as this" – and doing the right thing? What do we make of this in our own lives? What is God saying today in your own heart – your own life?

Esther could have protected herself and sold out her people.

Job could have lost his faith in God.

Mordecai and Daniel could have bowed down to other gods.

There are a host of other examples, not just in the Word of God historically, but in the lives of Christians living today. That's the example we should be. They could have! Esther could have protected herself and sold out her people. Job could have lost his faith in God. Daniel and Mordecai could have bowed down to the king – but they didn't! They didn't.

You could live a life for the flesh instead of a life for the Spirit. May it be said of you and me, "But they didn't." May that be the way history records our lives. Because, who knows, perhaps the Lord wasn't kidding when He said He would bless you abundantly and exceedingly, more than you could ask or imagine.

Who knows what that looks like?

Only God.

God will use so much in His Word to pierce our hearts and speak to us, if only we would listen. And when we don't, He always tells us the same thing. It was the first message from John, and then Jesus echoed it when He came, and that was… repent.

Repent and turn back to God, for the Kingdom is at hand! My prayer is that we would listen, that we would repent, that we would be at God's feet willingly, lovingly, excitedly, to partake and see and be a part of this life that He has in store for us.

My prayer is that we, too, would consider our trials and tribulations as pure joy, knowing that God is using them to build patience and perseverance so that we may be complete and lacking nothing and so that our joy would be complete. Scripture tells us to weep and rejoice, to be joyful always, to give thanks in all circumstances. His Will is that we trust Him no matter what.

Who knows? We know that God loves us because He's proven it with the Holy Spirit in our hearts. There's a purpose and a plan for your life.

Take hold of the promises and Kingdom of God. If you haven't yet, simply invite God into your life. It's an ABC proposition:

- Admit you're a sinner.
- Believe God died for you on the cross.
- Confess with your mouth that He is Lord.

The Word of God is alive. Jesus is the Word. God is so many things. God is the Father, Son, and Holy Spirit. God's Word is alive, and Jesus said if we eat of this Word, we will never hunger again. If we will drink of it, we will never thirst again.

Let that be the desire of your heart – to seek and find Him; not football, not fishing, not bowling, not business. It's not that there's anything wrong with those things – but the Father must be the first priority. We must only trust and believe.

No matter what happens on Earth, our life in eternity is secure. We are secure. He has said, "As far as from the east is from the west, I'll remember your sin no more" (Psalm 103:12).

There is a difference between knowing the message and being the message.

May we be the message God has called us to be.

Who knows?

The result might be more than you could ever imagine. Who knows? You might never question your destiny or the "who knows" ever again.

Chapter Five

EXAMINING PURPOSE AND PLAN PERSPECTIVES AND THEIR SHIFTS

When Jesus spoke, His disciples and apostles and followers couldn't wait to hear His next word because the truth of God was flowing out of His mouth. It was so alive; they were just dying to hear the next word; they couldn't wait. I pray that we never take the Word of God for granted.

When your heart is open, you will hear the Word of Jesus, the Word of God, specifically speaking to your heart, individually and uniquely. That's what the Holy Spirit who lives inside of our hearts does for each and every one of us.

I had the flu about three or four weeks ago and I was wiped out. I felt cruddy just lying there. Of course, there are sicknesses that are a lot worse than the flu, but when you're not feeling good, everything is off. You can't enjoy anything, you can't do anything, and your only focus is on getting better. You say, "Man, if I could just feel better again!" You also realize, "Perhaps I've taken for granted how important it is to feel good. Perhaps I've taken my eyes off how wonderful it is to be able to get up and get out and do things."

Well, as I thought that when I was sick, God spoke to my heart, and He said, "Jack, you can have a spiritual flu too. You could be walking apart from the Holy Spirit." You could have the spiritual flu and then you're wondering why things aren't right in your life spiritually.

Have we taken for granted the opportunity to be able to walk with the Holy Spirit of God? We wonder why our lives aren't going the way we want. Why am I not filled with the joy and the peace of the Lord? The joy and the peace of the Lord comes from the Lord, which comes from the Holy Spirit inside of you. Not only do you walk with God, but God is inside of you; He is an infinite part of your life every single day.

If you don't have that, you are missing what God intended with the abundant Christian life. Do not miss that. The blessing of the Lord is not something you have to wait for. You don't have to wait until you get to Heaven. The blessing of the Lord is right now. You have it in your life right now. We are always thinking of the future in our own lives.

When I'm in high school: "I want to be in college."

When in college: "I want to get a job."

When I get a job: "I want to get married... have kids... retire."

It'll always be better later, later, later – once I get this or get that or reach that goal – and then you wonder why you never feel satisfied or content. It's because you weren't satisfied with what you had. The blessing of the Lord is now. It's every minute in every day you walk upon this earth and it will be for all eternity in Heaven – but don't miss it now.

Do you know what a trust fund baby is? It's somebody who did nothing and got everything. You see, their parents or grandparents or great grandparents worked their butts off and built something so amazing – usually financially or in some asset rich way and the kid gets the benefit of every single thing that those parents or grandparents or great grandparents worked for, even though the kid did nothing.

Sometimes we resent trust fund babies. We say, "Aw man, look at that trust fund baby. He had everything handed to him on a silver spoon and didn't have to work a day in his life! This isn't fair. I work for what I get."

Yet, we are God's trust fund babies. God has given us everything – we didn't do anything for it – we didn't deserve it – and we have it – all of it.

I had a dream the other night. I'm not saying my dreams are prophetic. I'm saying this one applied to me. I dreamed I was playing tennis. I like to play tennis; however, in my hand I didn't have a racket, I had something which was very ineffective – it was a pair of glasses – and I was trying to hit the ball. As you could imagine, I didn't have much success hitting the ball without a racket.

God woke me up and I thought about the dream. God said, "Jack, I'm your racket and without me in your hand, you can't do anything. You're never going to be effective. You might have talent and ability, but without the right equipment, without the Holy

Spirit, you're never going to be effective." That was a reminder to me.

God has ordained you. You were created for a purpose. God is with you and He has filled you with the Holy Spirit. Look at this example in Exodus 31: Then the Lord spoke to Moses, saying: "See, I have called by name Bezalel the son of Uri, the son of Hur, of the tribe of Judah. And I have filled him with the Spirit of God, in wisdom, in understanding, in knowledge, and in all manner of workmanship, to design artistic works, to work in gold, in silver, in bronze, in cutting jewels for setting, in carving wood, and to work in all manner of workmanship" (v. 1-5).

God had given Moses specific details and instructions to build the tabernacle. He could instruct me to build an arena or coliseum, but I don't know how to do it. I'm not a skilled workman or craftsman. God said to Moses, "Don't worry; I have filled Bezalel with the talent he needs."

One minute, Bezalel was walking around, and he didn't have what he needed, and the next second, the Spirit of God reached down to touch him, and he had what he needed. We see it in healing miracles, we see it in turnaround-of-life miracles, and we see it in changes of attitude like salvation. One minute you're walking along – lost – and the next minute God takes the scales off your eyes. You see. You're transformed by the renewing of your mind. You're born again in the Spirit of Holy God and you are new and transformed in a flash. How's that for a great example of examining purpose and plan perspectives and their shifts. As you see when you learn and realize the truth of God things can change dramatically and instantly!

In the twinkling of an eye, when Jesus comes back, it's going to be the same thing. One second it isn't – and the next second it is – for all eternity. Just as God filled Bezalel with His purpose in an instant.

Remember, God knew you before you were formed in your mother's womb. He created you with a plan and with a purpose. He says in Ephesians 2:10 that you are to do the good works which He prepared in advance for you to do. God fills us with the Holy Spirit to do the good works He has prepared for us.

Exodus 31 goes on: "And I, indeed I, have appointed with him Aholiab the son of Ahisamach, of the tribe of Dan; and I have put wisdom in the hearts of all the gifted artisans, that they may make all that I have commanded you: the tabernacle of meeting, the ark of the Testimony and the mercy seat that is on it, and all the furniture of the tabernacle—the table and its utensils, the pure gold lamp stand with all its utensils, the altar of incense, the altar of burnt offering with all its utensils, and the laver and its base—the garments of ministry, the holy garments for Aaron the priest and the garments of his sons, to minister as priests, and the anointing oil and sweet incense for the holy place. According to all that I have commanded you they shall do" (v. 6-11).

God had a plan for their lives, and He equipped them to do it. It's the same for you. God has a plan for your life, and He will equip you to do it. You must be ready and willing, and He will make you able.

I was seeking God on a couple of issues a couple of weeks ago. I was praying and fasting. I needed to seek God because I had two very specific issues and I needed answers from God. Two very specific prayers I wanted God to answer. I figured I would give it a few days.

I was waiting on the third day, and I still didn't have an answer. I was thinking, am I doing this right? God, you know, it's time! You got to show up by the end of the third day, right?

God did show up – well, He's there all the time, but He spoke to me and said, "Jack, the things you're praying about are not your problem."

I said, "God – no, no, I assure you those are my problems. As a matter of fact, if You would just fix those problems, I assure you everything would be fine."

He said, "No, Jack, that's not your problem. Your problem is a lack of gratitude for what you have."

I said, "Okay, God."

That very morning, I was reading Exodus 16, where God is talking about the manna. It's the first time He poured manna down from Heaven. The Israelites were hungry, they didn't know how they were going to eat, and God gave them manna. They describe the manna as wafer-like, and round, and it kind of tastes like honey.

That's when God reminded me that I was murmuring and complaining just like the Israelites were. I was focusing on what I didn't have and not what I had. God said, "Have I not always provided for you? Have you ever gone hungry? Have I not always provided manna in your life? And I don't just mean food; I mean in every area. Have I not always been with you?"

Of course, the answer is yes. It's yes for me and it's yes for you. So, I said, "Thank you, Lord. Thank you for your love and may I rejoice and be satisfied and rejoice in the love and provision of the Lord." That's a reminder for all of us. May we rejoice in Him and be satisfied with the love and provision of the Lord.

Let's look at a great Old Testament example about trusting the Lord with the timing and provision of your life. It's found in Leviticus 25. Moses was getting ready to lead the people into the Promised Land after 40 long years, and the Lord spoke to Moses on Mount Sinai: "Speak to the children of Israel, and say to them: 'When you come into the land which I give you, then the land shall keep a sabbath to the Lord. Six years you shall sow your field, and six years you shall prune your vineyard, and gather its fruit; but in the seventh year there shall be a sabbath of solemn rest for the land, a sabbath to the Lord. You shall neither sow your field nor prune your vineyard. What grows of its own accord of your harvest you shall not reap, nor gather the grapes of your untended vine, for it is a year of rest for the land'" (v. 2-5).

God had a requirement. "Hey, listen, I'm giving you the Promised Land – it's like the greatest ever. Here's what I want you to do: for six years you can harvest and on the seventh year, I don't want you to plow the land. Don't do anything." That's interesting. Leviticus 25 goes on to say: "So you shall observe My statutes and keep My judgments, and perform them; and you will dwell in the land in safety. Then the land will yield its fruit, and you will eat your fill, and dwell there in safety" (v. 18-19).

There was a requirement for them. They had to observe God's statutes. They had to keep His judgments and perform them and then they would dwell in safety and then the land would yield fruit.

You might say, "Well, that's nice, but that was the Old Testament, when there were laws and requirements. Didn't Jesus die on the cross so we wouldn't have to fulfill the law because Jesus fulfilled them for us? So, we're free to do anything we want."

Not quite. Yes, Jesus did die and fulfill the requirements of sacrifice in the law once and for all for you and me. But there are still requirements. God said, "Seek first the kingdom and its righteousness and all these other things will come" (Matthew 6:33). God said, "Trust in the Lord with all your heart, and lean not on your own understanding; acknowledge Him in all your ways and then He will direct your paths" (Proverbs 3:5-6). He instructs us, "Be joyful always, pray continually, and give thanks in all circumstances" (1 Thessalonians 5:16-18), and, "Be anxious for nothing" (Philippians 4:6).

There are things that you need to do, instructions that you need to follow if you want to prosper. They're not laws we must follow – but they're things that will help you and bless you, so why would you possibly ignore them? Even salvation has a requirement. It's a free gift, but you must take it! There is a requirement: You must accept Jesus into your heart – there's something you must do.

God knew their thoughts in advance. He knows your thoughts and mine before we even think them. He knew in advance what they were going to say. And he says this in Leviticus 25: "And if you say, 'What shall we eat in the seventh year, since we shall not sow nor gather in our produce?' Then I will command My blessing on you in the sixth year, and it will bring forth produce enough for three years. And you shall sow in the eighth year, and eat old produce until the ninth year; until its produce comes in, you shall eat of the old harvest" (v. 20-22).

"Hey God, okay, I get that you gave us the Promised Land and that's a pretty good thing – we waited 40 years and you delivered – that's awesome. This sounds good, but you probably haven't thought of this, God. See, if we do what you say, if we just eat for six years and not the seventh – what are we going to eat the seventh year? We might starve."

You could just see God shaking His head, "Ye of little faith." I see God shaking His head at me sometimes, just like I shake my head at my kids and I'm thinking, I can't even believe you guys. I can't believe after everything I've done for you, everything I've given, all the times when your mother and I have proven our love for you, we've proven that every single thing we do is for your benefit and blessing and still, I say something and you don't believe it! Are you guys kidding me? And I sigh in disbelief and at their ignorance and lack of faith and trust in me.

I think God sometimes thinks that about us.

Let me ask this, does God not say the same thing to you and me? Does He not say in Luke 22 and Matthew 6, "Do not worry! Do not worry about what you will eat or drink. Do not worry." God has provided all of these things for you? Yet we do worry. We let Satan kick the crap out of us when we do exactly what God told us not to do – as if we don't believe Him.

Matthew 6:33 is a life verse for me: Seek first the kingdom of God and his righteousness and all these other things will be given to you as well.

But lately, I've had to examine my heart. I said, "God is it possible that I was seeking first your Kingdom and your righteousness so that I could get all of these other things? And is it possible that my motive for seeking You and your righteousness was so that I could get all of these other things?" I had to look at my heart. And when I did that I saw what effect my examining purpose and plan perspectives and their shifts had on my reality my truth and my life.

I hope you look at your heart… because this other stuff is meaningless. God is everything. If I have God, I have everything. Without Him, I'm nothing – even if I have those other things. So, what's my motive for seeking God? It's always about motive. May God help us to see our lives through His eyes and may we respond accordingly.

In Joshua 22, we find an interesting story. There were 12 tribes in Israel, but before they went to battle to take the Promised Land, two and a half tribes – the Reubenites, the Gadites, and half of the tribe of Manasseh – said, "Listen, Moses. We have a big idea. Look, we know we're going to the Promised Land, but this land – across the river here – this is beautiful. Why don't you just give us this land, we will stay here and settle here, and there will be more for you over there?"

Moses sought God, and God said, "Yes, they can have this land but there's a requirement. First, all you guys are going to come into battle with us. You're all going to fight with us and when we win, you can go back and take this land."

They said, "Great."

They went into battle, they won, they came back, and they took the land. So after they're settled in, here's what happened in Joshua chapter 22. The Reubenites, the Gadites, and half of the tribe of Manasseh left the Israelites at Shiloh and Canaan to return to Gilead – that's where their land was. Then Ruben, Gad, and the half-tribe of Manasseh built a separate altar to God apart from the Tabernacle in Israel. This alter was of a calf and placed by the Jordan River, where they had settled.

So, the Israelites, (the other nine and a half tribes) heard about this and they were furious. When the Israelites heard that they had built the altar on the border at Canaan, the whole assembly of Israel gathered to build a war against them. They said, "You guys have done something terrible, so we're going to war and we're going to kill you guys."

Well, what was their motive for building what the others considered an unholy alter? They didn't know, so they wanted to find out. The Israelites sent Phineas, the priest, to the land of Gilead to speak to Ruben, Gad, and half of the tribe of Manasseh. He took with him one leader from each tribe and they went up to Gilead and they talked to them, saying, "How could you break faith with the God of Israel like this? How could you turn away from the Lord and build to yourselves an altar in rebellion against Him now?"

Basically, they were calling them out, asking, "Are you guys crazy? How could you do this? You're nuts! Don't you know there's one God, one law, and one tabernacle? How dare you be disrespectful." They had an ulterior motive because they also said, "If you rebel against the Lord today, tomorrow he'll be mad with the whole community of Israel." Meaning, "He's not just going to take you guys out; He's going to take all of us out because we're all part of the same community. You guys are going to destroy us! This is like the worst thing you could ever do."

At that point, the two and a half tribes – the Reubenites, the Gadites, and half tribe of Manasseh – got to share their story in Joshua chapter 22 they said this:

> The Mighty One, God, the Lord! The Mighty One, God, the Lord! He knows! And let Israel know! If this has been in rebellion or disobedience to the Lord, do not spare us this day. If we have built our own altar to turn away from the Lord and to offer burnt offerings and grain offerings, or to sacrifice fellowship offerings on it, may the Lord himself call us to account.
>
> No! We did it for fear that someday your descendants might say to ours, 'What do you have to do with the Lord, the God of Israel? The Lord has made the Jordan a boundary between us and you – you Reubenites and Gadites! You have no share in the Lord.' So your descendants might cause ours to stop fearing the Lord.
>
> That is why we said, 'Let us get ready and build an altar—but not for burnt offerings or sacrifices.' On the contrary, it is to be a witness between us and you and the generations that follow, that we will worship the Lord at his sanctuary with our burnt offerings, sacrifices and fellowship offerings. Then in the future your descendants will not be able to say to ours, 'You have no share in the Lord.'
>
> So, you see that's why we did it. We built it as a memorial so that your children and grandchildren would never say to us; hey we don't have a part in the Lord. (v. 24-27)

In essence they were saying, and I'm paraphrasing now, "We would never do it to be disrespectful to God. We love God. As a matter of fact, we didn't build this altar to make sacrifices and burnt offerings. We know that's what the altar in Israel is for; we built it as a replica so that you guys would never say that we don't have our part in the kingdom."

So then Phineas, the priest, and the other leaders said, "Oh. No problem. We had no idea, but now we understand why you did what you did and it's OK. It's all good." They went home and told the other tribes, and everybody said, "That's great; that's right."

One minute the ten tribes were going to kill them for what they did. The next minute, after they listened to their perspective and their motive, it was fine. Wow! So, our job is to understand God's motive and to also understand our motives in life. God's not asking you to die on the cross, but He is asking you to live for it. We need to have an understanding. That should be our godly perspective. We should be praying, "Lord, your will be done. Give us this day our daily bread. Forgive us as we forgive others. Deliver us not into temptation."

We should be looking at Ephesians 6 and believe we have victory over Satan, believe Jesus defeated Satan at the cross, believe we have victory by putting on the full armor of God and standing against the devil's schemes. If we resist the devil, he'll flee from us. We know that! We know that there will be trials and tribulations. The Bible says it in James, in Peter, in Romans. And it also says to consider it pure joy when you face trials; to rejoice in your suffering. Why? Because it pales in comparison to the glory that will be revealed. You know you've been saved by faith, through grace and not of yourselves; it is a gift of God. You can read about it in God's Word.

Many of these things we have to take by faith. We walk by faith and not by sight. If you saw me holding a dollar in my hand, you'd know the money is there. If I told you I had a dollar in my wallet, you would have to believe me. You would have to take it by faith.

Once you know something for certain, it's not faith. God asks you to have faith. God says, "Now you know in part, but then you'll know in full." Right now, you need to have faith in God and what God is doing in your life.

I love when Jesus said to Peter, "Get behind me, Satan. You're a stumbling block to me. You don't have in mind the things of God, but the things of men." I believe God was speaking to you and me through that, as well; it's not that Peter was Satan. It's just that he was doing the Satan-like thing because he wasn't doing the God thing. Anytime you're not doing a God thing, it's a Satan thing. That's how it works.

I was thinking about my life lately and some issues I've been having – business, health relationships – and then I realized, "Oh my gosh, I'm thinking about this all wrong because if those things could make me happy, it means God is not the one making me happy. If the outcome of those circumstances could determine my happiness, then it means I'm not satisfied with God."

Examine your own life and your own heart and ask yourself that. If any circumstance could rob you of the joy of the Lord, there's a problem. It doesn't mean that you have to like the circumstances. It doesn't mean they're fun. We know we'll face trials and tribulations, but it means I focus on the treasures of the Lord, not on earthly things, not on Satan's illusions, lies and distractions, and not on my own heart and thoughts. I must take them captive and focus on the treasures of the Lord.

God calls us to live holy lives – lives that will glorify Him – to have a positive impact for His Kingdom in this world. We are called to be a light in this present darkness and salt to a tasteless generation.

A friend and I were in a conference and the speaker spoke to the leaders, saying, "How can you lead people without repenting yourself? We need to get right. We need to change our hearts. We're going to sin next week, and we need to be repenting. We need to be on our knees before God. We need to be asking God to cleanse us and purify us… and He will; but remember there's action required on our part. We need to go to God and ask Him to do this.

God is planning our lives; He wants to accomplish great things through us. How do we respond? Do we respond sometimes like Moses in Exodus chapter 3? Moses met God at the burning bush. God told Moses, "I'm going to use you to free the people and take them to the Promised Land." And how did Moses reply?

He said, "Who am I that I should go?" Moses didn't respond the right way. God said, "I have sent you."

Do you not believe that God has sent you to live your life for His Kingdom's purposes? I believe that for each and every child of God. Then Moses said, "Well, all right God. You're with me but when I go, who am I going to tell them sent me? Are they going to believe me? Are they going to hammer me? I have no credibility. Who am I going to tell them sent me?"

God said, "Just tell them 'I Am' – Yahweh – sent you. Don't worry about it. They'll know. Just say 'I Am' sent you and they'll know."

So, Moses was going, "Well, all right. I don't know if that will fly but let me ask you something else, God. I know you sent me, and I'll tell them you sent me, but what do I do if they don't believe me? What do I do then?"

God said, "Moses, take your staff, throw it down." He threw it down; it turned into a big snake. God said, "Pick up the snake." Moses picked up the snake and it turned back into his staff. God said, "Moses take your hand." His hand was perfectly fine. He said, "Put it in your jacket." He put it in his jacket, and he pulled it out and it was leprous. God said, "Put it back in." He did it again and he was healed. How's that? You'd think that would be good enough. Remember, we do the same thing to God sometimes. We question His authority and power.

The Holy Spirit of God is inside of us and we walk around sometimes saying we're not sure or we don't know. Moses was still not done. He said, "Okay, I trust you sent me and you're with me and you'll give me all this power, but you see, God, I don't speak so well." Like that would be an impossible thing for God to fix; like all things aren't possible with God. Like there's something that God couldn't do. "I just turned this staff into a snake and back, a normal hand into a leprous one and then back to normal in an instant, and you don't think I can help you speak?" I think God experiences this same lack of faith in Him by us sometimes and I think that's a tragedy.

God sometimes says to me and you, "All right, I'll work with what you give me. I love you and I'll work with what you give me." When Adam and Eve sinned in the garden, God didn't say, "You're done. There's no purpose left for you. I can't work with you. You disobeyed me." He said, "come here, put these clothes on. Here are some clothes for you. I am disappointed. Is this what I envisioned? No. I thought you believed me! But I'll work with what you'll give me." The Word of God reminds us "according to your faith it will be done for you" (Matthew 9:29.)

And to us, He says, "I thought you walked in faith. I thought that the Holy Spirit living inside of you would be enough." We need to live a life that glorifies God, trusting He's with us every step of the way, that all things work together for our good, that He'll never leave us nor forsake us, that no weapon formed against us would prosper.

So how does God handle Moses' lack of faith? God gave Moses his brother, Aaron, to speak for him. "Yeah, we'll let Aaron go and talk. I'm not going to take you out of the game or remove you from action for your lack of faith."

Do we make excuses with God? God was angry with Moses at the water at Meribah because Moses didn't trust God. I'm not going into the story now, but Moses had done everything right and then he didn't trust God on a certain issue. And God must have been in disbelief. How could you possibly question me now after all this stuff I have done for you?

I think that's the question for us: how can we possibly question God after experiencing the Holy Spirit of God? Not on a one-time basis, but inside of you? The living God is inside of you.

In the New Testament, there's the story in John chapter 6 of Jesus feeding 5,000 men (plus women and children). God gave me a new perspective and a new understanding of this miracle. Every time I've read this story, I've seen it being about this great miracle Jesus did. Jesus turned the water into wine, He fed the 5,000, He healed the paralytic... He did all these miracles.

That's how I've read it so many times before, but not this time. Here's the story. Jesus is crossing the Sea of Galilee; the crowd follows Him. He performs signs and they wanted to see more. Jesus says to Phillip, "Where shall we buy bread for these people to eat?" Now, Jesus knew. He tested His disciples so that He could prove their faith was more genuine than gold; that's the currency that has value to God – faith. Not money, but faith. God needs to prove that within us. God says that he who will be faithful with little will be faithful with much.

God says, "I want to prove to you so that I can give you more. I want to prove that you can handle it. I desire to give all to you." The Word of God says that Jesus only asked this to test Philip for He had already in mind what He was going to do.

Philip said, "Well, it would take more than a half-year's wages to buy enough bread for each person to have one bite."

Jesus talked to Andrew, Peter's brother. Andrew spoke up and said, "Here's a boy with five small loaves and two small fish." But even Andrew doubted and the next line out of his mouth was, "… but how far will that go among so many?" He doubted.

You can just hear Jesus sighing. "Oh, Andrew, ye of little faith." Sometimes I hear him sighing at me, "Ah, Jack, ye of little faith." I believe He's saying the same to all of us. So, Jesus told the people to sit down. You know the story. There were 5,000 men, plus we don't know how many women and children, and the Word of God says Jesus took the loaves. He gave thanks and distributed them to the people who were seated so that everyone had as much as they wanted.

I've read it a thousand times. But it wasn't about Jesus and the miracle He did this time. It was about my life and about your life and about the miracle that He wants to do in us. You see, we are the bread! But we need to put ourselves in the Master's hand. We need to give ourselves, put ourselves in His hand so He can use us, so He can break us, so He can distribute us, so that we are used to feed the people with the Word and gospel and message of the Kingdom of God, so that we have the privilege of making an impact for all eternity.

That's the message. We are the bread. Jesus took the bread, He broke it, and He distributed it. But we're scared to go. "No, Lord, I don't want that." We're so selfish. We're so sinfully minded. How could we miss this? How could we miss that that's what God wants in our life?

Put your life in Jesus' hands. You may have heard this analogy before: a piano in my hands is a bad thing. In Billy Joel's hands, in Beethoven's hands, it's magic. A basketball in my hands? I don't think so. In LeBron James' hands? Yes, absolutely. A dollar in my hand? Well, I could probably get you a cup of tea at 7-11 – it's on special today. In Warren Buffet's hands – you may have a fortune for the rest of your life. Your life in your hands? Hey, good luck with that. Your life in Jesus' hands – you'll be fulfilling your purpose. 1st Peter 2:5 tells us: "You also, like living stones, are being built into a spiritual house to be a holy priesthood, offering spiritual sacrifices acceptable to God through Jesus Christ."

Remember again, God isn't asking you to die on the cross. Jesus did that. He's asking you to live for it. Jesus says that our job is to "believe in the One who sent me." I believe in gravity, so I don't jump off the roof; I believe in airplane pilots, so I get on planes. I believe in Lipton tea, so I drink it; I believe it's not poison. How is it we believe in scientific law – other earthly things and principles that can fail us, yet we do not believe in the love and power of our Creator who will never fail us? How is that?

Jesus said, "Very truly I tell you, that whoever hears my words and believes him who sent me will have eternal life and will not be judged but is crossed over from death to life." In John chapter 5, He called out the people. He said, "You know, you study the scriptures because you think that in them you have eternal life and these are the scriptures that testify about me, yet you refuse to come to me to have life." It's always been about having a personal relationship with Jesus Christ.

That's what Christianity is. It's not about rules and regulations; it's not about coming to church; it's about knowing your Father, God, personally. If you have that, you have the Kingdom of God. Without it, you have nothing. It's not too late. You can choose to access God today. He's available. God says all who call upon the name of the Lord shall be saved.

You need to be looking. You need to be seeking. The Word of God is not a complicated manuscript. There are certain things that I don't understand completely and there are commentaries I can go read or people (pastors or other spiritually-intelligent people) I can ask, "Could you explain this or clarify that for me? I'm a little unclear." That's how I get clarity and I move on. That way I've come to my own conclusion on what God is saying to me; and you need to come to your own conclusion as well.

If you're not feeling like you are connected to God or in an individual relationship with Him, you need to go talk to God.

You need to seek and spend time with God. It doesn't have to be a three-day prayer fast. How about you start with 10 minutes opening the Word of God and seeking God's will for your life and walking with Him?

I don't always agree with God. But I know He's God, and I've come to the stage in my life where I've taken all the suggestions and promises of God and answered, "I'm all in. I'm not even questioning you anymore. I don't understand but I know how much You love me." If you are a parent, your kids know how much you love them by your actions, not by your title or your position. Kids love that they can count on their parents no matter what.

We have that with God. You may not have parents that gave you the kind of love that you needed. Maybe your parents abandoned you; maybe they weren't good parents. I get that. But God is good. Remember Jesus said, "If you eat of me, you'll never hunger again; if you drink of me, you'll never thirst again." You have this well inside of you, this Holy Spirit well that will never stop flowing unless you shut it down – unless you cap it off – unless you walk away. Then you won't get the benefit that God intended.

Remember that things happen according to God's way. He is in control. He anointed Bezalel and the workers knew exactly what they needed to perform the mission that God had called them to. He will do the same for you, enabling you to do the good works that He prepared in advance for you to do by His Holy Spirit power.

The Lord provides for all our needs, just like when He told the Israelites to eat for six years and then fast during the seventh year. They didn't know what would happen in the seventh year, but God had it taken care of.

From the beginning, to the middle, to the end, God is our Alpha and Omega. Everything has been planned before we were formed in our mother's womb. God knows you and has a plan for your life. He plans to give you a hope and a future – not to harm you, but to prosper you (Jeremiah 29:11). You only need to trust.

We are the bread. God will work miracles through us if we allow our lives to be placed in His hands. The bread was used to feed people. It was broken to feed others. Christ was broken to feed us, and we are to be broken to feed the world.

The Word of God also reminds us through the Reubenites, the Gadites, and the half tribe of Manasseh that we need to understand our motivation. If something is off, we need to align it properly because our motives are what matters.

Why do you do what you do? We need to be examining purpose and plan perspectives and their shifts in order to see reality and truth in order to understand ourselves, our motives and our actions in order to get closer to God.

Jesus said, "Many will come to me in that day and I will say 'Depart from me, I did not know you!'"

And many will say, "Lord, we did everything we were supposed to do!"

Jesus will answer, "Wrong, wrong, wrong. Your hearts were far from me."

Please examine the motives of your heart today.

We're meant to live a life that glorifies God. If we're going to be that witness, we need to share the gospel. It starts with us. It starts with our repentance and our returning to God.

I pray that we would seek God because He said we will find Him when we seek Him with all our hearts. I pray we would put as much effort into seeking God as we do into our finances, our recreation schedules, our health, our fitness, anything else – that He would be first.

If we do that, all these other things will come into God's perfect way and timing.

Chapter Six

DIFFERENTIATING THE DESIRES AND REALITIES OF WANTS AND NEEDS

What are you praying to God for? Are you praying to God for what you want and what you need? Or are you praying to God to get to know the will of His heart and get closer to Him?

I've had to examine my heart while asking myself these questions. I hope and pray the Holy Spirit will help you examine your heart and you'll ask yourself the same question: "What am I praying to you for? Is it to fix my needs and help me with the things I want or am I praying to get closer to you, Lord, and to get to know more of your will?"

There are some places in the Bible where the same story is told twice. In the New Testament, some of the parables are shared in multiple places; in the Old Testament, specifically in Chronicles and Kings, there are identical verses sometimes.

In one passage, King David has turned over the reins to his son Solomon, and then Solomon was the king of Israel. One of the first things that happened is described in 2 Chronicles 1 and also in 1 Kings 3. It says:

> Now Solomon, the son of David, was strengthened in his kingdom and the Lord, his God, was with him and exalted him exceedingly. And King Solomon went to Gibeon, to sacrifice there, for that was the great high place, and Solomon offered 1000 burnt offerings at the altar. At Gibeon, the Lord appeared to Solomon in a dream by night and God said, 'Ask. What shall I give you?' (v. 4-6)

Hey, that's a pretty good deal. I wouldn't mind if the Lord appeared to me and said, "Jack, what do you need? Ask. What shall I give you? What would you like?"

God spoke very specifically in the Old Testament through dreams, and the Holy Spirit may use dreams to communicate with you. The Holy Spirit is alive inside of your heart. Back then, Jesus had not yet died and risen, and His Holy Spirit wasn't available full time in people's hearts. It hadn't yet come to reside in the hearts of people forever and ever, it was a come-and-go thing. The Spirit of God would fall on people. The Spirit of God would anoint people. The Spirit would come and go upon people. God would speak through prophets and dreams.

But here in this passage, it was God speaking! It was God's Spirit – make no mistake about it. How blessed we are today to have the Holy Spirit living inside of us 24/7 – to have constant access to God Himself. It wasn't that way then.

So, God came to Solomon in the dream and said, "Ask. What shall I give you?" Solomon answered: "Now, Lord my God, you have made your servant king in place of my father David. But I am only a little child and do not know how to carry out my duties. Your servant is here among the people you have chosen, a great people, too numerous to count or number" (1 Kings 3:7-8).

Now, before we get to Solomon's request, let's look at how Solomon responded to God. The first thing he did was give all the credit and glory to God for everything! He knew he was responsible for nothing. He knew it was God who ordained David to be king and blessed him through his reign. He knew it was God who ordained him to the throne to be king and God who would bless him through his reign. He knows he was 100% dependent on God: for life, for success, for everything.

Do we know the same thing? Because it is 100% true in my life and in your life. We are dependent on God for everything. I have faith that the Word of God is true in all things. I hope you've found that in your life. It's the Word of God that tells us we are dependent on Him for all things! It is in John 15:5, when Jesus says, "I am the vine, you are the branch. Apart from me, you can do nothing." I believe that's true in this life and I hope you'll come to that realization. God doesn't want you to miss the blessings, the abundant life He has in store for you. He says, "Listen, I want to tell you this for your benefit. You can't do it on your own. You can try, but I have eternity in my hands. I have the keys to the Kingdom, and I want to share them with you now – in this life – and in the one to come."

It is God's will, as He said in His Word, that you are blessed abundantly, and exceedingly, more than you could ever imagine – that you'll receive from God an abundant life. So, how does Solomon respond? He acknowledged God's great mercy, and then he goes on to say this: "So give your servant a discerning heart to govern your people and to distinguish between right and wrong. For who is able to govern this great people of yours?" (1 Kings 3:9)

God had promised Abraham, "Your seed will be too numerous to count – like specks of sand, like stars in the sky." And Solomon said, "Therefore, give to your servant an understanding heart to judge your people – that I may discern between good and evil – for who is able to judge this great people of yours?" Solomon knew the power came from God. He said, "God, listen. I'm now the king of Israel. Holy cow! Here are all these people, and I don't know how to be king. God, do me a favor. Please, grant me the wisdom to fulfill this task. Grant me power, knowledge, and wisdom, so that I can accomplish the task that you've called me to."

Is that the prayer of your life? It needs to be the prayer of your life. Wherever God has placed you – whether you're a bus driver or a teacher, or you're the CEO of a company or a housewife – it doesn't matter; your job is to glorify God with all your heart and soul, to live a life that glorifies God.

In order to do that, you need to depend on God and be connected to God for the power and wisdom to do that on a daily basis. The Holy Spirit is with you, inside of you, and is the One who guides you – that is your GPS to the Kingdom of God. Solomon knew the power came from God and that it was God's to give. It goes on to say: "The Lord was pleased that Solomon had asked for this. So God said to him, 'Since you have asked for this and not for long life or wealth for yourself, nor have asked for the death of your enemies but for discernment in administering justice, I will do what you have asked. I will give you a wise and discerning heart, so that there will never have been anyone like you, nor will there ever be'" (1 Kings 3:10-12).

God gave it to Solomon and God gives it to you and me. God gave Solomon even more than he asked for or ever imagined. God gives you and me more than what we ask for. God gave you both life on earth and life in eternity. God gave it to you.

You might say, "Well, Jack. That's interesting. Then how come I don't have what I want?" Well sometimes we need to be differentiating the desire and realities of wants and needs.

Well, what do you want? Are you asking God to take care of your needs and wants? Or are you asking God that you would come closer to Him and know His will? James tells us in James 4:2, "You do not have because you do not ask God. When you ask, you do not receive because you ask for the wrong motives. That you may spend what you get on your pleasures."

God says, "You're asking me for stuff that you want for yourself. I know you have needs. I'll provide for every need." It's God's wonderful desire to bless us. What parent doesn't want to bless their children? But God says, "Listen, I have more for you, but you can only get the more from me when you're walking with me and you seek me. You'll find me when you seek me with all your heart."

That's the life we have. That's the life that is exceedingly and abundantly more than you could ever imagine. But you must come to it. It's yours, but you must grab hold of it.

Let's look at another lesson from the Word of God: "As Jesus looked up, he saw the rich putting their gifts into the temple treasury. He also saw a poor widow put in two very small copper coins. 'Truly I tell you,' he said, 'this poor widow has put in more than all the others. All these people gave their gifts out of their wealth; but she out of her poverty put in all she had to live on'" (Luke 21:1-4).

This poor woman gave all she had into the church treasury because she loved God. She so trusted God, she was so totally encompassed by the Holy Spirit of God pouring on her life, she was so showered and loved by the Spirit of God, that it was her joy to give all she had to the Lord.

Do we live like that? Do we love God like that? How much do you love God? By the way, everything I'm sharing with you in this book is what God is asking me. I'm not looking at you and saying, "Hey, Christian, you better look at your own heart." This is God saying to me, "Jack, I'm looking at your heart. Do you love me that much? And how much do you love me?" So how should we live?

In Luke 22, Jesus gives us another example. There was a dispute among the disciples. The dispute was which of them should be considered the greatest. Jesus had said, "Hey, I'm going to die." And they kind of understood it even though they hadn't seen it happen yet. And they said, "Well, you know, we're the disciples, we're the team – which one of us is the MVP? Who's the all-star? Who's the franchise? Which one of us?" They start to compare notes, "Oh, I've done this; I've done that," and, "Which one's it going to be?" Here's what the Word of God says: "The kings of the Gentiles exercise lordship over them, and those who exercise authority over them are called 'benefactors.' But not so among you; on the contrary, he who is greatest among you, let him be as the younger, and he who governs as he who serves. For who is greater, he who sits at the table, or he who serves? Is it not he who sits at the table? Yet I am among you as the One who serves" (Luke 22:25-27).

"He's saying, 'Look, you guys are arguing about who is the greatest – listen, you got it all wrong. Who is the greater: the owner of the house – the one who gets served – or the one who is serving? Of course, it's the owner of the house,' he said, 'But yet, I am among you as a servant. I've come as an example – as a sacrificial life – as a life lived of service to God.'"

That's how we're to be. We're called to be about other people. Jesus gave us an example, as He washed the disciples' feet. He gave us this parable and many others throughout the Bible. Of course, most importantly, He gave Himself when He died on the cross as a sacrifice for your life and my life, so we would have the assurance that when our time on earth is up, we are going to be welcomed into the Kingdom of God. We are going to hear, "Well done, good and faithful servant... Come and share your master's happiness" (Matthew 25:21).

I don't understand some Christians. Why can't you just be part of the great Super Bowl team that rallies around the great quarterback to win the Super Bowl?! We can all relate to that. "Oh, yeah! We're banding together – we're the Super Bowl team; I do it all for the team – we rally around our quarterback and we win; we're Super Bowl champions!" Why can't we be like that great corporate startup who rallies around their visionary CEO to build this great company that's going to change the world? Why can't we do that? I don't understand why the purpose of our lives isn't to serve others and rally around God who has given us everything.

Look at the reward God talks about for living a Godly life: "But you are those who have continued with Me in My trials. And I bestow upon you a kingdom, just as My Father bestowed one upon Me, that you may eat and drink at My table in My kingdom, and sit on thrones judging the twelve tribes of Israel" (Luke 22:28-30).

God has bestowed the same thing on you and me. We are children of God, heirs to the throne of Heaven. We are brothers and sisters of Jesus Christ; this is what we have. This is the abundant Christian life. This is what should make you go out and sing and dance and say, "Hallelujah! This is amazing!"

This is what should make life a breeze even through the trials and tribulations – even through the suffering. God said, "In this world, you will suffer. But take heart, for I have overcome the world" (John 16:33). He said, "I'm going to use your trials and tribulations. I'm going to mold you and shape you; you're going to learn from them. They're going to make you better and better, and they're going to bring you closer to me so I can bless you more and you can have more of this abundance of the love and mercy and peace and grace that only comes from Jesus Christ."

God told us He's coming back. We see end times signs all around us: we see nation fighting against nation; we see earthquakes, famine, and changes in world currency. I don't know when He'll return. That's up to God. Only God knows when. Do you believe Jesus about the things of this life and of the world – and what the true treasures are?

God asked me that, so I'll ask you. He said, "Jack, do you believe Me about the things of this life and what the true treasures are?"

I said, "Yes, Lord, I believe you."

He said to me, not audibly, but in my spirit, loud as thunder, "Then live like it. Live like you believe it." Then learn to live differentiating the desire and realities of wants and needs. God calls us to be sober, to be vigilant, to be alert: for Jesus will return at the hour we do not expect. God loves us and wants a relationship with us. He's not telling us these things to make us slaves, or robots, or for us to be fearful – quite the contrary. He's telling us these things because He wants us to be safe and secure and not miss His blessings.

On Friday, my daughter wanted to go to the Central Florida Fair. The fair is in town. I said, "You can go, but here's a couple of things to keep in mind: the fairgrounds are not safe. The neighborhood is not safe. I've been there before. It's a sketchy neighborhood. And not only that, but there's a carnival in town and some carnival people (no disrespect) are not necessarily the most trustworthy. Not all of them, but some are sketchy – on the run from something and they're leaving town the next day. So, it's not a safe atmosphere. I'm not comfortable with you going there."

She said, "But Dad, I'm going to be with a group of people, and there's going to be a mother there."

I said, "Okay, you can go for a while under those circumstances." I told her this because I love her and want to protect her. If I thought it was too dangerous, I wouldn't have let her go even if she thought I was a mean daddy or didn't care. It would have been because I loved her too much and I wanted to protect her.

The parable here is that God is doing the same thing with us. God is telling us stuff, and giving us warnings, and guiding us, and directing us – not because He doesn't want us to have pleasure and experience things – quite the opposite. It's because He wants to love us and protect us and help us and save us even if that means saying no. God loves you enough to say no. How lucky you are to have a Father in Heaven to say no when it's not in your best interest and yes when it's in your best interest.

You can know God's purpose for your life – it's in the Bible. God promises in Romans 8:28 that all things work together for your good. He tells us in 1 Thessalonians 5:16 that we're to be joyful always, we're to "give thanks in all circumstances, for this is God's will for [us] in Christ Jesus."

One of the most powerful examples in the Bible is something Jesus said to Simon Peter: "Simon, Simon! Indeed, Satan has asked for you, that he may sift you as wheat. But have prayed for you, that your faith should not fail; and when you have returned to Me, strengthen your brethren" (Luke 22:31-32).

Jesus was talking to Peter and he said: "Listen, I have a warning for you! Satan has desired to sift you like wheat. Be on alert! Satan, who prowls around like a roaring lion looking to find whom he can devour; the same Satan, the thief, the dark angel who comes to kill and destroy – he's here! He's out for you specifically! He's coming for you. He's asked to sift you like wheat – to destroy you."

Satan has that same desire for you and me. There's nothing better Satan would like than to sift us like wheat. But Jesus goes on to say to Peter, "But! I have prayed for you."

What's that? Satan's going to sift me like wheat? All right, are you going to knock the crap out of him, Jesus? Maybe now's a good time to just shoot him.

No.

"No. I have prayed for you." You know why? Because it's not time yet for Satan to spend eternity in the lake of fire. That day is coming. It's not time yet. We're still in the game. But there's a battle going on. There's a war going on.

So, Jesus was saying, paraphrased, "I did the most important thing I could do for you, Peter, because I love you so much. I prayed for you because my prayers are not empty; I'm praying to the Father. The Creator. God. I know the Father; I'm the Son of the Father, and so are you. You're sons and daughters of God."

Jesus said, "I have prayed for you." Jesus is praying for you no matter what trials you're going through. No matter what tribulation you're going through, no matter what attacks from the devil you're facing right now – Jesus has prayed for you. Here's His answer in the first part of Luke 22:32, "I have prayed for you, that your faith should not fail!"

That's the prayer – because your faith is your weapon. The prayer is that you wouldn't fail, that you wouldn't fall short, that you wouldn't give up, that you wouldn't think you can't win. "No, I pray, Peter, that your faith should not fail," then He adds this most beautiful line, and probably one of the most beautiful, encouraging lines from the Word of God: "I have prayed for you that your faith shall not fail. And when you have returned to me, strengthen your brothers." (Luke 2:32)

Get this right. Jesus didn't say, "If you return to me ..." He didn't say it might happen. No, He said it will. He said, "There's a battle going on, Peter. But I'm praying that your faith is strong and when you win the battle – when you have returned to me – use what you've gone through to strengthen your brothers. That's the purpose, Peter! That's why I'm letting you go through this. So that you can learn and be stronger, and so that you can use what you learn from this to strengthen your brothers. Because you see, Peter, that's the purpose of your life. It's to serve. It's to help others. It's to give of yourself – to give to others so they can use it and be blessed by it."

All of the gifts of the Holy Spirit are for one purpose: to edify the body of Christ, to encourage and strengthen the brothers and sisters – that is the purpose. It's a done deal. We have the victory. It's not if you come back, if you return, but when. This is how you overcome – with faith. You're to stay strong and courageous. God says, "Be strong and courageous. (I am with you always.) I will never leave you nor forsake you" (Deuteronomy 31:6).

You know the definition of faith. It's being certain of what you hope for and sure of what you can't see. But you need to understand, it's not about you – it's about God. God has a purpose.

Before my father passed away, he lingered in a hospital bed for a little over a week. Those were ugly days for us as a family. We had to watch our father passing away and the life being sucked out of him. It was horrible by human standards. I think it would have been much better for me if I didn't have to see that happen to my father, but here's what God said to me: "Jack, it's not about you. What if I'm using that time? See, now you know in part, but then you'll know in full. You're supposed to trust me and have faith in my plan because I'm God. Your father who lingered in that hospital what if I used those eight days to bring him to the Kingdom of Heaven? What if I was using that time to speak to your mother and brother who didn't know Jesus – to bring them to the Kingdom of Heaven? What if it was for a doctor or a nurse or an orderly or a patient or a relative of a patient in the next room? Oh, you'll know in Heaven what it was for. You don't know now, Jack, because you're just thinking about yourself. You need to trust Me. You need to trust Me."

God is not surprised by anything. Not by times, signs, happenings. He knows you'll face trials, but He has guaranteed your victory and that's a hallelujah moment.

I struggled with drug addiction for 10 years. I have asked God, "Why did I have to suffer through those years? That was a waste of time. Imagine what I could've done!" By the way, I was a functioning drug addict, so I still had a career and everything. But I'd say to God, "Imagine what I could've done with those 10 years if I wasn't wasted the whole time."

God said, in my spirit, "It wasn't my desire that you be a drug addict. That was your choice." And He was right. I made the wrong choices. He added, "But I'm using everything. You repented." And I did. God says in 1 John 1:9, "If we confess our sins, He is faithful and just and will… purify us from all unrighteousness." As believers, we're forgiven. When we sin, we just go right back to God, and we're forgiven instantly. But God used that; I got to see how God used my life to be able to impact the lives of others who are struggling with addiction. God has let me see many who have found victory and healing as a result of what I've gone through. So, I understand. I see how God has used that for His glory. I don't consider it a waste anymore. I don't believe that there's anything in our lives that we should consider a waste. We should be asking ourselves, "How can we use it for the glory of God?"

God has called us to fight a war! Joshua, Moses, David, and Solomon had physical battles they had to fight; they fought wars on behalf of the Lord. But even though their victory was assured and ordained by God, they still had to go out and fight the battle!

We are fighting spiritual battles! God said it's a spiritual warfare. It's not a physical battle; it's a spiritual battle. And we are to fight this spiritual battle. Our victory is assured, but we are still to fight the spiritual battle on earth with our sword of faith. We have a guarantee from God that we'll overcome what we go through – the trials and tribulations. There is a purpose for the trial. There's a purpose to the spiritual gifts God has given each one of us. I pray that you and I would understand the will of God so that we would receive the blessing of God in full both on Earth and in Heaven.

Let's look at Jesus' example for you and me. Jesus – like Solomon, like the widow who threw in two mites – knew that all things come from God, the Father. Let's look at how Jesus handled adversity. Maybe that will be a clue for you and me. This passage takes place right before His arrest and crucifixion. "Coming out,

He went to the Mount of Olives, as He was accustomed, and His disciples also followed Him. When He came to the place, He said to them, 'Pray that you may not enter into temptation.' And He was withdrawn from them about a stone's throw, and He knelt down and prayed." (Luke 22:39-41)

Jesus often withdrew to kneel and pray, personally and individually, to the Father. Because even though He was Jesus, and He was God's Son. He still knew that His Father was God. He knew what was going to happen, but He still prayed through everything. His victory and honor were assured, but He still fought! And here's what He said: "Father, if it is Your will, take this cup away from Me; nevertheless, not My will, but Yours, be done" (Luke 22:42).

Jesus knew He was going to have to go up on the cross and be crucified; He was going to die the most horrific of deaths! If you're not sure about that, just go watch the movie *The Passion of the Christ*, and you'll see how horrific it was. He knew He was going to suffer, and He said, "Wait a minute, Father. If there's another plan, if there's a plan B – I know this was the original plan: I'm going to die for all mankind and then I'm going to be one with you and then the veil will be torn and I'll repair the chasm that existed because of Adam and Eve's sin. Mankind will be able to go to you individually and have a one-on-one love relationship with you as their God – those are great plans. But now that I actually have to do it? Is there a plan B?"

But His next line was amazing: "But not My will – Yours be done."

What happened next? "Then an angel appeared to Him from heaven, strengthening Him. And being in agony, He prayed more earnestly. Then His sweat became like great drops of blood falling down to the ground" (Luke 22:43-44).

What did Jesus do? First, He prayed. Then when He wasn't answered, He was in agony, so did He quit? Did He say, "Oh, God. I can't believe you're putting me through this. How could you? If you really loved me, you wouldn't make me do this." No! He prayed more earnestly. He pressed into the Spirit of God.

That's exactly what you and I are supposed to do in our lives. Hey, times get tough. But what if they get tougher? Then you're supposed to come closer to God – not run away. You're supposed to draw closer and press into the Spirit of God. That's the lesson we need to learn.

What are you praying for? And when things get tough, what do you do? Do you pray harder? Do you press in? This is where the rubber meets the road with God. When a believer has fallen into temptation – we need to ask him, "How much have you been praying lately?" If you're living for the flesh, it's easy to fall into temptation.

The appeal, or pull, of temptation is going to be there every day of your life until the day you die. That's when the temptation will leave, that's when the smell of sin will leave, but right now it's here and sometimes it smells good. "Hey that smells pretty good. Maybe I should get some of that." Yeah, if you want to die, maybe get some rat poison, too, if you want to die. I've heard rat poison smells good, too. That's exactly what Satan does. He lies to us about sin being good. We need to press into God.

So, here's the bottom line. The bottom line can be found in John 15:5, "I am the vine; you are the branch. If you remain in me and I in you, you will bear much fruit. Apart from me, you can do nothing."

That is the bottom line of the gospel. There's a call, all through the Word of God (the Bible), it calls us to die to our flesh and live to our spirit. Many have phrased it as, "Die to self." We must die to self: meaning that we must forfeit the things that we want and live for God.

I have been praying about this a lot. I'm not there yet. I haven't died to myself. I want to. I know that's what God wants. I know that's the bar – that's batting 1000. I know that there are more blessings in store for those who do, and I've met some who have. I can see it. I can see they're 100% sold out to the Lord. They believe everything and do everything and there is a great reward in store for them. I want that. But I haven't done it completely. I haven't yet mastered differentiating the desire and realities of wants and needs, but I assure you I am working on it focus on and trying hard to get better in that area

It's something I am praying toward. And I suggest you do it as well. I think it should be instant. I think we should receive the salvation of the Lord and be willing to drop everything as the disciples did, as so many people today do – drop everything and live a life sold out 100% for the Lord. I think that's what God wants. I'm falling short, but I am praying that I get there.

John said about Jesus, "He must increase, I must decrease." That is a prayer each of us should have. He must increase, I must decrease. I'm doing that. God is increasing in my life, and I'm decreasing. And I want to get to the point where I'm done – where I've died to myself. But you better make sure that, if you haven't died to yourself yet, that at least God is increasing, and you are decreasing. If you miss that, you're going to miss the blessings of God, and it's possible you could miss the Kingdom of God. It's possible. I pray that never happens to anybody, but God said, "The path is narrow... The road is narrow... The gate is narrow..." We're to enter by the narrow door, which is through Jesus.

The Lord said if we examine ourselves, we won't be judged. If we look at what we're doing and clean it up, we won't have to be judged because we did it ourselves. We cleaned up what was messy. I pray that we would make it a mission, a commitment, a passion – out of gratitude for what God has done for us – that we would make sure that He is increasing, and we are decreasing.

Our focus needs to be more on Him than it is on us. Our desire needs to be more to hear the Holy Spirit than it is to hear the evening news. If we are listening to the Holy Spirit, He will warn us and speak to us – as I did with my daughter on Friday night – and tell us where it's safe to go and where it's not.

Remember, there's an enemy out to get you and he's subtle. He's not coming at you roaring like a truck; he's subtle, he's under the radar. He wants to get you off base; he wants you to miss the mark so he can laugh at you for all eternity when you miss out on the blessings that God, your Heavenly Father, has for you. I pray that you would desire to die to self, that you would desire for Christ to increase in your life and your heart.

Solomon loved God, and he knew all things came from God. Because of this, he prayed to God for wisdom and knowledge... and he received so much more. I pray that you and I would have that same prayer.

The widow gave all she had into the offering plate because she loved God so much, and she knew all came from God; I pray that you and I would live like that.

Jesus came to serve. Jesus reminded us to pray always – when things got tough and when things were great; I pray that you and I would live like that.

Jesus reminded us that Satan has desired to sift us like wheat. But not if we get back up! He may knock us down, but when we get back up, we're to use that trial and tribulation, we're to use that fight with Satan, we're to use what we've learned, we're to use that knowledge and courage and wisdom to strengthen the brethren – to edify our brothers and sisters. I pray that you and I would live like that.

Lastly, John reminded us that Christ must increase, and we must decrease. I pray that you and I would live like that

Chapter Seven

FOCUSING ON COURAGE AND STRENGTH WITH SPIRITUAL ENDURANCE

As Christians, we need to grow in maturity and completion. God tells us that, yes, when we're saved, we're spiritual babies and we need milk to grow. Babies can't handle meat; we choke on meat as a baby, so we don't feed our babies meat. But God says that as we grow and develop, we're supposed to understand and take more of the Word and truth of God and chew on it. It's supposed to satisfy you like your favorite food – whether it's filet mignon or pizza – whatever it is for you.

Recently in my life, I have felt like the Word of God is coming at me like a 3D movie blasting into my life. I'm just taking it in as it swarms over my heart and soul. It just gets more and more and better and better. When God said in Scripture, "Come closer to me, and I'll come closer to you," He is not lying. He is telling the truth.

I'm a reader of the *New York Post*. I usually go for the sports section first, but I want to highlight an article I recently read. Here's the title of the article: "West Village Woman Posts Suicide Note Online." Something really caught me about this article. This woman, in her late twenties, was working as a dietician. She was found dead with a cloth strap around her neck in her apartment. She left a suicide note and here's what she said:

"Truly I have a great life on paper. I'm fortunate to eat meals that most would only imagine, I travel freely without restriction. I live alone in the second greatest city in America, San Francisco. However, all of this seems trivial to me. Oh, I know; it seems like the ultimate first-world problem. I get it.

I often feel detached while I'm in a room of my favorite people. I also felt absolutely nothing during what should have been the happiest times of my life and yet I felt darkness. No single conversation or discussion has led me to this decision. So, at what point do you metaphorically pull the trigger.

I'll miss great food, I'll miss authentic street tacos and pork belly. I'll miss unexpected hugs, I'll miss… beautiful cherries in July, tracing the sleeping eyebrow, smoking cigarettes, the Golden

Gate Bridge at sunset, the first sip of ice cold brew in a sticky August, making eye contact with people walking down the street, Jeopardy, saying I love you, late night junk food, shooting the bull, and especially the no destination in sight in long walks … it's time for me to be happy and I hope you can get down with that."

This girl had everything by the world's standards, yet she was empty because she didn't have the one thing that she needed for life, happiness, peace, and joy – God. She didn't have a relationship with God. She didn't have the Holy Spirit in her heart telling her how much she's loved, how much she's cherished, that there was a perfect plan for her life, that there's a place for her in Heaven, that the Holy Spirit is with her. She didn't know that the love of God is enough. She figured out that the things of the world and the love of people weren't enough. And they're not. First, people's love for us is conditional. That's just the way it is. It shouldn't be – but it is. And the things of the world – they rust, moth, and decay; they're here temporarily just like we're strangers on this earth. But the eternal things of God, the Holy Spirit of God, your spirit that God has breathed into your life – that's what lives on for eternity and that's the joy and peace you can't get from the world. That's what I pray you would not miss.

Well, sometimes there's some funny stuff in the *New York Post* newspaper, but what I'm sharing in this chapter isn't. A couple of days later, there were three sobering headlines:

"Subway Hate Slash"

In this first article, a guy walks up to a girl on the train and he says to this 28-year-old woman, "I hate you. I'm going to cut you," and he cuts her with a box-cutter. He was a complete stranger.

"Rockland-Flint Suicide"

Keith Flint, lead singer of the dance-electronic band *The Prodigy*, was found dead in a suicide in his hotel room at the age of 49.

"Alabama Devastated: 2 Kids Dead Among Twin Tornadoes"

There was a tornado in Alabama, and 23 people died, including a couple of kids. Many of the deaths were from the same family.

Tragedy is everywhere. We're dealing with life and death on a daily basis. Life is sometimes hanging by a thread. This is the world.

It's a part of life. Not all of it is pretty. Our job – your job and my job – is the same as God instructed Joshua. It's the same as David instructed Solomon. It's the same as Jesus instructs His disciples and all of us – be strong and courageous!

Complete the task. Finish the job. Be an ambassador, a son, a warrior, a representative of Jesus Christ on this earth so that people may see your light shine in the darkness of the world. There's plenty of darkness, yet we need to be the lights that shine for Christ. So how do we do that? I have a couple of favorite Bible verses along these lines.

Judges 14 gives us the story of Samson. Now there are many stories about Samson in the Bible and much we could glean from Samson's life and walk with God. We can learn about his disobedience and obedience, and what God accomplished through him. However, I could write an entire book on that single topic. So, I'm going to simplify it a little bit.

We're just going to look at just one aspect of Samson's life, but I don't want to short-change any of it. I encourage you and urge you in your personal studies to go deep with the Word of God.

This might not seem directly related, but I'm a Bruce Springsteen fan. I'm also a Bob Dylan fan. I also like Al Pacino, and I like Brad Pitt, and I like Leonardo DiCaprio. I can't imagine if I first started listening to Bob Dylan when he released his 20th album, not going back and listening to the first 19 albums and listening to them. It would be absurd. Imagine if I said, "Well, I heard him here, so I'll only listen going forward." No! I love the music. I want to hear all of it! Because each song is different. It's all great. And who would see one Al Pacino movie and say he's a great actor and not want to watch the other movies he acts in? It's absurd. Likewise, I want to encourage you to study the full counsel of the Bible. It's God's desire that you know the whole story. You don't have to know every word – you don't have to be a scholar. But man, you should watch the movies, listen to the songs, and know the story. You should read the book; you should know the stories. It shouldn't be that your pastor or your teacher is the first guy telling you about Samson or things of the Old Testament.

We know that Jesus loves us and that's the most foundational thing to know. But there's more to the story. You can see Jesus throughout scripture – all through the Bible, He's there – I assure you. Just like you hear the same voice in Bruce Springsteen's music, no matter what type of music he's playing; just like Al Pacino; you know it's Al on the screen, but he's playing different roles. You know its Leonardo DiCaprio on the screen; but he's playing different roles, and he's great at what he does. So is God! God is amazing and I don't want you to miss any of it.

Let's get back to Samson. Here's the message that I take away from Judges Chapters 14 and 16: Samson is in some interesting situations and it dawned on me how easy it is to resist temptation – the first time.

In Judges 14, Samson went to Timnath. He saw a woman down there and he wanted her as his wife. He went to his parents and said, "Go get her for me as a wife," because that was how marriage was done back then. It was the tradition of the day. He went down and talked to the woman and Samson liked her. Not only did he like her after he saw her, but after he talked to her, he continued to like her. I'm paraphrasing and taking you through the story quickly.

It was customary to give a feast if you were going to marry somebody. Samson gave a feast and there were 30 young men there. Samson said, "Let me pose a riddle to you; if you can correctly solve and explain the riddle within seven days of the feast – I'll give you 30 linen garments and 30 changes of clothing. But if you can't explain it to me in the seven days, then you give me 30 linen garments and 30 changes of clothes."

Samson thought he had an easy score. Have you ever done anything like that – made a friendly wager with your friend that you were sure you would win?

Now he got the idea of the riddle because of something that happened to him. A lion had attacked Samson, and he killed it with his bare hands. He tore it open because he was Samson – the strongest guy in the world at the time. He saw a swarm of bees inside the lion's carcass and honey, so he grabbed some of the honey and ate it. So, the riddle was: "Out of the eater came something to eat and out of the strong came something sweet." That was the riddle they needed to solve.

Samson wanted the payoff. Linen garments and clothing were valuable at that time. Thirty linen garments were very valuable.

That would be like saying, "Hey, if you can solve this riddle, I'll give you each a thousand bucks; but if you can't, each one of you gives me a thousand." That'd be a pretty good day for me if you couldn't solve the riddle.

Three days go by and they cannot explain the riddle and the 30 companions are stumped. On the seventh day, they tell Samson's wife, "Entice your husband that he may explain the riddle to us or else we'll burn you and your father's house with fire."

Tough spot. "Hey, listen, you brought this guy in. You brought Samson down here among us Philistines. He's coming after you. He wants you. You brought him into our town."

"So, you go entice him, so we'll know the answer to the riddle. Otherwise, we're going to kill you and burn down your father's house."

Judges 14:16 tells us that Samson's wife wept on him and said, "You hate me. You do not love me. You posed a riddle to the sons of my people, but you haven't explained it to me. Oh, honey, if you love me, you'd tell me everything."

What did Samson say? He looked at her and said, "I haven't explained it to my father or mother, so I should explain it to you?" She wept for the seven days while the feast lasted. And on the seventh day, he told her because she pressed him so much.

Get this right. For seven days she's been hammering him, "Tell me, tell me, tell me, and tell me!"

He resisted her for the first six days, "No, no. I can't tell you." Why? I assume he's not an idiot. I assume he doesn't want to take any chance that he would be compromised in any way because then he would lose the bet and have to pay off a huge amount. He said, "Look, I haven't even told my mother or father. I know that we're married, but I just met you. I've known them all my life; if I were going to tell somebody something, it would probably be them."

On the seventh day, he caved. Why? Because she pressed him so much. I have news for you. You and I are going to be pressed so much in our life by Satan. He's going to press you so much to get you to break, to get you to give up what you have, to get you to give up the treasure and trade it for something. It is going to come at you at your weakest point, at your Achilles' heel, and he's going to keep coming like Chinese water torture. It's drip by drip. They don't take you and slam you and beat the crap out of you like they did with John McCain when he was a political prisoner and so many others who have suffered for our country so valiantly. No, it's drip by drip. You sit there tied up till the pounding drives you crazy. We would think it's nothing, just a little drip of water. Eventually, the pounding is like an anvil slamming on your head until you can't take it and you go insane! That's how they get you with Chinese water torture.

That's what Satan does. He keeps coming. He's prowling around like a roaring lion and looking to devour you, but he'll use any tactic he can. He'll come, and he'll keep pressing you and pressing you. God tells us we're to be strong. Scripture tells us to put on the full armor of God. He says, "Resist the temptations of the devil." He says, "Resist the devil and he'll flee from you." He doesn't say invite him in and party with him and you'll tell him when it's time to leave. It doesn't work like that. We must resist. We have to be strong.

So, here's how the story ends. The wife tells the people the riddle. Samson comes on the day and they tell him the answer to the riddle. Samson realizes he's been betrayed by his wife and he says, "Well, if you didn't plow with my heifer, you would not have solved my riddle." That's exactly what he said. It's a Bible quote. Then he went down to Escalon, he killed 30 of their men, he took their clothes and he gave the 30 changes of clothing to those who had explained the riddle.

His anger was aroused, and he went back up to his father's house and Samson's wife was given to his companion who had been his best man. He gets so angry that he kills 30 people and he loses the wife who had been given to him; the wife goes to the best man.

Clearly, we can see by the results it wasn't a good thing for Samson that he gave in to this temptation. And it's not a good thing for you and me when we're not strong and courageous and we give in.

A couple of chapters later, Samson went to Gaza and he slept with a hooker. Right after that, he met Delilah, the love of his life. He was in love with Delilah; now Delilah was a Philistine and she said to Samson, "Please tell me where your great strength lies and what you may be bound with to afflict you." By the way, Samson's great strength was given to him by the Holy Spirit. God had given Samson his strength, just as the Holy Spirit gives you gifts today to use for the Kingdom of God. It was God's desire that Samson use his gifts for the Kingdom of God because it was God who made Samson that strong.

But Delilah said, "Tell me what makes you so strong. What is your weakness?" And what did Samson do?

We notice this trend; it's easy to resist temptation the first time in this story. Here's what happens. The first time, Samson said to her, "If they bind me with seven fresh bowstrings, not yet dried, then I shall become weak and I'm like any other man." What did Delilah do? Well, she was committed to her people, the Philistines, even though she was with Samson, and she told the Philistines, "This is how we're going to get Samson."

So, they snuck up on Samson and they bind him with seven fresh bowstrings, not yet dry. The men were lying in wait and Delilah said, "The Philistines are upon you Samson!" The Word of God tells us Samson broke the bowstrings like they were a tiny piece of yarn when it touches fire; it was easy. In other words, the secret of his strength was still not known.

Then Delilah said to Samson, "You've mocked me and told me lies. Now please tell me what you are bound with that will reveal your strength!"

Samson said to her, "Well, all right. If they bind me securely with new ropes that have never been used, then I'll become weak and I'll be like any other man." Basically, he was saying, "This is really what it is, Delilah. You're bothering me, you're pestering me, here's the thing: bind me with ropes that have never been used and I'm just like any other man."

So, Delilah took new ropes and she bound Samson with the ropes and she said, "The Philistines are upon you Samson!" The men were lying in wait, but he broke them off his arms like a thread.

Delilah then said to Samson, "Until now you've mocked me and told me lies. Tell me what you may be bound with!"

You would think at this point Samson would kind of get the idea. It's easy in hindsight to be a Sunday morning quarterback. But there's a message here for you and me: we're to be awake and alert. God says in 1st Peter, "Be strong, be sober, be alert; you do not know the hour which I come." We're to be ready and prepared like a servant waiting, taking care of his master's goods while the master is away, so that when the master comes back, we'll hear, "Well done, good and faithful servant." That's our job.

Here's how the story ends. When Delilah kept pressing him, he said, "All right. If you weave the seven locks of my head into a loom then I'll be like other men."

So, Delilah did it, and Samson woke from the sleep, and he's fine – just as strong as ever.

The story from the Bible goes on like this:

> Then she said to him, "How can you say, 'I love you,' when your heart is not with me? You have mocked me these three times, and have not told me where your great strength lies." And it came to pass, when she pestered him daily with her words and pressed him, so that his soul was vexed to death, that he told her all his heart, and said to her, "No razor has ever come upon my head, for I have been a Nazirite to God from my mother's womb. If I am shaven, then my strength will leave me, and I shall become weak, and be like any other man."
>
> When Delilah saw that he had told her all his heart, she sent and called for the lords of the Philistines, saying, "Come up once more, for he has told me all his heart." So the lords of the Philistines came up to her and brought the money in their hand. Then she lulled him to sleep on her knees, and called for a man and had him shave off the seven locks of his head. Then she began to torment him, and his strength left him. And she said, "The Philistines are upon you, Samson!" So he awoke from his sleep, and said, "I will go out as before, at other times, and shake myself free!" But he did not know that the Lord had departed from him.

> Then the Philistines took him and put out his eyes, and brought him down to Gaza. They bound him with bronze fetters, and he became a grinder in the prison. (Judges 16:15-21)

They gouged his eyes out and put him into prison. Why? He gave in. He knew what was happening and yet he got worn down.

Are you worn down? Are you worn down by the frustrations of life? Are you worn down by situations? Are you worn down waiting for promises? Are you worn down by other people and what you think should be yours to have? Are you worn down by frustration, by anger? Are you worn down by pressure, obligations, fear, pressure, temptations in your life? Well, God has a message for you. God's message is, "Be strong and courageous." There is a prize at the end. We need to be focused on the prize at the end.

I just love God's Word because it's so relevant today. This Old Testament stuff is as relevant to us today as when it happened. There's an important point in 1 Samuel, chapter 12, where the people of Israel wanted God to appoint them a king. God was upset at this because the people didn't trust Him enough to deliver them. God pointed this out to the prophet Samuel. He said, "Look, I've delivered you in the days of Moses, I've parted the Red Sea, I've delivered you from Sanai, I've brought you out of Egypt, and I've brought you to the Promised Land; how could you possibly not trust me now?" But the people said, "No, we want a king," so God said, "All right, I'm going to give you a king.

We pick this up in 1 Samuel, chapter 12, verse 12: "And when you saw that Nahash king of the Ammonites came against you, you said to me, 'No, but a king shall reign over us,' when the Lord your God was your king."

This was the wickedness of Israel. They didn't trust God. Sometimes we do that. We don't trust God's timing in our life, or somebody else's life, with things that are happening. We don't trust God's timing. Samuel says to the people that they've sinned against God.

Have you ever been in that spot? Have you ever realized you've sinned against God? I hope, if that's happened to you, that you've stood on the Word of God. 1 John 1:9 tells us that if you confess your sins, God is faithful and just, and He will forgive you and purify you. God will wipe your sin away if you confess it.

So, the people of Israel replied to Samuel's warning and they said this: "Pray for your servants to the Lord your God, that we may not die; for we have added to all our sins the evil of asking a king for ourselves." "Sometimes in order to see our sin in order to see our weakness we need to focus with courage and strength and spiritual endurance".

They knew they had sinned. They knew they had sinned previously, but they've added on to that sin by asking for a king. Listen to what God tells Samuel to say to the people. This is God speaking to Israel, but this is a message He has for us as well. This message is for you and me: "Do not fear. You have done all this wickedness; yet do not turn aside from following the Lord, but serve the Lord with all your heart. And do not turn aside; for then you would go after empty things which cannot profit or deliver, for they are nothing. For the Lord will not forsake His people, for His great name's sake, because it has pleased the Lord to make you His people" (1 Samuel 12:20-22).

Serve the Lord with all your heart, as Jesus did. Jesus was our example. He was an example of a perfect life of sacrifice, of service, of eyes focused on His Master's business. He knew who God was – His Father.

You and I have that same confirmation through the Holy Spirit of God through our faith in Jesus. Don't go after empty things that cannot profit or deliver. They are nothing! God constantly tells us to work for treasures of the Kingdom of God, not for the things of the earth that will rust, moth, and decay. I love these few verses:

> I, even I, am He who blots out your
> transgressions for My own sake; And I will not
> remember your sins. (Isaiah 43:25)

> I have blotted out, like a thick cloud, your
> transgressions, And like a cloud, your sins.
> Return to Me, for I have redeemed you. (Isaiah 44:22)

> For as the heavens are high above the earth,
> So great is His mercy toward those who fear Him;
> As far as the east is from the west, So far has He
> removed our transgressions from us. (Psalm 103:11)
>
> Through the Lord's mercies we are not
> consumed,Because His compassions fail not.
> They are new every morning; Great is Your
> faithfulness."(Lamentations 3:22)

God has forgiven you so He can have a relationship with you for His sake. If you can't get up in the gratitude of that, if you can't get excited by that, if you can't get fired up by that, something is wrong. These are the promises of God. This is what God is telling you to do.

There's a line in Revelation chapter 3 that talks about the Church, about serving, and it asks, "When are you going to wake up and strengthen the things that remain?" When are we going to wake up and really give ourselves to God? When are we going to truly believe that God is who He says He is – not a slot machine, not a genie in the bottle, not a Magic 8-ball who we go to when we need an answer or have a question. No. May that never be so with you and me.

God created us for a daily relationship with Him. I have a friend who couldn't grasp the concept of Jesus as God; he just couldn't grasp it. So, I asked him about his relationships with his kids. I said, "Look, how would you feel if your kid that you love so much only came to you when they needed something?"

That was it. That was his relationship with God, "Hey God, I need something. Can you give it to me?"

"Well yes, I'll give it to you because I love you, but I want to spend time with you. I just want to be a part of your life. I just want to be there for you."

I was sitting in Texas Roadhouse one day with Jackson, my son. My wife and daughter were away at my daughter's dance competition. I was sitting there and just looking at him. He's 16 years old now, so he's not a kid. He was looking at his phone, and I was eating my bread and just looking at my son. I was so happy just to be in that moment. It was simple, but the most beautiful of moments. I prayed in my heart, "God, thank you. I'm just in this moment looking at my son. I worry and pray for his future, as we all do for our kids, but just to know I'm part of his life, to be with him – I get no greater joy than being a part of all of my children's' lives. Thank you, Lord."

Just being there with him, and seeing, and communicating with my son – that's what God wants from you and me. God's greatest heartbreak is when we run the other way. I believe my children come to me in joy, in fear, in anything that's going on in their lives because I love them no matter what. And I'm just an earthly father. If you are a father, you know that you're just an earthly father. Imagine God, our Heavenly Father, whose love is perfect and unconditional and forever.

That's what we're supposed to be excited about!

I love the promise from 1 Timothy chapter 2 that says that even if we are faithless, He is faithful because he cannot deny Himself. A part of Him is in us; the Holy Spirit is in us. We need to see Jesus in everything.

There's a powerful story in 2 Samuel chapter 9. David was king. His good buddy, Jonathan, had died before David became king. Jonathan was Saul's son; David and Jonathan were not just buddies, there was this close brotherly relationship. They swore an oath to each other to be true to each other and each other's families when Jonathan had died. David was king, the battles were won, and he was sitting in his kingdom, and this is how the question goes:

> Now David said, "Is there still anyone who is left of the house of Saul, that I may show him kindness for Jonathan's sake?" And there was a servant of the house of Saul whose name was Ziba. So when they had called him to David, the king said to him, "Are you Ziba?"
>
> He said, "At your service!" Then the king said, "Is there not still someone of the house of Saul, to whom I may show the kindness of God?" And Ziba said to the king, "There is still a son of Jonathan who is lame in his feet."

> So the king said to him, "Where is he?" And Ziba said to the king, "Indeed he is in the house of Machir the son of Ammiel, in Lo Debar." Then King David sent and brought him out of the house of Machir the son of Ammiel, from Lo Debar.
>
> Now when Mephibosheth the son of Jonathan, the son of Saul, had come to David, he fell on his face and prostrated himself. Then David said, "Mephibosheth?" And he answered, "Here is your servant!"
>
> So David said to him, "Do not fear, for I will surely show you kindness for Jonathan your father's sake, and will restore to you all the land of Saul your grandfather; and you shall eat bread at my table continually."
>
> Then he bowed himself, and said, "What is your servant, that you should look upon such a dead dog as I?" (1 Samuel 9:1-8)

Here, Mephibosheth thinks he's going to die. He's going to get slaughtered, As a result, there will be no lineage of Jonathan left. But King David was sincere, and he spoke to the servant, Ziba, saying:

> I have given to your master's son all that belonged to Saul and to all his house. You therefore, and your sons and your servants, shall work the land for him, and you shall bring in the harvest, that your master's son may have food to eat. But Mephibosheth your master's son shall eat bread at my table always." (v. 9-10)

So, Mephibosheth dwelt in Jerusalem and ate at the king's table – just like one of the king's sons. Mephibosheth did nothing deserving of what he received – not one thing. He couldn't do it on his own. He couldn't work for it, knowing it was impossible for him to do anything to get any of this. David, in his grace and mercy, and for his love of Jonathan, he bestowed all of this on Jonathan's son, and he gave it all to him.

What does that remind you of? Jesus. God, through Jesus, has bestowed upon you and me and the whole world His love and grace and mercy so that forever we would know that we are eating at the King's table. Jesus says that we're heirs to the throne of Heaven. We're brothers and sisters of Jesus. Our place is at the King's table in Heaven and we need to live and walk in that freedom every day.

I don't understand how you can walk through this world miserable as a Christian! I don't get it. I get that there are hard circumstances. I get that parents may die, children may die, and I couldn't imagine anything worse. You may lose money, relationships, power, titles, health – I get all of that. It's part of the game, but we have the Kingdom of God. We are God's kids – a gift freely given; we did nothing to deserve it.

Do you know how happy Mephibosheth was? Can you imagine? He was sitting there thinking the king was going to kill him because he was crippled and lame. But, no! Instead, King David extended love and grace and gave him more than he could have expected.

"Why? Why would you treat a dog like me? I deserve to die; I'm crippled and lame – why would you do this for me?"

"Because of Jonathan."

Why do you do things? Because of Jesus?

You go through the Word of God, and you will see Jesus everywhere in it – in all the stories. You will see Jesus in everything. All of this is for our teaching and edification and joy and knowledge.

> Therefore we must give the more earnest heed to the things we have heard, lest we drift away. (Hebrews 2:1)

In other words, we need to pay attention to what God is saying lest we drift away and miss it.

> The word spoken through angels proves steadfast; and every transgression and disobedience receives a just reward. How shall we escape if we neglect so great a salvation, which at first began to be spoken by the Lord and was confirmed to us by those who heard him? (Hebrews 2:2)

We've been ordained with the gift and Spirit of God to live this life. How can we escape if we neglect it, if we toss it away?

> "For in that He put all in subjection under him,
> He left nothing that is not put under him. But
> now we do not yet see all things put under him. But
> we see Jesus, who was made a little lower than the
> angels, for the suffering of death crowned with glory
> and honor, that He, by the grace of God, might
> taste death for everyone." (Hebrews 2:8-9)

Everything is under Jesus, but we don't see it. Why? Because now we know in part. One day, we will know in full. We're not God; we can't see and understand the mind and heart of God because He created us. When we're in Heaven, face-to-face with the Lord, we will understand; there will be nothing hidden from you at that point. Now, you have the Holy Spirit, you understand a lot of it, but not all of it.

God has shown us all through His Word that He is God; He can and will perform according to His Word; you don't need to rely on anybody else. You don't need to rely on me or what I say; it's the Holy Spirit of God speaking into your heart.

God is alive!

He's alive in your heart – but you need to seek Him. He says, "You will find me when you seek me with all of your heart" (Jeremiah 29:13).

Did you ever wish you were a lawyer? Or wish you'd been a doctor? Or maybe a policeman? Or maybe started a business? But you didn't do it, so you think, "Aw, man, I wish I'd done that," and now you regret it. Why? Well, why didn't you do it? Maybe it's because it takes seven years of college and law school combined. That's a long time! Medical school takes around 12 years. The police academy requires some intensive training. Starting a business requires another skill set and often some money to start out. So, let me get this right: You wish you'd done it because you wanted the benefit of it, but you weren't willing to do what it took to get there. Others were. There are plenty of lawyers, doctors, policemen, and business owners out there; I just used those as an example.

The bottom line is, if you aren't willing to do what it takes, you will regret not having the benefit. I pray that that's never the case for you and me with our walk with God. I pray that we will be willing, that we won't have to say, "We didn't know what to do." Sometimes it takes us focusing on courage and strength with spiritual endurance to see the truth.

God is saying, "Be strong and courageous."

He said in Ephesians 2:10, "I want you to do the good works I have prepared in advance for you to do." Jesus tells us in John 15:16, "Go and bear fruit, and fruit that will last."

That's what you need to do. Hebrews 2:14-15 tells us "Inasmuch then as the children have partaken of flesh and blood, He Himself likewise shared in the same, that through death He might destroy him who had the power of death, that is, the devil, and release those who through fear of death were all their lifetime subject to bondage."

You are free from death. A true believer does not need to be scared of dying. You know where you are going. You know Jesus paid the price; you're free from death. Death is only the beginning of the second – and the eternal – part of your life. We all have a terminal illness. It's called aging. We all have it. What we need to learn on earth is how to live in freedom. Titus 3:4-7 shows us how:"But when the kindness and the love of God our Savior toward man appeared, not by works of righteousness which we have done, but according to His mercy He saved us, through the washing of regeneration and renewing of the Holy Spirit, whom He poured out on us abundantly through Jesus Christ our Savior, that having been justified by His grace we should become heirs according to the hope of eternal life."

This is the gospel! The kindness and love of God appeared, not by our righteousness that we have done, but according to God's mercy, through Jesus Christ who saved us. He poured out the Holy Spirit on us abundantly through Christ. Have as much of it as you can take! It's being poured out abundantly; how many jars are you going to bring? How much of your heart are you going to bring for God to fill with His Spirit? Because that determines how much you get. You can have as much as you want of the Holy Spirit of God. We've been justified – not by our works, but by Christ. Therefore, we are heirs to the throne of the hope of eternal life.

The key to life is to make sure God's Holy Spirit, who is inside of you, is on the throne of your life. In other words, God is not just your Savior with your ticket into heaven, but He is Lord of your life and, as such, you are listening to, heeding, and obeying His every instruction, guidance, and advice which, for you the believer, is always available to you directly and consistently and is always for your blessing and benefit. This Holy Spirit of God's counsel comes to you directly from your Father God, realized by you through and in the form of His Holy Spirit, a part of Himself He deposited in your heart upon salvation to guide you and teach you all things as His words tell us in John 14:26. His Word also says in John 7:37-39, "'If anyone thirsts, let him come to Me and drink He who believes in Me, as the Scripture has said, out of His heart will flow rivers of living water.' But this He spoke concerning the Spirit, whom those believing in Him would receive…" So, it is our listening to and following God's Holy Spirit in us guiding our hearts and minds that allows us to receive the living water of God and allows it to flow out of our hearts to impact others for the Kingdom of God (as long as you do not drown out the Holy Spirit's voice by taking your focus off God and placing it on the things of the world).

This next story from Luke 19:12-26 is a familiar one, but I hope to bring a new perspective to it for you. It's often called "The Parable of the Talents." Jesus tells this parable that encourages us to do business until He returns:

> A man of noble birth went to a distant country to have himself appointed king and then to return. So he called ten of his servants and gave them ten minas. 'Put this money to work,' he said, 'until I come back.'
>
> But his subjects hated him and sent a delegation after him to say, 'We don't want this man to be our king.' "He was made king, however, and returned home. Then he sent for the servants to whom he had given the money, in order to find out what they had gained with it.

The first one came and said, 'Sir, your mina has earned ten more.' "'Well done, my good servant!' his master replied. 'Because you have been trustworthy in a very small matter, take charge of ten cities.'

The second came and said, 'Sir, your mina has earned five more.' "His master answered, 'You take charge of five cities.' "Then another servant came and said, 'Sir, here is your mina; I have kept it laid away in a piece of cloth. I was afraid of you, because you are a hard man. You take out what you did not put in and reap what you did not sow.'

His master replied, 'I will judge you by your own words, you wicked servant! You knew, did you, that I am a hard man, taking out what I did not put in, and reaping what I did not sow? Why then didn't you put my money on deposit, so that when I came back, I could have collected it with interest?'

Then he said to those standing by, 'Take his mina away from him and give it to the one who has ten minas.' "'Sir,' they said, 'he already has ten!' "He replied, 'I tell you that to everyone who has, more will be given, but as for the one who has nothing, even what they have will be taken away.'"

By the way, please do not use this parable to mean you should go trade the stock market, or that Jesus wants you to gamble because you're a gifted gambler – that's not what it means. The master gave talents to each of the servants and He said to do business until He returns. I believe that the symbolism of that is salvation. Jesus gives salvation to all who believe. It's available to all.

Jesus says, "With that salvation, with this life I've given you – use it! Do business until I return. Until I come again; until you meet me in Heaven; do business for the Kingdom of God." We're not meant to do selfish business that will rust, moth, and decay.

We are meant to do Kingdom business – where you build your treasuries up in the Kingdom of God.

There is going to be a judgment day – when you're going to be called to God and He is going to look at your life and say, "How did you do with the life, with the talent I gave you?"

The gifts of the Holy Spirit can be the key to your Christian life and walk; He wants you to lead a life that is exceedingly and abundantly more than you could ever ask or imagine. He doesn't want you to miss it. God offers salvation to all – but He gives different gifts to each of us.

Apostle Paul told us in Corinthians that we're given different gifts. Some have multiple gifts while some have one gift. Some have encouragement, some have prophecy, some have giving, some have faith. In Matthew, Jesus told a parable about investing your life in the Kingdom. One guy takes his 10 talents given to him by his master and using good business sense he turns it into 20. With the talent that God gave him, he used it to the best of his ability, to fulfill his purpose for the Master's Kingdom. Another guy took his five talents given to him by the Master and turned it into ten. With the talent God gave him, the amount he returned to the Master was different from the talent God gave the other man, but he was able to accomplish 100% of his purpose.

See, it didn't matter how many they got. It doesn't matter what God's gifts to you are or how many you get; it matters that you use the ones you have to the fullest. It matters that you use them 100% in the Kingdom of God. It doesn't matter if you're the one who got ten or the one who got five if you made the most of what you were given, each of us will be blessed to hear, "Well done, good and faithful servant!"

It won't be a case where we're saying, "Oh, wait, you got more than me." It's about our obedience to God with the life we have. Will we give it? Will we surrender it? Will we live it for the Lord?

But there was one who had the gift. He had a talent – and what did he do with it? He was too scared to use it. He feared judgment. He was scared.

God doesn't want you to fear Him. I have three kids. I would like them to fear me in reverence. I'm the dad, after all. I do have the authority to give and take certain things away, because they're not at the right age to be able to do it themselves; but it would break my heart if my kids were scared of me and didn't do something because they were scared, that if they would fail and that I'd be upset or disappointed. I would only be upset or disappointed if they didn't try.

Through the grace of God, I want my children to use the lives they are given to the best of their ability! If you're an artist, go paint; if you're a doctor, go save lives; if you're a teacher, teach; if you're a truck driver; drive trucks. I don't care what you do – but whatever ability you have, just use it to the fullest. My heart would break if my wife and I were standing back, looking at the lives of our children, and seeing that they wasted it. "You had this potential, but you didn't use it. Scared of me? I love you the most! Not only did I create you, not only did I feed you and clothe you and sacrifice everything so that you could have this opportunity, but I love you more than anybody ever will on this earth." That's a parent's love for a kid; and that's God's love for you.

There are many who will come before the Kingdom of God on the day of judgment and God will say to them, "Depart from me, I do not know you."

Those people might say, "Lord! Hey, we sang in the praise team, we were ushers in church for you, we came to church, we went to Bible study, we gave money, volunteered to feed the homeless on Thanksgiving, we did all this," and God will say, "Yeah, but your hearts were far from me. I never knew you."

I pray that God would do spiritual surgery in your heart so that you would hear, "Well done," instead of, "Depart from me." Have you ever taken the time to consider the value of focusing on courage and strength with spiritual endurance to make sure you get the desired outcome of your life both on earth and in heaven.

I pray that we would take God's words of wisdom that He has told us, to "Be strong and courageous." We already have the Kingdom, and we're already rich; we're free to live in grace and not fear. By God's grace, may we live out of gratitude for what God has done, out of the certainty of Heaven.

Each of us will come to that moment when we face our last breath, when we rejoice in the certainty of Heaven. We will realize that's just the beginning of our time in eternity forever. My prayer is that we will rejoice in the fact that our lives mattered for the Kingdom of God, that we stayed the course; that we resisted temptation – not just the easy times, but the hard times too – because we were focused on the prize. We believed God. We believed there was a Heaven. We believed it mattered what we did here on earth.

The Apostle Paul said, "One thing I do: I forget the past and I press on to the task at hand." Let "press on" be the words that motivate you and your life from here on out. Remember to press on to the higher calling of the Lord, because God's calling, the calling of Heaven, the calling of the Kingdom, is the reason you were born. Don't miss it.

Make it your goal to grow toward maturity and completion by the power of the Holy Spirit each day.

Regardless of the newspaper headlines around the world, you can be strong and courageous, for God is with you.

Chapter Eight

CHECKING AND ALIGNING YOURSELF WITH YOU, GOD OR BOTH?

I was brought up Jewish. We were not very religious growing up. I was also a business guy – a Madison Avenue guy – and I worked in advertising. I also had a major drug problem, which started in high school and continued through college and followed me through part of my early adult life.

I was 33 years old, walking along in my life, when Jesus Christ started knocking on my heart and I said, "Wait a minute. Excuse me?" First, I'm Jewish so I was thinking, what's going on here? Second, no one ever handed me a Bible and said, "You need to follow Jesus." It was Jesus Himself knocking on my heart.

I didn't really know what was going on, but I knew it was God. I sensed it was God, and I started to search and dig into the Bible and see what was happening. Two months later, I basically ran out of questions for God and accepted Him. That was a long time ago, and my life has gotten better every day since then – literally, every day. So, I give God the glory.

I just want to share with you how amazing God is. He Himself came to me, the Holy Spirit of God, and revealed Himself. I don't know that I necessarily have a message in this chapter that in itself can set your heart on fire, but I believe that God can; I believe that God can change your life today – and that He wants to.

As you probably gathered by the name of the chapter, I want to discuss aligning with God. When we think about alignment, we often think of a wheel alignment that we have done in the car shop. But I want to have a real alignment with God, not a wheel alignment. I want to encourage you to let God align your hearts a little more with Him, as well as share how He's aligned mine a little more. If you have a vehicle, you know that when your tires are out of alignment – if you let go of the wheel the car veers to the left or to the right – that's a bad thing. You can get into an accident. Plus, you must work a lot harder to drive. When the wheels aren't aligned, you have to make sure you're grabbing the wheel so that the car goes straight. Plus, your tires wear out quicker and you get lower gas mileage. So, everything about it is wrong.

Of course, you want to have your wheels aligned properly, just as you should want to have your life aligned with God properly. I don't know if you are familiar with Lasik surgery; I haven't had it done, but my understanding is that you go in and in a second they realign everything in your eyes with a little laser, just like that. One minute you couldn't see clearly and the next minute you can. I believe the Holy Spirit is going to realign your heart just like that. That's how quick it can be. When you allow God to be your surgeon and the Holy Spirit to be your GPS, He can show you exactly what the truth of God is. Have you ever considered the importance or necessity of checking and aligning yourself with you, God or both?

Alignment is an interesting thing. It's all about perspective. There was a point in time in history where they thought the world was flat. Then Columbus sailed (or someone else depending on whose version of history you want to believe... 3rd century BC) and all of a sudden we had new evidence, new proof, and we said, "Oh. Now we believe it's round. I used to think it was flat, but now I believe it's round."

There was a fairly recent news story about a girl in Britain who won the lottery. She won over a million dollars. She was 21 years old when she won the lottery. Her name is Jane Park, and she said, "At times, it feels like winning the lottery has ruined my life. I thought it would make me 10 times better, but it made it 10 times worse ... I wish I had no money. I say to myself, 'life would be so much easier if I hadn't won.'" She's sick of shopping. She misses working for a paycheck and she struggles to find a boyfriend that isn't using her for money. She used to work as a $10/hr. administrative clerk and lived in a small apartment with her mother; now she owns a flashy Range Rover, owns properties, and travels the globe ... but she says her lavish lifestyle has made her feel empty inside. She says people look at her and say, "I wish I had her lifestyle," but she responds, "They don't understand my stress ... I have material things, but apart from that my life is empty." The article says she pondered, "What is my purpose in life?"

How's that for a perspective? She had everything by the world's standards, yet she didn't understand what it meant to be aligned with the Spirit of God and therefore she had nothing. She was empty. Sometimes, as Christians, we can walk along not aligned with the Spirit of God. Of course, we have God. If you are a believer, and you were to die on this particular day, you would be in Heaven with God forever and ever; but if you walk through life not aligned with God, you can miss not only God's blessings, but you miss God's peace and so much of His unending love. God promised that He would give us the peace that transcends all understanding and He promised we would have rivers of joy and love flowing from us. That's absolutely the truth when we're aligned properly with God.

When my son was 14 years old he came to me and said, "Dad, I want an earring in my ear."

I said, "Absolutely not."

He was not very happy with my decision or my authority. He asked, "Why not?!" He was demanding an explanation.

So, I gave him an explanation. I said, "Look, son. I don't think there's anything wrong with you having an earring, but you know, the world's kind of a funny place. I know I grew up a long time ago, but in some places where you grow up, a guy might get ridiculed or beat up for having an earring in his ear. It shouldn't be that way, but it is, and I'm just trying to protect you. So, here's the deal: when you're 18 you can have an earring in your ear. No problem."

He was furious at me, so I said, "Let me get this right; I said yes to what you asked for. But it's not in the time you wanted, so you're miserable?" Yes, he was.

God spoke to my heart and He said, "Exactly like you, Jack." Don't we do that with God sometimes? God has promised us and has given us everything we want, and when we don't get it quickly enough, we complain about the timing – that's because we're not aligned with God's perspective.

Here's a new perspective for you – a new alignment with the Spirit of God. When were you born? You might be thinking about your birthday. I would say May 8th, but that's not when I was born. I understand that's my physical birthday, but that's not when I was born.

Let's see God's perspective and if we can align our hearts with God on this issue:

> Blessed be the God and Father of our Lord
> Jesus Christ, who has blessed us with every
> spiritual blessing in the heavenly places in
> Christ, just as He chose us in Him before the
> foundation of the world, that we should be
> holy and without blame before Him in love.
> (Ephesians 1:3-4)

What's that? You chose us, God, before the foundation of the world? Yes!

> You formed my inward parts. You covered
> me in my mother's womb. I will praise you.
> I'm fearfully and wonderfully made. Marvelous
> are your works, and that my soul knows very
> well. My frame was not hidden from you when
> I was made in secret and skillfully wrought
> in the lowest parts of the earth. Your eyes saw
> my substance being yet unformed and in Your
> book, they were all written – the days fashioned
> for me – when yet there were none of them.
> (Psalm 139:13-16)

God had a plan for you and created you in His mind before the foundation of the Earth. That's when you were born. David says in that Psalm, "… all the days were fashioned for me when as yet there were none." If you don't believe that God has a plan for your life, then you don't believe God's Word. David said, "The days were fashioned for me before I was formed."

God says the same thing to you. He said to Jeremiah, "Before you were born, I set you apart and appointed you to be a prophet." God has a plan and purpose for our lives, but we need to align with it.

Now I have another question for you: When did you die? We talked about when you were born – but when did you die? You might say, "Well, Jack, come on. Don't be crazy. I'm sitting here reading this book. I'm not dead yet." Wrong. Sorry about the bad news. Look at Romans 6:4: "We were therefore buried with him after baptism into death in order that, just as Christ was raised from the dead through the glory of the Father, we too may live a new life."

You died with Christ on the cross. You're already dead. Oh, I understand we're all going to have a physical death and I understand we'd all like to go peacefully in our sleep, but at the end of the day, we're already dead. Your physical body has an appointed time to die but you're going to live forever in eternity. Your spiritual life is for eternity. So why are you worried about when you're going to die? What's the difference? I understand you'd like to spend more time with your family and do good – so would I – but at the end of the day, God has given us this gift of life and He's given it to us for a purpose and He has ordained the length of our days.

He said, "I have a purpose for you – that you would do the good works I have prepared in advance for you to do," as written in Ephesians 2:10; and, "I have a purpose; that you would bear fruit – and fruit that would last," as Jesus said in John 15:16; and that our purpose is to declare the praises of Him who brought you out of darkness into light in 2 Peter 1:9. You don't have to be a theologian, you don't have to go to seminary, you don't have to be a pastor – all you have to do is tell people, "This is what my life was like before I met Jesus, and this is what it's like now." That's how you declare the praises of God.

The Apostle Paul confirmed that we're already dead. He said, "I've been crucified in Christ, it is no longer I who live, but Christ who lives in me." In Timothy, he wrote that it's a trustworthy statement, for if we died with him, we will also live with him. And, of course, you know you have your guarantee of eternal life: "God so loved the world He gave His only son, that whoever believes in Him will never perish but have eternal life" (John 3:16).

I mentioned how I came to know Christ. It wasn't through the church. Of course, I study God's Word in the Bible intensely now and I went back and read the Old Testament multiple times. I wish I had gone to Hebrew school; I made a mistake not going, but I know that God had a plan in it all. God has a perspective for us; God has a plan for our lives, and I want you to understand the world's perspective.

I don't know if you know who Will Wheaton is, but he's an actor on *The Big Bang Theory* and also appeared in a *Star Trek* movie, and when the Texas shootings happened in the Sutherland Springs church in Texas and 26 innocent people were murdered, he made a horrific comment. Paul Ryan, then the Speaker of the House, sent out a tweet that said, "Reports out of Texas are devastating. The people of Sutherland Springs need our prayers right now."

Will Wheaton tweeted back, "The murder victims were in a church. If prayer did anything, they'd still be alive." That's the world's perception. The world is not aligned with the Spirit of God. We are. We're Christ's representatives; we're supposed to be aligned with the Spirit of God.

On his deathbed, David Cassidy, Television star and the lead singer from The Partridge Family, surrounded by his family said, "So much wasted time." That's how he looked back on his life. Wow. What a tragedy; what a perspective; what a misalignment with the Spirit of God.

When my father was in hospice dying, I made many trips to see him from my home in Orlando to Boynton Beach. One time when I saw him he couldn't swallow anymore; I stopped on the turnpike to get a slice of pizza – I was hungry. I sat down with the slice of pizza and I thought, "Never ever again will I take for granted the ability to swallow." Seeing my dad lying in a hospital bed, not being able to swallow, I said, "I'm not taking anything for granted ever again; not food, not swallowing, not walking, not breathing, not hearing, not anything."

And when my father passed away, my attitude, was, "Thank you God for the 85 years he had. Thank you for giving me this great, amazing, father." It wasn't, "Oh, I can't believe I couldn't have more time!" and "How could you take him, Lord?!" No, it was, "Thank you for the gift of life that you had given him." It's all about alignment with God. It's an attitude, a perspective, that we bring in line our thoughts/thinking with God's.

We've seen tragedies in Charleston, South Carolina where nine innocent people were murdered in a church shooting, the Sutherland Springs church shooting in Texas, and in Las Vegas where a deranged man opened fire killing 58 people and wounding 413 at a music festival; we see the world going to Hell in a handbasket, as the saying goes. But how do we respond? We need to respond aligned with the heart of God. We need to respond by loving people and showing God's love. We need to be the ambassadors, the representatives, the warriors, the sons and daughters of God, and we need to love people whether they're worthy to be loved or not – just as Christ loves us. Christ loves us and died for us "while we were yet sinners."

I don't believe that Christ has called every child of God to be a martyr. I hope that's not the case for you. It was the case for our brothers in Charleston and in Texas in those churches, and it's the case for many believers worldwide who are being persecuted and killed for their faith, but it's not the case for everyone. I will say it again, God might not have called you to die as a martyr, but He called you to live as a Christian! That's a fact. God's called us to live as Christians.

Let's talk about God's perspective a little bit. When my daughter was 13, she wanted to be a dancer. So, I wrote a letter to a famous Broadway singer/dancer who she admires very much, and I asked if he would consider meeting her and investing a few minutes in her life on one of his tours down here in Florida. He agreed to do so, and I was so psyched. It was a surprise for my daughter. I was thrilled. This would be like for me when I met Bruce Springsteen – it was a very good thing. So, I knew how excited she was going to be, and I was sitting there thinking, Oh my gosh. She has no clue! As I was bringing her to the show, I was thinking, she has no clue! This is going to be amazing! This is going to be so great!

And it was! It was a blow-away. He spent an hour with her pouring into her life about her career and future. At that moment, God laid a truth on my heart: this is how God looks at us. You think my daughter was excited? She was thrilled beyond belief. God spoke to my spirit and said wait until you see what I've got in store for you. God says, "No ear can hear, no eye can see, no mind can conceive what God has in store for those that love Him." (1 Corinthians 2:9)

I saw little babies and 2-year-old kids in the church nursery on Sunday; can you imagine talking to them about 529 plans? They would say, "What? 5-2-9? I can't even add. What are you talking about?" They might not know much, but you know how much you love them. Everything you do as a parent is for your child's blessing and benefit. There is not one thing you do that's not for their blessing and benefit. Even when they don't know it!

I'll never forget my little son trying to stick his fingers in an electric socket, or the time he reached over to touch a burning hot stove. I pulled him back in nick of the time, so he wouldn't burn his little hand and yet he would always start crying when I wouldn't let him do what he wanted to do. He must have been thinking, "You are the meanest father in the world. You must really hate me, because if you loved me – you'd let me do what I want; you'd let me touch that beautiful hot red stove."

"No, son; it's because I love you that I don't let you touch the stove or stick your finger into the socket." It's the same way with God in our lives – that's the perspective and alignment we need with the heart of God. God says that all things work together for the good of those that love Him. Not a few things, not most things, not some things – all things. Yet we argue with God about things and circumstances as if we knew better.

You get a flat tire and you're mad. You go, "Aw, that flat tire ruined my day. Now I have to buy a new tire for $200, and I missed my important job interview. This is horrible. This is the worst thing that could've happened today!" Well, no it's not, you might have died up ahead in a car crash. You don't know.

God says, "You're to trust me," like our kids trust us. That's why we're supposed to accept the Kingdom of God as little children do – with unquestioning belief.

When my kids were little they loved miniature golf and when I said, "We're going to play miniature golf!" They never said, "Daddy, are you sure they are open? Dad, do you have enough money in your pocket to pay? Dad, is there enough gas in the car?" No. All they knew is: Daddy said we're going. Daddy said it – it's happening. To God be the glory.

Let's look further at this alignment with God:

"Be joyful in hope, faithful in prayer, and patient in affliction" (Romans 12:12).

I love it when God says, "Be joyful." In 1 Thessalonians 5:16, God says, "Be joyful always!" Is there any part of that verse that is unclear? Be joyful always.

"But God, what if things aren't going good?"

Still you are to "Be joyful always. Give thanks in all circumstances for this is God's will for you in Christ Jesus." (1 Thessalonians 5:16-18) He tells us to pray continuously in that same passage. We're to trust God; we're to be joyful always.

The Psalmist says, "This is the day the Lord has made. I will rejoice and be glad in it" (Psalm 118:24). Well "this is the day the Lord has made" is a fact. No believer would dispute that. "I will rejoice and be glad in it" is a choice; I believe we have to make that choice each and every day to align ourselves with the heart and Spirit of God.

I have to get up in the morning and do it. I have the same issues as you: I'm worried about my kids, I'm worried about my future, health, money, relationships, work – everything. Being a good Christian, I'm concerned about every single thing… but I know I have a choice to make in the morning and I want to make that choice first thing in the morning before the tsunami of the world starts crashing in on me; before I read all the garbage in the newspaper, before I hear everybody complaining about everything. I want to have that attitude right in the morning. I want my heart aligned with God, and I have found that makes a tremendous difference in the way I live and who I am.

In James chapter 1, the Word of God says, "Consider it pure joy, brothers and sisters, when you face trials of many kinds. You know the testing of your faith produces perseverance. Let perseverance finish its work so you may be mature and complete, not lacking anything" (v. 2-4).

"Let me get this right, God. Could there be a typo? You're telling me that I'm supposed to consider it pure joy when I'm going through trials and tribulations?"

"Yeah."

"Oh my gosh." Based on that I think now would be a good time to make sure I know and you know if your checking and aligning yourself with you, God or both.

I know buddies of mine who went into the military. They were so psyched to get into boot camp.

"Well, wait a minute. Isn't that where they are really tough on you and beat you up and beat you down?"

"Oh, no – it toughens me up!"

You see those pro football players who leave their families for two months to train vigorously to prepare for the upcoming season. They bang the heck out of their bodies and go on strict diets and exercise all day long. Why? For a trophy that will rust, moth, and decay – for the praises of the world. God says we're to work for things that don't rust, moth, and decay – for treasures in the Kingdom of Heaven. They consider it joy to train and fight for an earthly prize, but we look at life as if, "Oh! I can't believe I have so many troubles. This is so terrible! God, I can't believe you gave me a life and I must go live it! This is so hard! And let me get this right; in the end I go to Heaven to be with You forever and enjoy peace with no more pain, no more suffering?" We should be jumping up and down, excited, every minute of every day. The Christian life should look different to the rest of the world! It is different... If we're aligned with the heart and Spirit of God.

We should be joyful; we should be grateful; it should be unbelievable to us that we are alive – unbelievable that we have a life and get to live. I know that 10 out of 10 people die; I know we disagree with God sometimes on the circumstances: "God, how could this happen to a baby? A young mother?" I don't have an answer for that today. I know God says, "My ways are higher than yours." (Isaiah 55:9) I know God says, "I have a perfect plan." Whatever time God ordained for each person is the time He ordained. Whatever time He ordained for me and you, that is the time we have.

It goes back to the parable of the talents. We're supposed to take this life God gave us – out of gratitude, not out of obligation. We should say, "Oh, goodness! I've been given this life and it's such a blessing to be alive! Whatever time I have, I want to make the most of it because when I get to Heaven, I would love to hear: 'Well done good and faithful servant. Come and share your Master's happiness.'"

When I look at life, I believe Romans 8:28. God says, "All things work together for the good of those that love God,." All things – not some things, not a few, not most – all. Well, if everything is working together for my good, what do I have to worry about? God told me He wants me to be joyful, always, out of gratitude for this life I've been given. If you're not joyful in all things, you're failing the test! I believe it's a test of our faith.

Jesus asks, "Why do you call me, 'Lord! Lord,' and not do the things which I say?" (Luke 6:46) How do you answer God on that one? I need to look at the things I'm going through in joy – trusting that God is using them, trusting that His Word is true, trusting that when He said He's going to use these trials and tribulations to mold me and shape me so that my joy would be complete, He's doing it for me, not for Him; He's using it all for my good. If I believe that, then I would definitely be joyful through it.

If someone said to you, "Listen, do me a favor. We're going to do a Habitat for Humanity house. For the next 36 hours straight, we're going to work on this house, and at the end of it, I'm going to give you $10 million."

It's an inconvenience for you not to go home, but would you sacrifice 36 hours building a house for someone who needed a house for $10 million? The answer would be yes, naturally. Oh, wait a minute: It's inconvenient, you might go hungry, it's hard work. "I know ... but the reward is amazing! I'm going to get $10 million!" Right! That's your life here on earth! God says the reward is amazing, yet we take it for granted, as if Heaven was just this afterthought. We take it for granted that we get to have the Holy Spirit walking with us through life.

Hey, the same things happen to the non-Christians that happen to us; our family members die, we'll lose money in the stock market. The difference in our lives is that we have God with us. That should be the difference. We have the Holy Spirit inside of us and people should see it. So, if you're not looking at this stuff with pure joy – you're doing it wrong. Remember "This is the day the Lord has made. We will rejoice and be glad in it."

We're the beneficiaries of Jesus' sacrifice and death on the cross. We did nothing to earn it, nothing to deserve it, and we get the full benefits and blessings of it. This is how we're to align ourselves with the Spirit of God – by looking at the truth of God and the Word of God and knowing that it's true.

I got to meet rock and roll legend Bruce Springsteen backstage at a concert set up through this charity I was involved in. The concert organizers said to me, "Look, you're going to meet this guy, Tom Rye, he is a member of Bruce's road crew and Tom is going to bring you back and introduce you to Bruce." Now let me tell you something, every single thing Tom Rye said to do, I did. He said, "Walk like this," and I'd walk like this. He said, "Don't touch that," and I didn't touch that. Why? Because I knew he had the key to get me to where I wanted to go.

That should be our life and attitudes toward God. We should know for a fact that Jesus and the Word of God and the Holy Spirit can get us to where we want to go, and we should be aligning our self with every single thing the Word of God tells us.

God's been putting a thought on my heart lately: "Jack, you need to do something more."

I asked, "What's that, God?"

He said, "You need to love people more."

I said, "Well, come on. I love people. I'm a good guy. I write books about you, Lord. I preach. I minister."

He said, "No, you need to love people more. You see, everything you do, you do for you." And He's right – really. I mean, at the end of the day I think about myself and my family. Oh, I love to preach, I love to teach, I love to write books, I love to minister – but they are things of comfort, not things of sacrifice – so I'm taking that thought into my life. I'm listening to God and what He's saying to me specifically.

What is God saying specifically to you today?

I had a wonderful pastor, Truman Herring, who preached a great sermon, and this was the crux of the message: "Where was the last time you said 'no' to God?" He said, "Wherever it was in your life that God asked you to do something and you said 'no,' you need to go back to that place and meet God back there – whether it was 20 years ago or yesterday because you cannot advance forward spiritually until you say 'yes' to God."

He added, "Now, that doesn't mean God doesn't love you; that doesn't mean you're not going to Heaven; it just means you've hindered your spiritual growth because you've been disobedient to God."

I hope that you will investigate your heart and ask, "Where did I last say 'no' to God?" That is the place you need to go back and meet God.

If you make this alignment with the heart of God, you're just so far ahead of the game it's amazing. Consider Ephesians chapter 3. The Apostle Paul is on his knees praying for the saints and the church in Ephesus. Here's what he prays: "For this reason I kneel before the Father, from whom every family in Heaven and on Earth derives its name, I pray that out of His glorious riches He may strengthen you with power through His Spirit in your inner being" (v. 14-16).

Paul is praying that God strengthens the people through God's power. It's not your power; it's the power of God that will strengthen you through the Holy Spirit of God that came in you upon salvation. Here's what he says in the next verse: "So that Christ may dwell in your hearts through faith" (v. 17).

God must strengthen you in your inner spirit with His Holy Spirit because it's God who calls you to Him. You accept God's call. Christ dwells in your heart through faith. The next verse says: "And I pray that you will be rooted and established in love" (v. 17).

Get this right. Unless Christ dwells in your heart through faith, unless the Holy Spirit strengthens you so that Christ is dwelling in your heart, then you can't be rooted and established in love.

"Well, that's great, Paul, but why do I have to be rooted and established in love?" He gives the answer: "So that you may have power together with all the Lord's holy people to grasp how wide and long and high and deep is the love of Christ and to know this love that surpasses knowledge" (v. 18-19).

If I'm filled in my inner being with the Spirit of God, then I can receive through the riches of God's power through God's Holy Spirit. With Christ dwelling in my heart through my faith, I will be rooted and established in love, then I'll be able to grasp how wide and deep and long and high the love of Christ is, which surpasses all knowledge. Here's the last line: "So that you may be filled to measure all the fullness of God" (v. 19).

If you want to have the fullness of God, you must grasp how much He loves you; that's how you get the fullness of God. That's been my prayer lately. I often pray about specific things, but I've stopped praying for specific things this past month. I've just prayed, "Lord, please strengthen my inner being through your Holy

Spirit so that Christ can dwell in my heart; so that I'm rooted and established in love; so that I can have power together with all the Lord's holy people to grasp how wide and long and deep and high is the love of Christ; so I know this love that surpasses knowledge; so that I'm filled to the measure of all your fullness because that's all I want, God – more of you." That's how you grasp the love of God.

God's Word tells us, "I'm persuaded that neither death nor life, nor angels nor principalities, nor things present, nor things to come, nor height, nor depth, nor any other created thing shall be able to separate us from the love of God which is in Christ Jesus, our Lord" (Romans 8:38-39). That's how you align yourself with God - you understand the truth of God.

In Hebrews chapter 11 – often referred to as the Hall of Fame of Faith – Noah, Abraham, Isaac, and all these people of God died before they saw the promises of God fulfilled in their life.

"What? Wait a minute. Let me get this right: So, they did everything they were supposed to do, they lived this great life of faith, but they never saw the payoff?"

That's right. They never saw the payoff while they were alive. But can you see the payoff now? Yes, you can, big time! Noah, David, Abraham, Isaac, Joseph, and the 30 others that are listed (and some you can't even list) didn't see the promise of God in their lifetime.

"So, let me get this right: all we're supposed to do is live our lives in faith?"

Yes, that's exactly what you're supposed to do, then your reward in Heaven will be the same as the greatest teacher, preacher, pastor or minister you could ever know or any others who have responded faithfully to the call of God. You will see the effects of God in their lives. God doesn't judge you based on your accomplishments. He judges you based on your obedience. That's all He's asking, wherever He's placed you. You don't have to be a pastor, a teacher, or a preacher; you could be a shoeshine guy, you could be a housewife – it doesn't matter where you work. You just need to show the love of Christ to others in your heart. You need to see the world through God's lenses.

Remember, we're all going to die, but we don't all get to make a difference. Here's my personal challenge to you: what will you do today to change your life 30 days from now? We must do something different. We must make that alignment with God.

I pray that you will align yourself to the heart of God – not because you have to, not because you think, "Oh, God's going to punish me," but because you want to. If the wealthiest stock investor in the world was going to teach you about finances today, or the greatest basketball player was going to teach you about basketball, or the smartest computer programmer was going to teach you about the computer – I think you'd be running to them. "Oh my gosh, oh my gosh! These guys are amazing they are geniuses – I'm going to learn everything! This is great, I'm going to be so smart. These guys are the smartest guys in the world," and that's right. You wouldn't be able to wait to get to their feet to learn what they know.

How is it that we cast God aside? How is it that we don't have time for God? How is it that we're so busy – that we're aligned with the things of the world and not with the things of God – and then we wonder, "God, why am I not being blessed?" I don't mean material blessings here; I mean spiritual blessings. "God, why don't I have your peace that transcends all understanding? Why don't I have rivers of joy that flow through my heart?" Because you're not aligned with the Spirit of God.

Look at what God says. Consider this perspective. I want to show you God's view of you, how God looks at you: "God raised us up with Christ and seated us with Him in the heavenly realms in Christ Jesus" (Ephesians 2:4).

That's how God sees you: with Him. He sees you wholly blameless and above reproach, clothed in the righteousness of Jesus Christ. That's how God sees you. If you have a young child who stands next to you, your shadow covers him. We should be covered in that Psalm 91 shadow of God. Satan tries to condemn us. God says our hearts are "deceitful above all things" (Jeremiah 17:9), and our own hearts will try and condemn us. Still, God says, "I don't see you in your sin." God says, "As far as the east is from the west," He has removed our sins from us and He will remember them no more. God see you wholly blameless and above reproach because He doesn't see you as that sinful self in the human flesh… He see you wholly blameless and above reproach clothed in the righteousness of Jesus Christ.

Will you see yourself as God sees you? "The Lord is near to all those who call on Him in truth" (Psalm 145:18). So how do you see yourself? I believe this would be a good time to be determining and confirming if you are checking and aligning yourself with you, God or both?

God says, "You'll find me when you seek me with all your heart." If you don't have a close relationship with God, you're doing it wrong because God's made a promise: "You'll find me when you seek me with all your heart." He's near to all who call.

If I was dying of thirst in the desert and you brought me a bottle of water, that water is useless, meaningless, if I don't drink it. It can't help me if I don't take it in. The Word of God is alive, but can't help you if it stays unused; you need to take it in. It needs to be in your heart. God sent the Holy Spirit, and He comes upon salvation. God says, "I take out your old heart and put in a new heart. You're born the first time of your mother's womb; you're born the second time of the Spirit of God – when you accept God." And He says, "I put the Holy Spirit within you, who will teach you all things." The Holy Spirit will teach you the Word of God. It's your job to know the Word of God. God says, "If you drink of me, you'll never thirst again but if you don't drink of me, you will die of thirst." That's a choice we must make individually.

When I was 40 years old, my mother said, "Jack, I want you to have children not because I want to be a grandmother, I really do, but I want you to get married and have children because I don't want you to miss the blessing of having kids." Well, I've been married for almost 20 years now. I have three kids. She was right.

I want you to experience the Holy Spirit of God and a close, personal, relationship with Jesus Christ because I personally know God, and I know that He does not want you to miss out on His blessing. The blessing is not later in Heaven. That's a part of it, of course. But it's also right now as you're going through this life on Earth – secure, confident – knowing God is with you. God says, "I'll never leave you or forsake you; I'm with you always." All things work together for my good, no weapon formed against me

CHECKING AND ALIGNING YOURSELF WITH YOU, GOD OR BOTH?

will prosper. Your name is written in the palm of His hand. He has plans to give you a hope and a future and to prosper you.

So, ask yourself, when did you last say 'no' to God?

Romans chapter 8 says there's no condemnation for those in Christ Jesus. Satan would love to condemn us, but God wouldn't set us up to fail. God would not have us keep trying to obtain perfection because He knows we fall short. Only Jesus was perfect. We would be miserable if we believed we had to be perfect because we cannot be perfect; our whole lives would be filled with misery, lamenting our failure each and every day to where our joy would be lost or stolen. That is contradictory to the saving nature and grace and mercy of God, but it is a great trick and weapon of your enemy, Satan. He would just love to condemn you with that.

God wants you to be joyful always. Remember, this is the day the Lord has made.

You might ask, "Well, what should I do? How do I align myself with God?"

The answer can be found in 1 Corinthians chapter 10 verse 13. The Apostle Paul said this. It's a challenge to the church and to us today. It's very simple – just one line: "Whatever you do, do for the glory of God."

Can you imagine if you said this line every day, before you did anything? "This I do for the glory of God." Would your attitude and actions be different? That's how we need to align ourselves with God.

My prayer is that you would allow the Holy Spirit to speak to your heart and that you would also ask yourself, "Lord, is there a place where I said 'no' to you? Is there a place where I need to turn back and come to you and say 'yes'?"

I pray that you would make that decision to align yourself with the Spirit of God. So much did Christ love us that He came to guarantee we would spend eternity with Him together in Heaven – the best place ever.

Jesus said, "I've come so they have life abundant and life eternal," not miserable, not depressed, not sad, not anxious, not frustrated, not defeated. He wants to give you an abundant, joyful life – the greatest life ever; that's what God has in store for you, but you need to align yourself with God.

Think of the story that Jesus tells of the prodigal son. When the son wasted his inheritance and finally returned, the father didn't angrily say, "Oh, you rotten son, I can't believe you spent all the fortune! How dare you come back and try to be a part of this house again? Depart from me!" Absolutely not! He opened his arms. He couldn't wait. He ran toward the son to love him and embrace him, and he said, "Let's celebrate – we need to have a party! My son was dead, but now he's alive."

That's what God wants for you. God's not mad at you, God loves you and God wants to bless you. I do not bless my own children when negative actions and disobedience are prevalent in their behavior toward me... But that does not change my desire to bless them. Yet, because of disobedience they can either postpone or lose some of the blessings I had in store for them. The same holds true for us in our relationship with God. Remember, it is God's desire and heart to bless you. You bless God with your faith, love, and obedience.

I pray you take a time of reflection, inspection, and introspection in your own hearts. Simply pray, "Holy Spirit what would you have me do? How would you have me respond?"

Listen to the leading of God, and then act in order to align your heart with God.

Chapter Nine

ASKING BY SEEKING, CALLING AND TRUSTING SIMULTANEOUSLY

I'm a bit of an idiot. I've sold God short; I really have. I was standing in the Grand Canyon with my son Jackson. We had gone on a father-son trip – and I was looking in awe and wonder at God's creation. It was mind-blowing, breathtaking; no picture could do it justice, and I said, "God, I've sold you short, because if this is what You can do on earth, I can't even imagine what You can do in Heaven."

God's Holy Spirit spoke to me and He said, "That's right. You can't even imagine how great it's going to be." I don't want to be in a position of selling God short.

With God, you must choose whether or not you are going to ask and expect great things from Him. You have a choice.

My father always told me, "Son, you can ask me for anything. I may not always say yes, but you can ask me for anything." He also said, "I don't understand why you wouldn't. Not only ask me – but ask anybody for anything." He said in his great wisdom, "You see, if you ask and someone says 'no,' you're in the exact same spot as you were before you asked. But if you ask and they say 'yes,' you've got what you wanted. So, what do you have to lose?"

That advice has served me well. And I hope it serves us well with God.

In this chapter, I want to go back to the story of the prodigal son in Luke 15. Talk about a big ask! In verse 12, the prodigal son asked for something that was almost unbelievable in his day. Look at a few versions of his request:

> There was a man who had two sons. The younger one said to his father: 'Father, give me my share of the estate.' (NIV)

> Father, give me the portion of goods that fall to me. (NKJV)

> Father, I want right now what's coming to me. (THE MESSAGE)

I want my share of your estate before you die. (NLT)

A big ask. I'm thinking how comical it would be if my children said that to me. I can just imagine them coming up and saying, "Hey! Give me what's mine before you die."

After I was done laughing, I would basically say, "No! Are you crazy? No." But in this parable that Jesus told, the father gave the son what he asked for. That's mind-boggling. You see, he could have said 'no.' He didn't have to say 'yes,' but he so loved his son that he gave him what he asked for.

We have a Father who wants to give us what we ask for. I want you to understand - it was not the father's desire that the son leave him and miss the blessings that the father had in store for him. The father had worked so hard to pass these things on to the son and have the son be blessed and benefit from them. The father wanted his son close by his side. But this son chose to reject the father. He chose to go his own way.

The father could have said, "No. I'm going to keep you here, I'm not going to let you do that," but, no, he gave his son free choice.

You and I also have free choice. God is looking at us the same way. We have free choice in this life. God could have made us robots. He could have made us obedient robots who did whatever He said — but no. He gave us free choice. So, let's see what we should be asking God for by looking at God's Word.

> Do not let your hearts be troubled… Believe me when I say that I am in the Father and the Father is in me. Or at least believe on the evidence of the works themselves. Very truly I tell you: Whoever believes in Me will do the works I have been doing. (John 14:1, 11-12)

I think we take that one out of context a little bit. Let's look at one more verse and I'll show you why. Jesus goes on to say:

> And they will do even greater things than these because I'm going to the Father. And I will do whatever you ask in My name so that the Father may be glorified in the Son. (John 1:13)

Here's where we take this out of context. We say, "Jesus, you said I could ask for anything. So, I want a house, a job, a car, security, a future – everything that I think is good."

But Jesus said, "Whoever believes in me will do the works I have been doing."

The works Jesus had been doing was spreading the gospel message; it was doing the Father's will; it was living a sacrificial life for others – which He showed in many ways, including washing the feet of the disciples, and dying on the cross for our lives. It was sacrificial.

It's not what you or I want that glorifies God's purpose – it's what God wants. The line "I will do whatever you ask in my name" assumes you're already doing the work of Jesus. That's when you can ask anything in God's name and get what you desire. It also says, "So that the Father may be glorified in the Son." That's why you're supposed to ask – for the glory of God through Jesus Christ, His Son. When you ask, you're asking for stuff that glorifies the Father, not you. If you were asking for stuff that glorified the Father, you would be asking for the blessing of others. You wouldn't be asking for things for yourself.

God has been talking to me in my heart about some heavy stuff along these lines. In John 16, Jesus says: "Now is your time of grief. But I will see you again, and you will rejoice, and no one will take away your joy. In that day, you will no longer ask Me anything" (v. 22-23).

What's that, Lord? No longer ask?

"No."

Why? Why won't I need to ask you anything?

Because you will see God face-to-face. There will be no more questions; you will have the answer. You'll have the clear knowledge of the gospel mysteries. Your understanding will be complete; you won't need to inquire anymore.

That is the desire of God for every single believer – that is the promise of God for every single believer – the promise of Heaven. "Now you know in part; then you'll know in full. Trust me. Live in faith. Believe me." That is God's desire for you.

God assumes that you're going to ask nothing in vain. You see, it was taken for granted that the disciples were praying. They were Jesus' disciples. They were praying for the will of God. And God assumes the same about you and me. He assumes we're followers of Christ, that we're going to be matured in the gospel, and that our prayers are going to further the gospel of God. I also believe that He expects or at least assumes we are going to be asking by seeking, calling and trusting simultaneously.

Jesus taught us by His Word to be in prayer. We're taught to seek. We're taught to ask in the Father's name. God is our Father, and although we can come to Him as beloved children, we often come to Him as if He were a stranger, or as if we were a client of His and not His child. Jesus is the mediator with us to God in Heaven. We can come to Him with a sense of expectation of spiritual blessings – with a conviction, a knowledge, a certainty in our hearts that these things can only come from God. You can't get them anywhere else. We come to Him in confidence, believing that, as a Father, He's ready to help us.

We ask in His name, acknowledging that we are unworthy to receive any favor. It is only by His grace and kindness that we receive. I believe God is thinking, "You've asked me nothing in comparison to what I have to give and have promised to give you." That's why we're told to open our mouths wide with the expectation that God will fulfill those promises.

How do I know God wants me to ask? Well, He just said it. But He repeats it in Jeremiah 33:3, "Call to me and I will tell you great and unsearchable things you do not know."

That's a promise from God. So, what should we do about it? Let's look at God's Word and see what we should be asking God for. I think we get a glimpse in 2nd Corinthians, in a message given by the Apostle Paul.

Just a side note here: The Word of God is alive. The Word is God. When you take time to place it in your heart, the Holy Spirit expands it and blows you away. It's a waterfall of revelation, of truth, of knowledge, of love, pouring over you and washing you. It's amazing and unbelievable – but you need to be there in the Word. Twenty-something years of walking with the Word, I can tell you that God's Word is as real as ever. He speaks to me most loudly in my quiet time with Him – so don't miss that blessing. Here's what God was speaking to me in my quiet time: "He has made us competent as ministers of the New Covenant" (2 Corinthians 33:6).

That's the gospel of Jesus Christ; we've been saved by the blood of Christ. He's made us competent as ministers of the New Covenant – not of the letter of the law – which was the law in the Commandments, but of the Spirit. For the letter kills, but the Spirit gives life. What does that mean? It means that no one can keep perfectly the 630+ laws of Leviticus as well as the Ten Commandments. If that is your requirement for Heaven, you will die and not go to Heaven because you cannot attain perfection; you're not perfect. The only perfect person who walked on Earth was Jesus.

God says there's only one righteous, Jesus alone. But God says through the Holy Spirit, through the gift of the Spirit, we have life. We're no longer bound by 630 laws; we're no longer bound by the Ten Commandments. Of course, we should do good things out of the gratitude of our hearts for God. We want to strive to do those things – but those aren't a requirement anymore.

God says we're ministers of this. This is not just for the disciples and the apostles. This is for you and me in the church today; this is your purpose in life. 2 Peter chapter 1 tells us that we are called to proclaim the glory of Him who brought us out of the darkness into light. That is your purpose on this earth. That's our job. "Even to this day when Moses is read, a veil covers the hearts of those who hear. But whenever anyone turns to the Lord, the veil is taken away" (2 Corinthians 3:15).

Whenever anyone turns to the Lord, they are redeemed. Whosoever should call on the name of the Lord shall be saved. Whenever anyone turns to the Lord, the veil is removed; the darkness is removed. But that's a choice! You either choose to turn to the Lord or not.

Hopefully, you have chosen to turn to the Lord so the veil is off – and you can see the glory of God. I pray that we would ask God to remove the veil from those who are blinded. That would be the first ask of our heart.

There is freedom in Christ. "Now the Lord is the Spirit and where the Spirit of the Lord is, there is freedom" (2 Corinthians 3:17). It is for freedom you've been set free – free to not worry about life and death because Jesus conquered the grave; free to live this life with joy, hope, happiness – as Jesus said, "Be joyful always." Free to walk this life with our Father, together, protected, and blessed by the glory of God. It is for freedom you've been set free – so I pray that you would ask for more of His Spirit.

Now understand, you have the Holy Spirit of God. When you asked Jesus into your heart, God promised that He'd seal you with His Holy Spirit upon salvation. So, you have it, but how much of it will you use?

I have a guitar. How much do I play it? Well, I guess I haven't played it as much to be as good as Jimi Hendrix or Eric Clapton or some other great guitar players. I have access to play the same model guitars they do, but I am not a very good guitar player. Yet they've chosen to use their instrument, to devote their time and efforts to make sure they get good at it and practice because that's what mattered to them, so they accessed it and used it. They made it a priority in their life and became amazing with it.

We should be the greatest guitar players for Jesus. And I don't mean physically with musical instruments; I mean spiritually. That should be our lives. We should use this gift of the Holy Spirit we have. I pray that we would ask for more of the Holy Spirit. 2 Corinthians 3:18 tells us: "And we, with unveiled faces, contemplate the Lord's glory and are being transformed into His image with ever-increasing glory which comes from the Lord."

We're being transformed into His image with ever-increasing glory. I pray that you would ask God for more of His Glory. I pray that we would all want more of the glory of God. And I encourage you to be asking, calling and trusting simultaneously as we pray for that.

We have the ministry of the New Testament. Our salvation is assured and our place in Heaven is assured because the Holy Spirit is inside of us. "Therefore, since through God's mercy we have this ministry, we do not lose heart" (2 Corinthians 4:1). It's the deposit inside of us guaranteeing our place in Heaven. We know, we know, we know, we know – why? Not because you told me, not because

I told you, but because God is living inside of us. That's how we know our place in Heaven is assured. Therefore, because God has a purpose and a plan for our life, we don't lose heart – no matter what.

I pray that you would ask the Holy Spirit to help you not lose heart. "The god of this age has blinded the mind of unbelievers so that they cannot see the light of the gospel that displays the glory of Christ" (2 Corinthians 4:4). But they still have a choice! They still have a choice because if they look to God, the veil is removed. I'm not going to get into theology about election and predestination. My belief is that God certainly knows, in His holiness, who will choose to accept Him and who will choose to reject Him. I believe this because the Word of God tells us, and the Holy Spirit has confirmed in my heart, that it's God's desire that all be saved! He says, in first Timothy 2:4, "God our savior, who wants all people to be saved and come to a knowledge of the truth…"

It is God's desire that we all come to know the truth; it is God's desire that all His children would be saved. I cannot believe that any parent does not have the desire for all their children to be blessed to their fullest potential and live the best life they can.

No parent with three children would ever say, "Oh, it's only you two kids that I like; I hate my other child," or, "I'm just going to provide for two of you and not the other one." No way. Not possible. "For God, who said, 'Let light shine out of darkness,' made his light shine in our hearts to give us the light of the know-ledge of God's glory displayed in the face of Christ" (2 Corinthians 4:6).

I pray that we would ask God for more knowledge. The passage goes on to say, a little later: "Since we have that same spirit of faith, we also believe and therefore speak, because we know that the one who raised the Lord Jesus from the dead will also raise us with Jesus and present us with you to himself. All this is for your benefit, so that the grace that is reaching more and more people may cause thanksgiving to overflow to the glory of God. "Therefore we do not lose heart. Though outwardly we are wasting away, yet inwardly we are being renewed day by day" (2 Corinthians 4:13-16).

We're all losing this battle with age; it's a terminal disease. Ten out of ten people die. You have it. You're going to die too. The good news is you get to live in this life and have life eternal, if you choose to accept it. You get to live. Outwardly we might be wasting away, yet inwardly we're being renewed day by day. I pray that we would ask God for renewal of our heart, our soul, our spirit, our mind. "For our light and momentary troubles are achieving for us an eternal glory that far outweighs them all. So we fix our eyes not on what is seen, but on what is unseen, since what is seen is temporary, but what is unseen is eternal" (2 Corinthians 4:17-18).

I pray to God that you and I would see and look to what is unseen.

So, let's summarize:

> We ask God for more of His Spirit to be more like Him.
> We ask that we don't lose heart.
> We ask for removal of the veil for those who are blinded.
> We ask God for more knowledge, for renewal, so that we may look to what is unseen.
> We ask God to allow thanksgiving to overflow us.

Let's imagine God has answered "yes" to all your big questions. What if you've done everything right and not gotten the results you desire? What if it seems like there is no answer to your prayer – no change in your situation?

I asked my friend, Tom, that question. We were having lunch a couple weeks ago. He's a very mature Christian brother. I said, "Listen, what if I've done everything God told me to do – but I still don't get results?"

He said, "Well, my advice is to just do the next thing God tells you to do."

I said, "Well, what if you've done that? What if I did the next thing God told me to do for years, and I still don't have the results I want?"

Tom didn't have an answer at that point, but God did, and in my quiet time I believe God brought me to the key to life. I believe it's the key to life for you and the key to life for me. I came to this conclusion: No matter what I struggle with, and we all struggle with different things – physical, emotional, spiritual, relational, financial, whatever – God is God.

There's not a doubt in my mind. I believe I can say, like Peter, "Where would we go, Lord? Thou art the Christ." There's no question of that. I was reading in the book of Revelation and God is talking "to him who overcomes" and making a list of what He will give. Another version says, "to he who is victorious." "Overcoming" and "victorious" will make you assume there's a challenge, a fight, something I must overcome – something I must have victory over.

That's right! It is your flesh throughout this life; God has promised "to him who overcomes" He will give the Tree of Life. He won't get hurt by the second death. He'll give you hidden manna – food that you don't even know about that's so great. He'll give you a new stone, a white stone, with a new name. He'll give you power over nations. He'll give you white garments; your name will be in the Book of Life. You will be a pillar in the temple of God, and you will sit with Him on the throne. But that only comes to the one who overcomes – to the one who is victorious.

When God says your "light and momentary troubles" are nothing compared to the glory that will be – that's what He's talking about. You need to take hold of this victory. Yeah, there's a fight. Listen to the writer of Lamentations. If you're discouraged, if you're depressed, if you're not sure, if you're struggling, if you've done the right things and still don't have the answer you want – if you've done the wrong things and still don't have the answer you want, listen to this. I think he came to the same conclusion and here it is: "Yet this I call to mind and therefore I have hope! Because of the Lord's great love, we are not consumed. For His compassion never fails" (Lamentations 3:21-22).

My compassion may fail, yours may fail, but God's never fails. Because of His great love, we're not consumed; we're not going to Hell; we have victory over the grave. That's why we have hope! "God's compassions renew every morning; great is your faithfulness. And I say to myself, 'The Lord is my portion. Therefore, I will wait for Him'" (Lamentations 3:23-24).

David, Noah, Isaac, Abraham – all of them waited on God for His promise. God says the same thing to you and me. Understand that God's time is different from ours; a thousand years is like a day to Him and a day is like a thousand years. I thought I could put

God in a box my way and tell Him what He's supposed to do and what should be and, "God, you must not have this right." It's like my visit to the Grand Canyon, which I mentioned earlier. I sold God short. But then I looked out and saw what He created and said, "I don't even have a clue as to what is going on or what can be done." I don't have a clue – but God does. God made the Grand Canyon, He made the world, He made us – you and me – for a purpose.

What are you asking God for? Are you asking by seeking, calling and trusting simultaneously.

May we have the faith to believe and do and act and not just play and pretend, but to be real, to believe that all of God's promises are true, and to claim them for our lives.

Chapter Ten

REMOVING THE DOUBT BLINDERS TO CLEARLY REVEAL OUR CHOICES

I made a "big ask" of God that comes from the chorus of a famous gospel song: "Just a closer walk with thee." They play it a lot as a funeral song, although that is not the purpose for it. That I have a closer walk with Him – that's been my big ask from God.

I was thinking about "big asks" in life. A big ask in the work world might be, "Can I have a raise?" A big ask in the family world is definitely, "Will you marry me?" But I was thinking that you probably won't get a raise if you don't work hard. And you probably won't hear, "Yes, I will marry you," if you didn't show a lot of love, care, and concern for that person. There's action required on our part to get the response we want. The question is, what is your mindset? And what should it be as you ask God for the big ask?

I want to look at one facet of Daniel's life in the Old Testament. You probably know the story; Nebuchadnezzar, the King of Babylon, overtook Jerusalem. As part of his victory, the spoils of war, he said, "Let me take the young men that are in their teens and early twenties and let me groom them and teach them our language and our ways so that they can serve me as king."

He gave this order and among the men from Judah were Daniel and his friends Hananiah, Mishael, and Azariah, who later became known as Shadrach, Meshach, and Abednego; You've probably heard stories of them. But here's the important part—the king wanted Daniel to be fed the king's own food and wine and cause them to grow strong. Daniel did not want to do that because he wanted to continue to honor God. He didn't want to defile himself with food that wasn't holy. It tells us this in Daniel 1:8: "But Daniel resolved not to defile himself with the royal food and wine. And he asked a chief official for permission not to defile himself this way."

The New King James Version puts it: "But Daniel purposed in his heart, he would not defile himself."

The New Living Translation and Message Bible both say: "But Daniel was determined not to defile himself. He was resolved. He made up his mind. And he was determined not to let these things happen."

What about us? Are we determined?

Are we determined to live a life for God? There's a lot to be said for giving your all. In Nehemiah 4:6, Nehemiah is talking about the Israeli people rebuilding the wall of the temple and it says, "So we rebuilt the wall till all of it reached half its height, for the people worked with all their heart."

The people in Nehemiah were determined. They were resolved. They had made up their minds to work with all their hearts. God says in Jeremiah 29:13, "You will find Me, when you seek Me with all of your heart."

Ross Perot was a billionaire. You may or may not know of him. He ran for president once a long time ago, but his success and fame were in building companies and selling them. Here's what he said on his deathbed: "Most people quit one inch short of the goal line." Most people are right there but they quit, they give up.

Have you ever felt that way in your walk with God? Or perhaps in your trust and your faith with God? "Hey God, I've been doing the right thing, but it's just not happening for me. It's not going my way." Is it health? Is it financial? Is it relational? Is it spiritual? Is it emotional? There's something not going your way even though you've been trying and trying. What if you had been giving it your all? What if you'd been doing everything right? You'd been at God's feet, you've been walking closer to God, you've got a closer walk with Him and you're still not seeing a change in your earthly situation. What do you do? Well, there's only one thing you do... you keep going. You keep the faith. You live a life that glorifies God and you do not give in or shrink back or give up; you keep going in faith.

Even if you don't see the results you want, you keep going. That is the test of faith! – that you continue to trust God and love God even when you don't get what you want. So, are you determined? Are you resolved? Have you made up your mind? Are you willing to remove the doubt blinders to clearly reveal our choices

How do you handle adversity? Do you handle it with fear? Or do you turn to God? When you are overwhelmed by fear and doubt and circumstances in your life, what do you do? Well, let's look at what you should do. In Lamentations 3:17, the writer said this:"I have been deprived of peace. I have forgotten what prosperity is, so I say my splendor is gone and all that I had hoped from the Lord."

Here is a man who had given up hope! But he goes on to say this: "Yet this I call to mind and therefore I have hope. Because of the Lord's great love, we are not consumed. For His compassions never fail, they are new every morning. Great is your faithfulness" (Lamentations 3:21-23).

He's saying, "Look, I was beyond despair. I'd given up everything. I'd lost everything but you know what? Here is what I call to mind, here's what I think of, here's what I remember. I have hope because I remember that God's great love for me is with me always. It will never fail. His compassion and His mercy are new each and every day. Therefore, I am not consumed by the world because the love of God is stronger than anything the world, my flesh, and Satan can throw at me. I have the victory in God."

The statement closes with this thought: "I say to myself; the Lord is my portion and therefore I will wait for Him." (v. 24)

Are you determined in your mind? Have you resolved? Have you made up your mind to wait on the Lord? God is in control. Nehemiah 8:10 tells us, "The joy of the Lord is our stronghold." That's what we hang onto; that's what keeps us strong. That's why we're the light to a world of darkness; they can see the light of the joy of the Lord flowing through us because that's what we're hanging onto.

God promises in Jeremiah 31:13, "I will turn their mourning into gladness, I will give them comfort and joy instead of sorrow."

That's God's promise. You may be mourning through this life. You may not have comfort and joy in this world. But, God promises you're going to have in Heaven. He didn't say this life would be easy. He just said He would walk through it with you.

It's like the "Footprints" poem that you may know.

> One night I dreamed a dream. As I was walking along the beach with my Lord. Across the dark sky flashed scenes from my life. For each scene, I noticed two sets of footprints in the sand, One belonging to me and one to my Lord.

After the last scene of my life flashed before me, I looked back at the footprints in the sand. I noticed that at many times along the path of my life, especially at the very lowest and saddest times, there was only one set of footprints.

This really troubled me, so I asked the Lord about it. "Lord, you said once I decided to follow you, You'd walk with me all the way. But I noticed that during the saddest and most troublesome times of my life, there was only one set of footprints. I don't understand why, when I needed You the most, You would leave me."

He whispered, "My precious child, I love you and will never leave you Never, ever, during your trials and testings. When you saw only one set of footprints, It was then that I carried you."

We might ask, "How come you deserted me, Lord?"

God says, "I didn't desert you. When there was one set of footsteps, I carried you."

Look at this great promise from God for you. This is what the Lord says: "Restrain your voice from weeping and your eyes from tears, for your work will be rewarded, declares the Lord" (Jeremiah 31:16).

This is God's promise for you. Don't cry! Be joyful. Why? Because your work will be rewarded. It's a promise from God. You've already been rewarded for the work Jesus did on the cross. You are the beneficiary of everything Jesus did on the cross. When He died for you and shed His innocent blood for our sinful blood, it was so we would be covered in the blood of Christ. We are covered and clothed in the righteousness of Christ and therefore we are sin-free, guilt-free. We have that already. That's ours.

We're reminded that the work we do here on Earth will also be rewarded. It's not a case of God keeping score. This isn't a scorecard with base hits and singles and home runs – it's not about that. It's about your work being meant to glorify God in your life. That's it. You don't have to do that from the pulpit. You can do that wherever you are called to do it. That's your work. It's to share the gospel and glorify God with your life and then you will be rewarded.

That's your heavenly reward. If you don't get that, you've got nothing. It's everything. Jesus tells us to build up spiritual treasures that won't rust, moth, or decay; that the world can't take away – because the world is going to take away everything you have. You're going to die one day, and everything is going to be gone, including your body.

Recently, I was watching the news, looking at yet another shooting. It's the saddest thing. Twenty people were shot dead in a Walmart store in El Paso, Texas. They went to Walmart. They didn't know that that morning their lives would end. They thought they were coming home. They had plans and lives and futures and dreams and hopes and wishes and kids and grandkids – yet, that day, their time was up. The only thing that matters is, what were their decisions prior? Did they know God before they walked into the Walmart? They don't have the choice anymore.

They might have thought—and you may think, "Well, I've got time. I'll get to this God issue one day." No, no, you've got to get to this God issue now. You've got to decide now so that when your time is up, you know where you are going to spend eternity. I hope and pray every one of them is in Heaven with God today. Certainly, the little kids are in Heaven with God, those who didn't have a chance to make a choice are automatically covered by the blood of Jesus. But those who are old enough to make a choice, they live and stand by their choice... the choice to believe in God and spend eternity with God and have the Holy Spirit in them or the choice to ignore God and refuse God and spend eternity separated from God.

For us, we are to restrain our voice from weeping and our eyes from tears because we know our work will be rewarded. Here's the greatest news ever, God has declared you innocent. God has given you a white stone. In the old days, in trials, they would judge guilt and innocence by a white stone or a black stone. If you were guilty, they would push forward the black stone. If you were innocent, you'd get the white stone. The book of Revelation tells us that God will give us a white stone with a new name only known by Him. God has declared you innocent. You need to understand the true nature of God.

Back to the book of Daniel, look at what Daniel says: "We do not make requests of You because we are righteous. But because of Your great mercy" (Daniel 9:17).

Daniel understood. We do not make requests of God because we are righteous, or because we have earned it, or because of what we have done. No, we make requests because of God's great mercy. The character of God, our Father, is certain; it's the same yesterday, today, and forever.

God in His love, and Jesus in His sacrifice and victory at the cross do not change. Only our focus, our perspective, our commitment, and our love change when we are not certain of who we are in Christ. We are sons and daughters of Christ. Christ is our Rock, our solid foundation. He cannot be shaken and thus we who live in faith are not to be shaken by the events of this world. You are not to be shaken.

Let's look briefly at Martha's faith and Mary's faith. I love Martha and Mary. They were Lazarus' sisters. Lazarus was raised from the dead by Jesus after he had been dead for four days. But this is what I love… I was reading through the passage during my quiet time and God spoke to my heart.

Martha went up to Jesus as He came to the town where Lazarus had been buried for four days. She said this: "Lord," Martha said to Jesus, "If you had been here, my brother would not have died. But I know that even now God will give you whatever you ask" (John 11:21-22).

What great faith! First of all, she was saying, "Lord." She was addressing Jesus as God. She was saying, "Look, I know if you had been here, because You are Lord, my brother wouldn't have died." But then she added, I know God gives you whatever You ask because I know You are the Son of God." Jesus said to her, "Your brother will rise again." Martha answered, "I know he will rise again in the resurrection at the last day." Jesus said to her, "I am the resurrection and the life. The one who believes in Me will live, even though they die; and whoever lives by believing in Me will never die" (John 11:23-26).

Then He asked Martha this great question: "Do you believe this?" (v. 26)

I believe God asks every one of us this question today. Do you believe this?

She answered, "Yes, Lord. I believe You are the Messiah, the Son of God who has come into the world" (v. 27).

Martha's sister is Mary. This is the same Mary, the Gospel of John tells us, who was at the tax collector's house during dinner and wiped Jesus' feet with perfume. She took all she had and used it for God. The Pharisees and tax collectors were upset and said, "Oh, couldn't this have been sold to help the poor?"

Jesus said, "The poor you'll always have. But Me, you won't have. She's preparing me for burial. Therefore, everywhere that the Gospel is preached, she will be remembered." (Matthew 26:11-13) She will be remembered for her sacrifice. She took all she had – this perfume, and her hair. She wiped Jesus' feet and His body in this great act of sacrificial love.

This was that same Mary who was there grieving the loss of her brother, Lazarus. She saw Jesus come and she said the same thing.

> When Mary reached the place where Jesus was and saw him, she fell at his feet and said, "Lord, if you had been here, my brother would not have died." When Jesus saw her weeping, and the Jews who had come along with her also weeping, he was deeply moved in spirit and troubled. "Where have you laid him?" he asked. "Come and see, Lord," they replied. Jesus wept. (John 11:32-35)

Jesus, seeing the grief of Martha and Mary, said, "Take away the stone from the tomb." Even though there had been odor because Lazarus had been dead for four days, Jesus said what could be the most unbelievable line in the Bible.

I pray you will hear this. He says to Martha in John 11:40: "Did I not tell you, that if you believe, you will see the Glory of God?"

That is the gospel! That is the message of Jesus Christ. You can accept it or reject it, but that is the bottom line. God says if you believe, you will see the glory. Martha and Mary saw it right there. Jesus resurrected Lazarus from the dead right there, and there were many, many witnesses. At that point it was safe to say that removing their doubt blinders had been accomplished and they could now clearly reveal their choices based on truth and reality.

Wow, that sounds incredible. You're right, it does. Let me get this across to you, though. The same thing is going to happen to you! The same exact promise is going to happen to you. You are going to die. We're going to come to our El Paso day, and I hope it's not a death like that. I pray that you would go peacefully in your sleep at 104 years old like my wonderful grandmother Fanny Kornfeld did.

But even that day, is that it? Is that the end? No! If you believe, you will see the glory of God. You will spend eternity with Jesus in Heaven. That's why you should be rejoicing. God rewards faith.

In Daniel chapter 10, an angel came to Daniel and spoke to him; the Holy Spirit spoke through the angel and what he said to Daniel is a lesson for you and me, a reminder for you and me: "Daniel, since the first day you set your mind to gain understanding and to humble yourself before your God, your words were heard, and I have come in response to them. Do not be afraid!" (Daniel 10:12)

He was saying to Daniel, "Don't be afraid! Since the first day you did what? You set your mind to gain understanding! You set your mind! You determined! You resolved! You made up your mind that you were going to get understanding of the Lord, Daniel. You were focused! You did it since that day! And you humbled yourself before God! Since that day you sought to gain understanding and humble yourself before God – your words were heard! And I have come in response to them."

God makes that same promise to each one of us. He hears our prayers. We're His children. He loves us. He's coming in response to us. He's responding. The Holy Spirit is responding to your heart and your prayers today, whether it seems like it or not. He is guaranteeing you your place in Heaven and He's walking with you through this life; so, there's only one question – do we set our minds and hearts to gain understanding?

And do we humble ourselves before God? Humbling occurs when you're grateful to God. It happens when you surrender your will to His Life. That's humbling.

Setting your mind to gain understanding means you set your mind to work out. We set our mind to work. We set our minds to achieve the goals we want – cars, houses, money, stuff we want. We set our minds to make people think we're good and to impress them – either physically or emotionally – or with our words, or any way that we can. We set our minds upon this world because we're focused on what everyone here thinks about us. But we need to be focused on what God thinks about us.

So, God had a message for Daniel and the same message for you and me: "Do not be afraid. You are highly esteemed. Peace be with you. Be strong. You, during all your failures, and in spite of your frailness, humanness, and fragileness, you are highly esteemed – so much that God gave Jesus specifically for you." Here's the bottom line. Daniel was speaking to the angel and he asked: "I heard but I didn't understand. So, I asked my Lord, what will the outcome of all this be?" (Daniel 12:8)

"What's the bottom line, God? What does all this mean? What's the outcome?" And He replied to Daniel, "Go your way, Daniel. Because the Words are rolled up and sealed until the end of time. Many will be purified and made spotless and refined. But the wicked will continue to be wicked. None of the wicked will understand but those who are wise will understand" (Daniel 12:9-10).

God is very clear. Many are going to be purified – made righteous. We shouldn't be the ones who get up to Heaven and hear, "Depart from Me, I didn't know you." What do you mean depart from me, Lord? I was in church, I sang, I tithed; and God says, "Yeah, but your hearts were far from me." God says it's a wicked person whose heart is far from God. God says many will be purified and refined; that needs to be you and me. We need to make sure that we are in that category.

God says the wicked do not understand, but the wise understand. So today is a good day to ask yourself, do you understand? Are you willing to reflect a life that understands? For believers, I love Psalm 50:15: "Call on Me in your day of trouble. I will deliver you and you will honor Me."

Is there any believer who can say that God hasn't delivered him in his day of trouble? You may say, "Well, Jack, I still have financial troubles, marital troubles, relational troubles, spiritual troubles, emotional troubles…" Oh, I understand that, but God has delivered you from death. He's delivered you from the grave. He's resurrected you. He's giving you your inheritance in the Kingdom of Heaven. That's what you have. God has delivered you and He will continue to deliver you.

But He goes on to say, in Psalm 50:15, "But to the wicked person …" Here He is talking about the wicked and God's definition of wicked is one who doesn't believe in Him. When you don't believe in God, you're basically spitting in the face of Father God, the Holy Spirit, and Jesus. So, God says that's wickedness. It's not, "Oh, I killed, robbed, murdered, raped, stole." Those are all bad things of the flesh and the world. But God is defining wicked as those who don't acknowledge the Kingdom of God. He says this: "But to the wicked person, what right have you to recite My law or take My covenant on your lips? You hate My instruction and cast My words behind you" (Psalm 50:16-17).

God says you're not going to be able to come later and say, "Oh, I claim this now." God says you have no right to it! Because you hated it, you didn't pay attention to it, you didn't love it, you have no connection to Him. That's not for the believers. That's for those who don't believe.

A friend of mine called me up. He's married with some kids. They're planning a move. He told me, "Jack, I'm broke. I've depleted all my savings. We want to make this move to a better life and where we believe God is calling us. But we're broke. We've depleted all our savings. I don't know how we're going to do this."

So, I asked him a couple of questions, in love, and because I was curious. It turns out he has a house that he's had for a long time. The house has increased in value and he owes very little on the house.

I asked him, "So, wait a minute, pal, you have a lot of equity in this house, right?"

He said, "Well, yeah."

I told him, "So, I don't understand why you're compartmentalizing. You're not broke. You may have no cash flow, but you have assets you can turn into cash flow immediately."

I was thinking to myself, how could he be so blind? How could he have worked himself up into this frenzy of concern, worry, and fear when he had the treasure? The answer was there all this time. He had it already!

You have it also! If you're a believer in God, you have the Kingdom of God already. You have the treasure. You have it already. We need to live in that, and walk in that, and not succumb to fear. God has already delivered you. He says to you what He said to Daniel in Daniel 12:13: "As for you, go your way until the end. You will rest and at the end of days, you will rise to receive your allotted inheritance."

That's the same thing God says to you. Go your way, do your thing. Be the light, be salt to a tasteless world. Live a life that glorifies Me, and in the end you will rise to receive your allotted inheritance. It is the greatest promise, so how do we live? Do we live gratefully?

In Luke 17, there is a very famous story about Jesus healing ten lepers at one time. Lepers have a skin disease; they were considered unclean. They couldn't mingle with the regular population because if you were a leper, you had to distance yourself and live outside the city. If you came near somebody who didn't have leprosy, you had to scream, "UNCLEAN! UNCLEAN!" so that people would know you had leprosy and to stay away!

Jesus healed ten of them in one day. One came back, one of the ten, and he said, "Oh, thank you so much! You are amazing. You are God. I cannot believe You healed me. This is the greatest thing ever. I had leprosy. I was cast out of the city. Everybody hated me. My life was over, but you've given it back to me. This is amazing. Thank you so much. You are God. You're amazing..."

Then Jesus asks, "Where are the other nine? Did I not heal ten?"

The question I have for you and me today is, which one are we? Are we the one guy who came back, praising God for saving us? Or are we the other nine? They were basically like, "Thanks, a lot. That's great. Now I've got to go back to my other business. I've got to be all about me because I am all about me. I'm not grateful and giving glory to the One who saved me. To the One who has the power to have victory over the grave." I think we take that for granted sometimes.

Here's the tragedy and the problem in the Book of Ezra. Ezra is talking about intermarriage and the Israelites sinning against God because He told them not to intermarry, and yet they did. The

Israelites realized that God was mad at them and was punishing them for their sins. And they said in Ezra 9:1, "Because of our sins, we and our kings and our priests have been subjected to the sword and captivity. To pillage and humiliation at the hands of foreign kings as it is today."

Because of their sins, they were separated from God. What separates you from God and the Holy Spirit is your sin. You have the Holy Spirit if you are a believer. But our sin can separate us from God. Have you ever had a fight with a parent, a spouse, or a kid? You were still the parent, spouse, or kid. You still loved them, but guess what wasn't the same anymore? The love wasn't flowing. Something had happened that affected the relationship. It was the same in title, but it wasn't the same.

God is saying that's what sin does with your relationship with Him. "But see, we are slaves today. Slaves in the land you gave our ancestors, so they could eat its fruit and other good things it produces" (Nehemiah 9:36).

This is mind-boggling! God had given them this land so they would eat of its fruit and have the benefit and blessing of everything the land produced. But they recognized that they were slaves in the land God had given them. They weren't having the fruit, the benefit, or the blessings. They were slaves in the land because of their sin! It separated them from the blessing and fruit.

Here's my question for you. Are we slaves in the Kingdom that we are supposed to have inherited and ruled in? That is the Kingdom of God within us! God says, "Don't look for a sign. It's not somewhere else. The Kingdom of Heaven is within you." Are you a slave to your flesh and to this world? If so, know that that's not what God intended. God intended for you to have the blessings and fruit of the Spirit and of the Kingdom of God. He wants you to have it right now, not just when you get to Heaven.

When you get to Heaven, there will be no pain, no suffering. That's good news. Those people who recently died in El Paso, those who were believers, they're in Heaven. They're not feeling any pain and they're going to be in eternity with God forever. There will be no tears and no pain in Heaven. We grieve for them. In our humanity, we grieve, of course, but they're free. Whom the Son sets free is free indeed.

But are we slaves? Many live as slaves today to their fleshly desires, to their wants and the rules and the attitudes of society instead of following the Holy Spirit and the Kingdom of God. Here's the great news: "Though we are slaves, our God has not forsaken us in bondage" (Ezra 9:8).

God has not forsaken you. God wants to deliver you from whatever situation you're going through today. But remember the testimony of Daniel. You've got to be determined, resolved, and focused. You've got to set your mind on the things of God and on drawing closer to God. He says, "Come closer to Me, and I'll come closer to you."

Now I want to share some personal stuff with you. I got a text from a buddy of mine. This is very relevant considering I received it right after the senseless, tragic shootings in El Paso and Dayton. In El Paso, 23 people were killed and 23 more injured in a mass shooting at a Walmart department store. In Dayton, nine people died in a late-night shooting at a bar. My friend's son died in a tragic car crash a year ago. He and his wife are struggling with this, as you can imagine. I know other friends who have unfortunately experienced the loss of a child.

Here's what he texted me: "My wife and I have a tough day ahead. Not that all days are not tough. But today my son is gone one year. I still can't believe it. We're going out to the buoy where we put his ashes with some close friends and going to remember my son. When tragedy strikes, as it has stricken my wife and my family and myself, it changes your whole life. The pain of losing our son always weighs on me. I work and live but I am not the same person. You don't get over this. You don't accept this. You just survive it. A piece of me had died. I am very thankful for my grandson and my wife and my friends and family. It could always be worse. When something like this tremendous tragedy happens to someone, it is life-altering and forces you to think about eternity and makes you want so bad to believe in God and Heaven and that one day I will see my son again. And that life they call eternity can be all the Bible says it will be, which is a blissful life of love and vividness and high sensitivity, and no pain, no greed, no anger, and no jealousy and on and on. Enjoy your weekend, love your kids, love your wife and family. Tomorrow is promised to no one."

That's the bottom line. What are we going to do with the time that we have? I was at a party a few weeks ago. It was my uncle's 90th birthday. And he has a friend, Murray, who is a great guy. Murray's first wife Fran died of cancer. We watched her slowly die for four years of cancer. Murray said, "As I watched Fran suffer, over those four years, we learned what was really important and what wasn't."

I pray it doesn't take for any of us to go through a tragedy – financial or health or illness or losing a loved one – to realize what's important and what's not. I pray that we would focus our minds on the truth that every day we have is a gift from God and we need to treat it as such.

I've been talking to God lately. I talk to God a lot, but I want to share a few things that God has spoken to me recently. I have no different access than anyone else has to God. I am no more special or loved; I am just one of God's kids. I'm mentioning this because I have friends who say, "I don't hear from God like you." God has already spoken through His Word. You don't need to hear anything else.

A lot of people might go up to Bruce Springsteen or Bob Dylan or Harry Styles or Ed Sheeran and ask, "Hey, hey, what did that song you wrote mean?"

"The one I wrote?"

"Yeah, what did it really mean?"

"Well, look at the words. That's what it really meant. You don't have to go digging through my garbage to find some ulterior motive."

God has already spoken and is speaking to your heart each day. The Word of God is alive. If you're not reading the Word of God, then you're missing God speaking to your heart.

I was struggling, big time, a few months ago. I just get to that point sometimes. I, too, struggle. We all struggle. Anyone you can think of who seems to be all together… they struggle. We're all human, but we're trying to keep the faith. This time of struggling was very personal and very deep for me. It went on for at least a month, and it was getting worse.

Then I got a call one day from a guy in South Florida who I have known from men's ministry for about 20 years. I've never been to his house, never been to lunch with him, although we have spoken a couple of times. He usually calls me every couple of years for a reference for a job; if he needs something, he calls me. When you know someone from men's ministry, you might not know each other really well, but you still know each other, you love each other; you're brothers.

So, he called me, and I ignored the call for a couple of days, but I put it on my list that I needed to call him back. I was just very busy, and I knew he probably wanted something. I was getting to it. Eventually, I returned his call.

He said, "Jack, I had a dream."

I repeated, "You had a dream?"

He said, "Yeah, it was a dream about you." He went on to say, "You were struggling, and you were failing in your faith. Satan was attacking you determined to bring you down. And I said, 'No, not Jack!'" As I am a men's ministry leader, I believe this brother looked up to me. I've known him for years, so I take it as a compliment that he looks at me as a strong man of faith.

I was so amazed. I prayed in my mind, God, you've got to be kidding me. Frank Thomas of all people called me? Frank? Of all the people in the world, I'm walking along, and you give this obscure and sweet-spirited, humble brother a specific dream about me that is so chillingly real and accurate it left me speechless.

I was completely speechless and I didn't even know what to say. I told him, "No, no, everything is fine, Brother." I couldn't even speak! I was so blown away.

God was just demonstrating to me His power. He was basically telling me, "Watch! You don't think I got everything under control? You think you've got to worry? What's the matter with you, Jack? Watch, let me show you." He gave a dream to this guy who called me and told me about it as if it was the angel who came to Daniel. I was flabbergasted. I couldn't even speak.

So, the next day God puts on my heart that I'm supposed to go to Pittsburgh. God has done this two times in my life.

One time, years ago, God told me I was supposed to go to St. Louis. And believe me, I tried to ignore this. I was asking myself, "How do I know if it's God? Maybe it's Satan who is telling me that." But it wouldn't go away, and suddenly everything I heard, it felt was about St. Louis. It seemed for two weeks, every news story, every sitcom character, every waitress that served us was from St. Louis. St. Louis, St. Louis, St. Louis... God asked me if He could be any clearer and did I get the message yet! So, we made a scouting trip to St. Louis, then we wound up bringing a team back and doing a week-long ministry in the streets of St. Louis. That's something I usually don't do. This was just a God-directed thing that took place many years ago, but I never forgot how specifically God led me in that direction. We were blessed amazingly in St. Louis, as we got to minister in the streets for a week, leading people to Christ and praying for them. It culminated with a Friday night service in a theater in the Delmar Loop in the heart of St. Louis. We met and ministered with Vic Venezia and the Friends of Jesus band. It was an awesome, life-changing service with many coming to know the Lord, prayers answered and truly living up to the title God had given me for that night "A Night of Hope and Miracles." I know the seven of us from Florida had our lives changed dramatically by that opportunity to minister in a new city, with no holds barred, inspired, and empowered by the Holy Spirit's leading and call. It was a blessing I will never forget (and one I'd have to write about in another book to give you the whole story).

The second time God told me to go somewhere, was to move to Orlando. Very specifically, again, God was telling me, "You need to go to Orlando," and I was like, "I don't want to go to Orlando." For a month, God was pushing it my way; every waitress was from Orlando, every TV show was talking about Orlando, everything was Orlando, Orlando. And, of course, I moved to Orlando. God was in it. What an amazing blessing it has been to follow God in faith to Orlando. Thankfully, we didn't miss what God had in store for us as family and for our ministry here in Orlando, as fortunately we responded and followed the calling of God through His Holy Spirit speaking to our hearts.

So now I'm seeing this again. I'm like, "Oh no, not again, not Pittsburgh. Not again." This took place a couple of months ago;

every interview guy, every sitcom was about Pittsburgh; everything I picked up mentioned Pittsburgh. It felt like I was in a movie.

Then I got a call to do an interview on a TV show for an opioid thing because I help a lot of people who have drug addictions, and I've written a book called *My Addict Your Addict*. Where is the interview? Pittsburgh. So, I finally responded, "Okay, I'm going."

I flew up there by myself to the studio and there was a guy sitting next to me on the plane. There were three of us in a row. I nodded to the guy next to me and he nodded to me. We didn't say a word for the whole flight. The plane landed, we got up to get our luggage, and God spoke to me in the Spirit. He said, "Give him a book."

I had a few books in my suitcase, but I said, "No, God. Not today." Normally I wouldn't mind giving somebody a book. But I just sat with this guy for two and a half hours, and I just nodded at him, but didn't say a word. There were people standing in the aisle of the plane. I didn't want to give him a book. You know, it would just be too embarrassing.

So, I got off the plane. It was a Monday morning. I'm familiar with the Orlando Airport and LaGuardia Airport—those airports are always jammed with people. Yet on this Monday morning in Pittsburgh it was different, aside from people getting off our plane, there was nobody in the airport terminal when we landed. No other planes landing, no other people milling about. We came up the jetway ramp into the terminal and there were no other people around. It was eerie, like a ghost town or zombie apocalypse movie. Nobody else there!

God said to me again, through the Holy Spirit, "Give him a book."

I said, "No, no, I'm going to go to the bathroom." I went to the bathroom and in the bathroom, God very clearly told me again, "Give him a book."

So, I finally decided I had better give the guy a book. I got out of the bathroom, looked to my left, and didn't see anybody. I looked fifty yards in the other direction, half a football field, and I didn't see anybody. The others of us who had been on the plane obviously got off to leave had already headed down to baggage claim or to an exit to leave the airport while I had gone to the bathroom.

So, I said, "Lord, that's that. I'm off the hook." I walked toward the baggage claim. I took an escalator down to the tram. As I came down the escalator, I looked down on the tram platform. There were two tall guys, a lady, and a kid. Nobody else. I walked up to where the tram was going to be. I glanced at my phone for less than one second to see the time, I raised my head, and the guy who was sitting next to me on the plane was standing right there! I'm like, "Holy Cow God, you've got to be kidding me! Is this what Moses felt like at the Red Sea? Clearly you are real God and you are amazing." (Both of which I already knew, but clearly God felt it necessary to remind me and to prove to me at this point in my life!) I was crying with joy at God's supernatural power. He literally made this guy reappear out of thin air right before my eyes.

There was no way to get out of it now. I told him, "I was on the plane with you. God told me to give you this book."

He said, "Oh, thank you very much." That was that.

God spoke to me when I got home. He said, "You didn't go to Pittsburgh to give the guy a book. You went to Pittsburgh to meet me. I wanted to show you how powerful I am. I can wake up Frank Thomas in the middle of the night and have him call you with your circumstances that I showed him in a dream. I can send you to Pittsburgh to see Me personally and see My power in action if you doubted it for a minute."

Perhaps you have not had those exact same experiences, but I think we have all had experiences where we know God is real in our life. But what do we do about them? Too often, we forget the very next day. It's like the disciples in the boat when they got scared because of the winds and the waves; they had forgotten everything Jesus had done when He provided bread and did miracles in front of them. We do that in our own lives, too. We forget the power of God. We don't default to God's power and God's reality. That's what we need to do.

Jesus asked His disciples, "Do you still not understand? Are your hearts hardened? Do your eyes fail to see, and your ears fail to hear? And don't you remember?"

It's like He was a teacher quizzing them, and in a way, He was. He asked, "Don't you remember when I broke the bread? How many did I feed?"

"Five thousand."

"Then I broke it again; how many did I feed?"

"Four thousand," they replied.

He said, "Do you still not understand?"

I believe God was saying that to me through my personal experiences. "Jack, do you still not understand?"

So, I'm asking you the same thing today. Do you not know the Holy Spirit? Do you not have the Holy Spirit? Do you still not understand?

Perhaps you just need to choose to believe God. As we near the end of this book, I want you to linger on these amazing words of Jesus. I believe we've covered a lot of amazing words in this book. I'm especially drawn to the passage that says, "Do you not know that if you believe, you will see the glory of God?" The glory of God is available for all who believe and seek it.

But there's another amazing passage found in Mark chapter 9. There's a big crowd around Jesus, and a man brings his son to Jesus. He tells Jesus his son is demon-possessed by a spirit that has robbed him of speech; the kid can't talk. It seizes him, it throws him to the ground, and he foams from the mouth. He gnashes his teeth. He becomes rigid.

The father says, "I asked the disciples to drive out the spirit, but they couldn't."

Jesus looks at them and He asks a question to the boy's father, "How long has he been like this?"

The father says, "Since childhood. He's been like this since he was a kid." He adds, "The spirit often throws him into the fire or into the lake—to drown him or to burn him or to kill him." You know, if there's a guy throwing himself into the lake and the fire, he's clearly possessed. But this has happened since this son was a child.

Can you imagine being the parent of that child? You might be the parent of a special needs child; I know that can be a burden and not an easy life, but at the same time, you love your kids more than anything. This is a special needs kid. This kid is demon-possessed. He can't speak. The father says to Jesus that he's been this way from childhood. In Mark 9:21, the father says, "...But if you can do anything, take pity on us and help us."

He basically says, "Jesus, here's the story, my kid's been possessed since birth. It's just terrible and it's horrible. I came to your disciples and they couldn't cast the demon out. He's mute and he's throwing himself into the water; he's foaming; he's gnashing his teeth. But if you could do anything, please help me."

IF? Jesus looks at him and He says, "Everything is possible for one who believes" (Mark 9:23).

It's like Jesus is asking, "If I can?" Of course He can. God can do anything. "Everything is possible for him who believes." Not some things, not a few things, not most things. Everything is possible for one who believes. When we go about removing the doubt blinders to clearly reveal our choices, I believe we will clearly see the truth of God is not only the only choice but the best choice.

Either God is a liar, or He is Lord. You've probably heard that before – the logical conclusion that C. S. Lewis so famously made, both in his fantasy series, *The Chronicles of Narnia*, and in his book, *Mere Christianity*. Either Jesus is a lunatic, a liar, or He is Lord. He claimed to be the only living Son of God and said, "I am the way, the truth, and the life. No one comes to the Father except through Me" (John 14:6).

That's a bold claim. I added a couple:

> Either He's a goofball or He's God.
> Either He's a maniac or He's the Messiah.
> Either He's a chump or He's the Chosen One.
> Either He's a kook or He's your King.
> Either He's a jackass or He's Jesus, the Lord of your life.

You get to decide; but remember, your life depends on it.

I don't know where you are in your personal life today, but I encourage you to believe that God, the Holy Spirit, is working in your life. He is real and He is alive. His Word is alive. It is active.

Our Heavenly Father has promised He would never leave us nor forsake us. He is with us always. What great promises He has given us! But we need to ask ourselves a few questions.

Are we determined?

Are we like Daniel and like the people Nehemiah spoke about, working with all their hearts?

Are we determined, have we resolved, have we made up our minds to follow God and to live a life that glorifies Him?

When we pray, are we praying not based on our righteousness and our works, but praying to God because of His great mercy and love?

I hope that we would focus on that – that we would not think for one minute that we must do anything to earn the love of God. He loves us because we belong to Him. We're God's children. The wicked should not expect anything from God. But we, the believers, the family of God, should expect everything.

When a man dies, he leaves an inheritance to his wife and children and family, not to strangers, not to friends who claimed to have known him. No, his heirs are those he loved. Those are the ones to whom he leaves his inheritance. God is our inheritance, and He has given us an eternal inheritance above and beyond all we could ask or think.

May we examine our hearts and our faith in light of God's Word. I think about Martha and Mary; they were just ordinary people like you and me. No better, no worse. But they are remembered for their faith. They believed 100 percent that Jesus could do anything. Both of them told Jesus that if He had been there, Lazarus would not have died. Why? Because they knew and believed He had the power to do anything. And He did. He called Lazarus from the grave.

Whatever God says or ordains or calls into being, is. Whatever He blesses is blessed and whatever He curses is cursed. We can only thank Him that He has blessed us with an eternity in Heaven. He has blessed us with the Holy Spirit of God in our hearts. He has blessed us with His Word, which is alive.

It amazes me that people won't read the Bible. They consider it as if it were a chore or obligation, instead of a treasure chest to be opened. They would be filled with this treasure of God's Living Word if only they would open it. The Word of God is alive. Jesus, the Word of God, came to Earth and the Word was made flesh. Why? To set us free. To enable us to live in freedom.

We are called to be joyful always, to pray continually and give thanks in all circumstances; for this is God's will for us. Take a moment to reflect on your own life. Are you living in joy, in thankfulness, in prayer? If not, if you are living in fear and in slavery. Believe the promises of God and take hold of them for your very own.

God has given us this time here on earth to enjoy Him and love Him and others. If you are living in the fear of your mind, or heart, or thoughts, or emotions, and not in the freedom He has called you to, then you just need to claim His promises for your very own.

God has given us dominion over this earth and a place in Heaven. He wants us to live in it and be free in it. Whom the Son sets free is free indeed. I pray that our gratitude would be like the one leper who turned back to Jesus. Ten lepers were healed but only one turned back and gave God the glory. He didn't forget. The other nine forgot. Perhaps it wasn't so important to them. The gift of God that He's given us is of supreme importance, and we need to believe in it and value it above all else.

I pray that God would rest in your heart and speak to your heart very specifically about your life. I pray you would open your heart to what God would have you do, to what He would set you free from, to what He would have you change, to what you're doing right, that He would have you do more of.

God has given us the Bible like an open-book test in school. All the answers are there. Even if we've gotten the answers wrong, it's not too late. We've written them in pencil (our life actions so far). We can just erase them and fill in the right answers (our life going forward).

I pray that you would finish this chapter filled with joy, with knowledge, that your sins have been forgiven. Anything you've done wrong is covered with the blood of Christ. God loves you and forgives you. He just wants to see you blessed and fulfilled. He wants to pick you up and help you.

If I've learned anything in many years of walking with the Lord, I've learned that He is my joy. My joy and my peace come from being with the Lord, walking with Him, communing with Him, and living this life with Him. I like living on this Earth. I enjoy many of the things of the world. I love my family and my friends. I like life. I love it, in fact. I'd like to hang out a little longer and be a part of it. But none of that has ever given me sustaining joy and peace. Only God has done that. He's given me a certainty of Heaven. He's given me rivers of joy and the peace that transcends all understanding. And that's not unique to me. It's for each believer.

I pray we will rejoice, and that we would be determined and focused and set our minds to coming closer to the Lord so that we do not miss anything He has for us in this life and the one to come.

Chapter Eleven

CONSIDERING A GODLY DIRECTION WITH NO MORE HESITATION

I took a picture of my friend's newborn son last week when he was just two days old sitting in his bassinet. I looked at him and thought to myself, this kid has no clue how loved he is! He couldn't even begin to imagine how much love there is in this in his parents' hearts, in his friends' hearts, in his family's hearts - for him. As he lay there, he could not comprehend it. It would be unimaginable for him.

At that moment, God said to me, "Jack, that is the same love I have for you. You can't even begin to grasp and imagine how great My love is for you. You think baby Sean has no clue how much love there is for him? Well, he doesn't. But he's going to see it as his life unfolds."

The Lord added, "In the same way, you see My love as your own life unfolds." We see the love God has for us as His love unfolds every day of our lives. I pray that we would rejoice in the fact that when God says, "Now we know in part, then we'll know in full," it means He has so much love for us that it is incomprehensible.

Of course, we saw this love demonstrated on the cross when Jesus died for us. That was the greatest manifestation of His love, but it is also just the beginning of God's love for you. Just the beginning. I hope that excites and thrills you.

I have yet to meet the mother who said childbirth and labor pains weren't worth it. It is the same, spiritually, regarding the trials and tribulations we go through here on Earth. Our faith should be the same as Abraham, Daniel, Moses, Joseph, Paul, and so many other disciples and believers.

In God's Word, Jesus says, "In this world, you will have trouble. But be of good cheer; I have overcome the world." (John 16:33) The problem is, sometimes we are like the Israelites who were wandering in the desert. They got so scared in the desert, but why? It was because God's timing to fulfill their envisioned outcome took so much longer than they thought it should take. They couldn't visibly see the future. So, they gave up on God because of their own perception of what God's timing should be and what He should provide. They turned away from God because instead of trusting what was unseen, they chose only to believe in what they could see. The Bible tells us, they shipwrecked their faith. I pray that our faith would not be shipwrecked.

Let me share with you a parable that God shared with me that crystallized this truth for me. My family was up in Cazenovia, NY over the summer and I was looking out over Cazenovia Lake. You can see the lake, and there are trees beyond the lake as far as you can see. It's beautiful – absolutely gorgeous.

Behind those trees, I know there is a road. How do I know? Well, I've been down that road. You can't see it behind the trees when you are looking out from the lake, but behind the lake and the trees, there is a road. That road will take you out of Cazenovia into Manlius and if you continued on the road a few more miles, you'd get to Fayetteville. If you continued on the road another five miles or so, you'd get to Syracuse. See, I know exactly where that road leads because I have been down it. In that moment, God gave me clarity and visualization to show me a spiritual truth.

God has told us He knows exactly where the road leads and we are to trust Him when we can't see the way. When all we can see are the lake and the trees, we are to trust that God said, "I prepared a way for you. I have a plan for your life. You are to follow Me in faith and obedience." We are to trust in Proverbs 3:5-6, which says, "Trust in the Lord with all your heart, lean not on your own understanding. In all your ways acknowledge Him and He will direct your paths."

That was a realization for me. It's all about perspective. Considering a godly direction with no more hesitation was now my new perspective and thus became my new reality.

There was a teacher talking to a kids' classroom, and she was trying to get them to think about the Seven Wonders of the World. You probably know some of them: the Pyramids, the Grand Canyon, the Panama Canal, the Empire State Building, St. Peter's Basilica, the Great Wall of China, etc.

Well, there was one kid who couldn't make up his mind. All the other kids were ready. They had the Seven Wonders of the World in mind, and this kid couldn't make up his mind. The teacher asked, "Johnny, what's the problem?"

The kid said, "Teacher, there's so many!"

She answered, "Well, actually, there are only seven."

Finally, the kid said, "All right!" He made up his mind and here were his seven: touch, taste, sight, hearing, feeling, laughing, and love. That was his perspective of the Seven Wonders of the World.

A Few Stories of Faith

I want to share with you a couple of stories about faith. I believe our lives are dependent on our perspective and focus on God. You probably know of Justin Bieber. Justin Bieber came to know Jesus Christ as his Lord and Savior and this is something he recently shared on social media:

"By the time I was 18, with no skills in the real world, I had millions of dollars and access to whatever I wanted. This is a very scary concept for anyone. By 20 I had made every bad decision you could have thought of and went from being one of the most loved and adored people in the world to the most ridiculed, judged and hated person in the world! I started doing pretty heavy drugs at 19 and abused all of my relationships. I became resentful, disrespectful to women, and angry. I became distant to everyone who loved me, and I was hiding behind a shell of a person that I had become. I felt like I could never turn it around. It's taken me years to bounce back from all of these terrible decisions, fix broken relationships, and change relationship habits. Luckily, God blessed me with extraordinary people who love me for me. Now I am navigating the best season of my life, marriage! You learn patience, trust, commitment, kindness, humility and all the things it looks like to be a good man. All this to say even when the odds are against you keeping fighting. Jesus loves you. Be kind today! Be bold today and love people today! Not by your standards but by God's perfect, unfailing love."

That sounds to me like a transformed man. Our God tells us that He can create a new creation out of anyone who will give their life to Him. He says, "The old is gone. The new has come." God celebrates the new man, so we celebrate that.

Another example of faith in action is a man named Tommy Zurhellen. Tommy blew me away. This man spent four months walking twenty-two miles a day – a total of 2,866 miles in four months. He traveled from Portland, Oregon to Poughkeepsie, New York... walking 22 miles every day for four months in an effort to raise awareness about the scourge of suicide and homelessness among veterans. I was thinking, man, there is a committed guy!

In response, God said to me, "Yes, he is committed Jack! And how have you committed to Me in your life?" This is for you, too. What have you done for Jesus Christ in the last four months to show that you're sold out for the cause of God? Here's a man walking and living out his cause. I don't know if he's a believer or not, but I know he's a man focused on what is important to him. As believers, we need to be focused on what we believe in, which is Jesus Christ. Tommy was sold out for a cause. The question for us today is this: Are we sold out for Jesus? What have we done or sacrificed for Jesus?

This next story of faith will tear your heart out. It's an unfortunate one. Blake Bivens is a minor league baseball player with the Tampa Bay Rays Association. Tragically, his family was murdered by his brother-in-law. His fourteen-month-old son, his twenty-five-year-old wife, and his mother-in-law were murdered while he was away. His brother-in-law was mentally ill and killed his three family members. Here's what Blake said two days after this happened, on social media:

"Two days ago my heart was turned to ash. My life as I knew it is destroyed. The pain my family and I feel is unbearable and cannot be put into words. I shake and tremble at the thought of our future without them. Emily, my sweetheart, you are the best wife and mother this world has ever seen. You made me into the man I am today and you loved me with all of my flaws. You brought our precious baby boy into this world and made our family complete. Your love and kindness changed countless lives, including mine. My sweet little boy, dada loves you so much! I can't breathe without you here. I finally understood what love was when you were born and I would have done anything for you. You have changed my life forever; you are my reason why. I long to hold the both of you again in Heaven. I'm so glad you are with all your great-grandmothers now. I know they are eating you up. This earth did not deserve either of you; you were just too wonderful to comprehend. Joan, you were the best mother-in-law anyone could ask for. You loved your family more than anyone I've ever seen. You raised the most wonderful girl in the world. I'm so glad y'all are still together. You were the best Nana this world has ever seen and I will never forget you. Skip, you are a wonderful father and grandfather. We will get through this together as a family. We will not let the devil win! Thank you, God, for giving me the most wonderful family in the world! I've been blessed beyond belief. Thank you to all my family and friends who have reached out to me during this time of sorrow. Thank you all for your support through everything. I am comforted by all the messages and well wishes. I'm not sure what is next for me, but I do know God has a plan even though I can't see it."

Now that is faith in action and I believe a great example of considering a godly direction with no more hesitation and then acting on it. I pray and hope that would reflect the faith of every believer. In 2 Corinthians 11:3, the Apostle Paul talks about what our faith should look like. He's talking to the Church of Corinth and, I believe, through the Holy Spirit, that he is talking to you and me today. He says, "But I'm afraid that just as Eve was deceived by the serpent's cunning, your minds may somehow be led astray from your sincere and pure devotion to Christ." Paul was scared that, just like Eve was fooled by Satan, we would also be fooled and get pulled away from what should be a sincere and pure devotion to Christ. That is what our devotion to Christ should look like. It should be sincere and pure. That is the focus of our life: our devotion to Christ, which should reflect sincerity and purity.

The God Who Cares

Here are the questions we, as Christians, sometimes ask:
1. Does God care about our work?
2. Is there a reward for what we've done?
3. Are we responsible to be lifesavers?
4. Are we responsible to those we are called to minister to?

I want to take you into God's Word to consider the answers to those questions. We're going to look at Ezekiel the prophet. He got a message from the Lord and here is what God said: "Son of Man,

I have made you a watchman for the people of Israel; so hear the word I speak and give them warning from Me" (Ezekiel 3:17).

What about you? You might say, "Don't be ridiculous. First of all, that's from the Old Testament. We're not bound under Old Testament law. We're under New Testament grace."

Yes, that's correct.

And you might say, "Second of all, I'm not a watchman. I'm just me."

No, that's not true. You are a priest. You are an ambassador. You are a representative. You are a warrior. And you are a child of your Father, God. You are absolutely a watchman for the people of today. You have a purpose, as laid out in Scripture:

> "To do the good works which God created in advance for you to do." (Ephesians 2:10)
> "To bear fruit and fruit that will last." (John 15:16)
> "To declare the praises of Him who called you out of darkness and into the light." (1 Peter 2:9)

We absolutely have a purpose. It goes on in Ezekiel 3:18-19 to say this: "When I say to a wicked person, 'You will surely die.' And you do not warn them or speak out to dissuade them from their evil ways in order to save their life, that wicked person will die for their sin and I will hold you accountable for their blood. But if you do warn the wicked person and they do not turn from their wickedness or from their evil ways, they will die for their sin but you will have saved yourself."

I want you to understand that, as Christians, we are not under Old Testament law. You are not bound by that. You are not going to die if you don't tell the person about Jesus. You don't have to do it. Back then, Ezekiel had to do it. You don't have to do it. But you should want to do it out of gratitude and love in response to what God has done for you. We are still called to share the gospel. The Great Commission is for all of us. To go and share the gospel and make disciples. We are called to shine our light, the light of Jesus, to the world. We are called to not take a lamp and put it under a basket to hide the light. We're called to shine the light. We're called to declare what we heard in secret. We're supposed to take the things

God has put in our hearts and shout them from the mountaintops. That what we're called to do.

God was upset with the priest of the Old Testament. God was mad. He said, "Listen, if you speak out and tell them and they still don't come to the Lord, that's on them. But if you don't tell them and they don't come, that's on you. I'm holding that law on you." He was mad.

In Malachi 2:1-2, He gives an additional warning to the priests. He says, "Now you priests, this warning is for you." I want to remind you that God's Word says you are a priest of God. I don't mean a pastor or reverend; you might not have a title, but you don't need a title to preach for God. Not having that title does not exempt you from your responsibilities and duties to share the good news of Jesus Christ, to be a lifesaver to this world that is dying. Here's the warning: "Now you priests, this warning is for you. If you do not listen and you do not resolve to honor My name, I will send a curse on you. I will curse your blessings. Yes, I've already cursed them because you have not resolved to honor Me."

Understand what made God mad back then. The priests had not resolved to honor God. My question is, do we honor God? Have we resolved, committed, decided, made up our mind to honor Him? Every Sunday, when there's a sports game going on, you've probably made up your mind which football game you're going to watch after church. Every Sunday, you've probably made up your mind where you're going to eat lunch by the middle of the service. And you follow through on both those things. Is it too much to do the same for God our Father, our Lord, our King, our Friend, our Savior? Do we honor God with our words and actions? Do the actions of our life reflect our trust and faith in Him?

He goes on to say in, Malachi 2:7, "For the lips of a priest ought to preserve knowledge. Because he is the messenger of the Lord Almighty, and people seek instruction from his mouth." The world is open to you. You're God's messenger! People are seeking instruction from your mouth!

He then states in verse 8, "But you have turned from the way by your teaching and have caused many to stumble. You have violated the covenant with Levi." Let me ask you this: What is your life teaching the unbelievers of this world? What are we teaching them with our attitudes and our actions and our words? God is worthy of our love. Remember, this is the God of your salvation. In Zechariah, God says, "Jerusalem will be a city without walls because of the great number of people and animals in it and I, Myself, will be a wall of fire around it. I will be its glory within."

In Revelation 21:23, it says of Heaven, "The city does not need the sun or the moon to shine on it, for the glory of God gives it light and the Lamb will be its lamp." God's glory is greater than the sun and stars put together.

One time the car battery in my son's Toyota was dead. I called AAA, because that's the smart thing to do. The AAA guy came – an African American kid, maybe 25 or 30. I was talking to him a little bit. I will call him Sam. He said he grew up in the church. He started to tell me about John Isaac, who is a basketball player for the Miami Heat. He said, "Oh, John Isaac is so cool. He tells people about Jesus. He invited all his teammates to come to the Bible study. None of them came but he invited them."

I answered, "Yeah, that's really cool." As he was telling me this story, I could see how far away from the Father he was. It broke my heart. He knew about the religion, but he had no personal relationship with Jesus Christ. He didn't understand God as a loving Father who really, individually, loves him. He didn't understand that if he were the only guy on Earth, Jesus would have died on the cross for him, personally and individually. He didn't have that personal relationship with the Father. He had a knowledge of God, but he didn't have a personal relationship with the Father.

I talked to him a little bit and I think I explained that to him. God reminded me that it's not enough to be sitting back and listening. We have to be doing. The book of James says, "Faith without works is dead." Remember, "faith without works is dead" (James 2:26).

The next day God spoke to me while I was at a gas station. By the way, when I say that God spoke to me, do not think for one minute that I have any more access to God than you do. I am not any more special. It does not matter that I have the title of pastor or preacher. That's a professional job. You have the same access to God that I have. He speaks to me through His Word and through His Holy Spirit the same way He wants to speak to you.

So, I was at a gas station and it was a Sunday morning right before church. It was 9:01 a.m. and I was getting gas. I saw a well-dressed man and I thought to myself, "This guy is definitely going to church." It was not even a question on my mind. He was dressed in a suit and tie, so I thought to myself, "I'm a great Christian guy. Here's what I'm going to do. I'm going to bless him with one of my books." Isn't that nice of me? Here I am, a great, spiritual, Christian man.

Then I looked over and saw a ragged looking young man in a beat-up car getting gas in front of me. He wasn't going to church, that's for sure. I don't want to judge him, but he looked a little rough. And God spoke to my heart and spirit and said, "Give him the book! Give the young guy the book!" I hesitated and God pressed into my heart, saying, "The guy dressed up in a suit and tie going to church – he doesn't need your book! The young man who doesn't know Me, he's the one you need to be ministering to."

Jesus said the same thing when He walked the Earth, remember? He didn't come to heal the righteous. The righteous don't need a doctor. He came to heal the sick, the people who are lost spiritually, who do not know God." So, I did give the book to the young man. He was very grateful and very humble. Even though I thought he was going to say, "Get away from me," he didn't. But it doesn't matter what his reaction was. What matters is that we listen to the Spirit of God. That's what matters.

My focus was all wrong. I wanted to talk to the guy who would be grateful and thank me, not the one who might have had a negative response. But that's God at work. His ways are not our own, but we know He cares about everyone and is not willing that anyone perish.

How is Your Spiritual House?

Here is the question for you and me today. It's in the first chapter of Haggai and I believe it's a question God is asking you and me. It's the second year of King Darius. The Word of the Lord comes through the prophet Haggai and he speaks it to the rulers of the day. "This is what the Lord Almighty says, 'These people say the time has not yet come to rebuild the Lord's house.' And the Word came through the prophet Haggai and he said, 'Is it time for you yourselves to be living in your paneled house, while this house remains in ruin?'" (Haggai 1:2-4)

You see, in the Old Testament, we were talking about a physical house. God's temple had been destroyed. It was a ruin. It had not yet been rebuilt. And God was saying to the people, in effect, "Look, do you think it's okay for you to be happy in your house and enjoying all the comfort and luxury of your house while my house lies in ruins?"

There's a physical temple in the Old Testament. Today, He's talking about our spiritual house! Is our spiritual house in ruin? God is asking you and me if we think it's okay that we sit comfortably and do what we want and enjoy all of the benefits and comforts of home while God's spiritual house is lying in ruins? That's a question we each need to answer individually. I'm not talking about the world or about America. I'm talking about your heart and your spiritual house.

This is what the Lord goes on to say in Haggai chapter 1: "Give careful thought to your ways. You have planted much but harvested little. You eat but never have enough. You drink but never have your fill. You put on clothes but you're not warm. You earn wages only to put them in purses with holes… Give careful thought to your ways. Go up into the mountains, bring down timber, and build my house so that I may take pleasure in it and be honored" (Haggai 1:5-8).

What kind of life honors the Lord? The kind of life that is working and living and building for the Lord. That's what God says. He says bring down timber and build my house so that I may take pleasure in it and be honored. Are you building the house of the Lord with the timber of your life? That's the question God has for you and me. You are to build a spiritual house and you build it with your life.

I'm not saying there's not a spiritual battle. Ephesians chapter 6 reminds us that the war we wage is not against flesh. We face spiritual battles in the heavenly realms. God tells us we need to put on the full armor of God; that is how we win. In Daniel 11:31-32, speaking of Satan and his evil forces, God says, "His armed forces will rise up to desecrate the temple fortress and will abolish the daily sacrifice. Then they will set up the abomination that causes desolation. With flattery he will corrupt those who have violated the covenant. But the people who know their God will firmly resist him."

This is what's going to happen in the last days. This is what's happening now. The Antichrist is rising up. The world is going to hell in a handbasket. Everything is happening and God says, "But the people who know their God will firmly resist" (Daniel 11:32). To that I say, "Hallelujah!" Just keep working on your spiritual house and serving the Lord faithfully.

Just Do Something

Are you ready to do battle for God? Are you ready to firmly resist the enemy and do battle for God? You can start today by advancing the Kingdom of God, one soul at a time. You can hand out a Bible tract. You can give someone a Bible. You can share your salvation story. You can invite someone to church. You can ask someone what you can pray about for them. You'll be shocked at how many non-believers welcome prayer. They know they want it. They just don't know how they can get it and don't believe they themselves have access to, or are worthy of, God's love.

I pray that you would take time to ask God to reveal how He would have you specifically and personally advance the Kingdom of God. Is it more quiet time for you? Is it to work harder? Is it to increase your faith? Is it that you should give more? Is it that you should pray more? Is it giving something up permanently? Is it forgiving somebody? Whatever it is, you need to do it. I believe it starts with considering a Godly direction in determining you act and live with no more hesitation. That is what I call trusting God and moving in faith.

I was at a meeting for Project Opioid. It's a special project they're doing in Orlando to put business and faith leaders together to fight the opioid epidemic. The governor was there and other dignitaries. They had one woman there who lost her son to an overdose and they showed his story on the screen. It was heartbreaking; I won't take you through it. At the end of the meeting, they gave the microphone to the lady; I think it was kind of a spontaneous decision to do so. They said, "Listen, by the way, you have everybody assembled here – faith leaders, business leaders– is there anything you want to say to them?"

As she held the portrait of her son, dealing with this deep tragedy of her heart, she picked up the mic and without looking up, she said, "Do something. Just do something."

I believe God would say that same thing to you and me today. Do something! Just do something. God's promise in Psalm 126:6 says, "Those who go out weeping, carrying seed to sow, will return with songs of joy, carrying sheaves with them." When I first read that, I didn't know what a sheave was. I had to look it up. So, I did. It's a bunch of grain stalks bundled together. It's like this huge stash. You plant these little seeds and then you get this huge harvest out of it.

God's promise is, "Those who go out weeping, carrying seed to sow, will return with songs of joy, carrying sheaves with them." God promises you that if you invest in His Kingdom, if you invest your life in His Kingdom, you will receive 30, 60, and even 100 fold. You will receive more than you could ever ask for or imagine in this life and in the life to come. That's the promise of God, but you have to invest your life in God.

Are you carrying seed to sow? Your life, your faith, and your actions are your seed. That is the seed you need to sow. In Jeremiah 10:23 we read, "Lord, I know that people's lives are not their own; it is not for them to direct their steps." Yet God promises us in Jeremiah 29:11 that He knows the plans He has for us. He plans to prosper us, to give us hope and a future, not to harm us.

What's the bottom line? How can you be sure it's worth it?

In Matthew 16:13, Jesus asks the disciples, "Who do people say the Son of man is?"

They reply, "Some say John the Baptist, others say Elijah, still others, Jeremiah or one of the prophets."

Jesus looks at them and says, "But what about you? Who do you say I am?"

Peter answers, and you probably know the verse well. He says, "You are the Messiah! The Son of the Living God."

Jesus replies, "Blessed to you Simon, son of Jonah, for this was not revealed to you by flesh and blood but by My Father in Heaven. And I tell you that you are Peter and on this rock I will build My church and the gates of Hades will not overcome it!" (Matthew 16:13-18)

That is a promise from God! The outcome has been decided. There is no fear; we have the victory. In Luke 1:73, He says, "The oath which He swore to our father Abraham, to grant us that we, being delivered from the hand of our enemies, might serve Him without fear." This is God's desire – that you serve Him without fear: without fear of ridicule; without fear of condemnation; without fear of death; without fear of the outcome. The true currency of the heavenly realm is your faith and your faith in action.

Imagine if you knew the outcome of a football game that has not been played yet. Imagine if you knew the closing prices of the stock market tomorrow at 4 o'clock. Oh my gosh, you could make a fortune having that advanced knowledge. But here in life, in death, in Heaven, in Hell –you already know the outcome. You can live with certainty, with security, with joy, with happiness. God has the victory and you have the victory – live like it! Just do something for God.

What Are You Scared Of?

Either God is a liar or He's not... If He's not, you are an idiot to worry!

I was driving an older friend to the doctor one day. It was raining very, very hard on the way – brutally hard. It was hard to see even with the wipers going full speed. My friend was upset and praying as we drove, "Oh God, please don't let anything happen to us." I was reassuring him I had everything under control. I had driven in situations like that many times going to college in Syracuse, living in New York, and in tremendous thunderstorms in South Florida over the years. While this was an inconvenient driving situation and not what I prefer, it was not life-threatening, and I had it under control. The more I reassured him everything was under control, the more he worried and panicked, saying it was his fault for making me take him to the doctor and that he should never have come, which was pretty absurd since he needed to go and it was my pleasure to take him.

Eventually the rain subsided. The bottom line is he worried and panicked for nothing, just like the disciples in the boat when the waves began to crash around them, they panicked and thought Jesus had deserted them. Either my friend didn't believe me or didn't have enough faith in me to not panic. He got scared by his own fear and imagination of how the situation might end, with no faith in the assurance I was giving him, no faith in what the ending I assured him would be! No wonder non-believers are scared of dying! They have no faith in the assurance God has promised and not enough faith to believe in Him. I believe that is a tragedy.

Do we do that in our lives? Do we worry for nothing in our lives? What are we worrying about? In Galatians 5:1, God says, "It is for freedom that Christ has set us free. Stand firm and don't let yourself be burdened again by a yoke of slavery."

We are to remember that no matter what is happening in our lives, God's is saying to us, "I've got this; I am in control." It reminded me of when I learned to drive harness horses, learned to play professional Jai-Alai, went repelling down a 60-foot building, or was flying on a trapeze in circus school… Once you've learned it and done it well, you are not afraid. But in the beginning, it is terrifying!

So, here's the bottom line. It's found in Galatians 6:3-5: "Each one should test his own actions. Then they can take pride in themselves alone, without comparing themselves to someone else. For each should carry their own load." The New King James version says, "For anyone thinks themselves to be something when he is nothing, he deceives himself. But let each one examine his own worth and then he will have rejoiced in himself and not in another. For each shall bear his own load."

The point Paul is trying to get across is much like the Parable of the Talents. In Galatians 6:14, Paul says, "I never boast except in the cross of the Lord, Jesus Christ."

I had a buddy many years ago. He was a very close friend of mine, but then we had a disagreement. He didn't trust me about something. He used to work at the same company I did. I left. I sold my part in the company. He stayed on working at the company and he had a dispute with the new owners and then stopped talking to me.

I asked him, "Why aren't you talking to me?" He told me it was because his lawyer told him not to talk to me." I said, "But I've been out the company for two years and we're best friends." But he wouldn't talk to me.

Finally, twenty years later, I visited him in Nevada. I was still a little mad, but I saw him and he was sick. All the madness went away. There was no bitterness or resentment. It was like Prodigal Son time. I just loved him for who he was and hopefully encouraged him through his time of difficulty and walked with him again in those last months, as a true best friend.

For twenty years I thought this guy had wronged me, but the minute I saw him it just all disappeared. God wants to remind you that all that matters is God's love. We need to see the world and its people in that light. I didn't need to carry that burden for twenty years; I should have forgiven him instantly. It wasn't a big burden I carried, but it was there. When I thought of him that's how I thought. But then when I saw him, I saw him through God's eyes. And it was just about loving him and helping him as much as I was able.

A friend from church loaned me a book about the building of St. Peter's Basilica in Rome – its history and architecture, as well as the battles that went on personally and professionally to get it built. The book told of the different emperors and people involved in the church through the years.

I really did not have a desire to read the book; it wasn't my type of book. It sat on my shelf for six months. I was going to give it back to my friend without reading it. But I picked it up and started to read it and was fascinated – especially one part about Michelangelo and his battles with Rafael and Bramante and other artists of his time. Michelangelo was not his full name. His name, according to the book, was Florentine Michelangelo Buonarroti.

Reading about Buonarroti over a few days made me remember and think of another friend of mine, whose name is Mike and who has a last name that sounds similar to Buonarroti. I thought about a situation I helped Mike with a few years ago when he was in a dispute with a guy he worked for. Amazingly, I was thinking about Mike's situation that day and thinking about how I put a lot of time and effort into helping him. Then I realized that I hadn't heard from him in quite some time. Years had gone by.

I went to church that Sunday and I handed the book back to my friend and thanked him for loaning it to me as I really found it interesting. I was driving home that afternoon and I got a text from none other than Mike, the man I had been thinking about. Here's what it said:

"Hi Jack. I hope all is well with you and your family. I meant to send this message many times but this time I pulled over to do it. First of all, thank you again for your intervention with my ex-employer. A couple of months after you tried your hardest to help, an attorney from Coral Springs took the case on contingency. The court ordered them to pay me $143,000 but my ex-employer went bankrupt. The attorney was really mad. The story is a bit more involved, but I wanted to know that I really appreciated you and what you did for me"

How amazing is that! The Holy Spirit of God was there at work in his life and in mine – God reminding me that nothing is impossible with God!

How Do You Look at Life?

So, how do you look at life? How do you look at your circumstances and your trials and tribulations? The Apostle Paul saw his prison chains and his individual trials and tribulations as an opportunity to share the love of God and the saving gospel of Jesus Christ. How do you see your life?

I was talking to my buddy Craig who owns a pizza place. He said that the pizza place was his platform to interact with people and get to know them. He said it wouldn't matter if he was serving a slice of pizza or in the construction business selling or installing pipes. All that mattered to him was he had a platform to interact with people! How awesome is that!

Whatever platform you have in your life, remember that's your opportunity to interact with people and build relationships.

The Apostle Paul didn't live his life selfishly. He knew his purpose. He was called to proclaim the gospel of Jesus Christ and everything he did was to accomplish that purpose. He saw his life circumstances as his platform as his opportunity to share and spread the good news about God. How do you see your life? If you are a believer in Jesus Christ, there's a big difference between knowing the message and being the message!

The one thing we see that summarizes the Apostle Paul's life is that he was sold out to God; he was the message! Our lives, no matter what platform we have to live it out in, should reflect the same. That way, you can expect to be abundantly and exceedingly blessed more than you can ask or imagine, and you will hear, "Well done, good and faithful servant," when you meet God face to face.

I was talking to a friend of mine and he commented that he would die for a stranger in a heartbeat. I thought that was an amazing comment because I don't believe that I would. For a family member, yes; for a stranger, I don't think so. He's a Christian brother and he said he would die for a stranger because he knows for sure he's going to Heaven, so he has no fear of death. He asked, "What if the person who was going to die didn't know Jesus and isn't sure that they are going to Heaven? If I die for that person and keep them alive, they still have a chance to come to know Jesus and be saved for all eternity."

In my heart, I was astounded. I thought to myself, what great faith, what great love, what a Christ-like attitude! Like Jesus, this guy was living his life as love in its purest essence – sacrificial, putting others first. How amazing is that!

It was inspiring to see somebody so sold-out for God that they were willing to follow God's Word, but even more so than that, that they believed it 100% and knew for sure that they were spending eternity in Heaven! I am praying and striving that God continues to mold me and shape me so that I would be more like my buddy and have a godly attitude about all things.

Paul Allen, the co-founder of Microsoft, died. He was one of the world's richest men and people had wonderful things to say about his accomplishments here on Earth. But there was no mention of his eternal salvation or resting place. Here we have a man who, by the world standards, had everything, and yet when his time was up, where does he spend eternity?

Where will you spend eternity? I believe it's a choice. You can choose to accept God, His love, and His Son Jesus' sacrificial death on the cross and spend eternity with God in Heaven or you can spend eternity separated from God in what we call Hell. It is a choice.

I previously mentioned Stephen Hawking, the world-famous physicist who claimed there is no God. But one thing is for certain… he knows the truth now! I believe he now knows that he is separated from God for all eternity and that he regrets his decision and wishes he had made different choices on this Earth while he had the chance. I hope and pray that you will never have any regret about the choices you made here on Earth and especially those that impact where you will spend eternity.

Are You Satisfied?

I was reading Exodus the other morning in my quiet time. It was talking about how God gave the Israelites manna every day. That was the food they had to eat while they were in the desert. The passage was describing manna as a wafer-like substance that had a mild taste of honey and I thought, That's interesting. I probably could've eaten that.

I had recently been praying to God about two very specific issues in my life and I was seeking God for answers to these two issues. At the end of a couple of days of feverishly seeking God, God had still not answered me on these two matters. As I read in Exodus that morning, God spoke to my heart and reminded me that my concerns had nothing to do with the issues I was facing, but rather had to do with the condition of my heart. He showed me that the condition of my heart was not right. I, too, was just like the Israelites. I, too, had not been satisfied with the manna of God I had been receiving.

God reminded me, "I am your joy, and if you are not satisfied with me and my riches and joy, you will never be satisfied with the things of the world." I had to examine my own heart and realized that I had taken my focus off God. I was asking God for certainty and security and God was asking me to trust Him day by day.

God has always provided abundantly for me in my life. God has always given me manna. God has always been there. It was me who would take my eyes and focus off God. It was me who would get distracted by the things of the world instead of focusing on the things of God.

So, I took great joy in being refocused on God and remembering how much I love Him and how grateful I am for the life He has given me – both on earth and the one to come for all eternity. I had to refocus. I had gotten distracted and off-track.

I was not starving. I was not left wanting, but I, too, had begun to grumble and complain – not satisfied with the blessing and manna that God had given. Instead, I was desiring more of the things of the world I selfishly thought I needed or wanted. I am so thankful to God for the great reminder.

So, here's the last question, and I believe the most important one. Are you satisfied with God?

Oh crap, Jack. Just when I thought I was done with the book you ask me a question I have to think about. Yup! I pray you consider it a blessing that moves you forward and causes you to walk closer to and closer with God. Because that, my friends, when you take your blinders off, is what you will clearly see. And that, my dear brothers and sisters, is always the answer!

Special Thanks

My utmost and heartfelt thanks to the awesome people who continue to love me, encourage me, brainstorm with me, and help me through the book process. I am truly indebted to each of them for their individual contribution to this book and so many others I have done. So, in no order of preference, I want to thank the following:

John Rabe. Johnny, you just have a gift of clarity, classification, insight, and wisdom. Somehow you are able to shape things in a remarkable way that benefits the Kingdom in such an impactful way. I am so grateful that you've invested your time in me and in my work and you have made me a better person, a better writer, and I pray I have repaid you in kind. I am blessed by your friendship, love, and support through the years. It means the world to me. Blessings to you and your family, brother!

Downtown Scotty Brown. The man and the legend. A man whose train has finally come into the station. We are so excited about your move to Orlando to continue to minister and help us to build the Kingdom. You are a valued, trusted, and loved friend. You and your family are a tremendous blessing. I so much appreciate being able to pick your brain and having your writer insight. Your comments, thoughts, and suggestions have been invaluable in this book and the others you helped me with. So once again, thanks! Blessings to you and the family. I'm excited to be doing life and ministry with you and so excited that not only are our trains finally on the same track, but if I'm not crazy (definitely a subject that's open for debate), I believe we are actually on the same train! You got to love that!

Russ Womack. Thanks for investing your time and energy in this book. Thank you for sharing with me your own journey and the amazing victories and insight God has given you in your life. I know it was no accident that God brought us together to have you help me with this book and it has been a tremendous blessing to me. I look forward to the beginning of our continued lifelong friendship, fellowship, and ministry together.

To my mom, Marcia Levine. Best mom I ever had! Mom, now it's your turn; in this cycle of life you are Grandma Fanny now! Now you know how Gram felt… isn't it great! We love you so much.

My wife, Beth. Honey, thank you for your love. Thank you for doing the final edit of this book. You did an amazing job. Perhaps you missed your calling. You should've worked for major publishing companies, but I am so grateful that you chose to work for God and to put the kids and me first. Along with the kids, you are my cherished and valuable possession. Thank you for giving me the freedom and flexibility to write and your encouragement to continue on. I am excited to see what God is going to do with this exciting crazy upcoming season of our lives! And I'm so thankful that I am getting to spend it with you!

My children, Jackson and Talia. You both continue to inspire me beyond belief. I love you guys so much and I am so impressed by your passions and zeal for life. I love to see how quickly you learn and how wonderful and kind your hearts are. You are both amazing. I am so excited to see what God is going to do with your lives going forward and I am so grateful to be a part of it. You have been such a great joy and blessing to me. To be your father is truly the best blessing I could ever imagine. God must really love me.

My brother Mike, Leslee, Zac, Alex, and Dylan. We love you guys so much. You are the greatest family; the kindest, sweetest, and most loving family a guy could ever have. I am so blessed to be a Levine and so blessed to have you guys as my family. I have never doubted and have always felt your undying love and support... it means the world to me. I hope and pray you have all felt the same back from me.

Scott Wolf. Your talents and time are a priceless treasure and I value them more then I could ever thank you for in words. I hope and pray the books we do together will speak louder about your amazing creativity and design gifts then any compliments I could pay you. You are the man. I truly appreciate all you do for me and most importantly your friendship.

DEDICATION

I dedicate this book to some people who have inspired my life greatly. This year I asked my wife to make me a picture frame as a Christmas present with three pictures of people I know personally who have inspired me greatly for many years and continue to do so.

The first is **Richard Headrick.** He was an amazing person. He died in October of 2020 after battling cancer. I was introduced to Richard by my first pastor Truman Herring as he and Richard were friends back in Mississippi. Richard was a true renegade early in his life and an adventurer, as well, not always with good intentions. Richard would rob treasures and artifacts from foreign countries and was involved in other unscrupulous dealings. He was a pilot back then and became completely dissatisfied with himself and his life. One day he was flying his plane and was ready to commit suicide. He began to purposely plummet downwards in a straight suicide spiral. As the plane was going down, he heard God speak to saying, "I'm not done with you yet, boy." He did not commit suicide that day but instead accepted Jesus as His Lord. Richard ran a very successful sign company, Headrick Signs, a pioneer in outdoor billboard advertising. One of the company's divisions Headrick Crosses built some of the world's largest crosses, monuments and church steeples. He sold the sign company for many millions and invested those proceeds and his life in building the Kingdom of God and bringing lost souls to the cross.

Richard's life story and what he did for God is amazing. He was 100% sold out for Jesus. God used him in such a mighty and magnificent way for the glory of the gospel it is mind-boggling. From the time God spoke to him, just like the apostle Paul heard from God, he was instantly and radically saved. Richard used his life to spread the message of the good news and love, mercy, and forgiveness of Jesus. Richard had time for everybody. He was one of the most incredible, generous and kind people I've ever met and one who has influenced me so much. I was only together with Richard a handful of times over the years, but had an immediate, special, ongoing bond with him in my heart and a solid friendship. I was proud to call him and his wife Gina my friends. His picture reminds me that people are what is important to Jesus and our job is to convey that message forward. The joy, happiness, and peace that radiated from Richard was a direct result of his love for Christ. I am reminded that my life should reflect the same.

My prayers and blessings to Gina and all of the Hellfighters and Mission at the Cross family. Richard's impact was felt across the world, but none of it more important than the personal testimony and love he shared with every individual he met. Richard wrote many amazing books. His book *America's Churches Through The Eyes Of A Bum* detailed experiences when he and his wife would dress up as bums and hang out outside of churches. He wrote about the reaction they received from the churchgoers coming into church. Imagine the shock of congregations around the country, as the hobo/bum they shooed away (many of the churches, not all) went up to the alter and began to preach the morning message about how he was treated. Another one of his books *Letters From Hell* is a chilling firsthand account by many of the recovering addicts Richard ministered to at Mission at the Cross, one of many great ministries started by Richard. Mission at the Cross, a 24-hour mission in Laurel, Mississippi is open to all, but is especially for the hopeless, homeless, and those caught in Satan's bondage of drug and alcohol addiction. Another was the Hellfighters motorcycle ministry, motorcyclists devoted to riding for and living for Christ. They are some of the toughest but kindest, most sold out sons of God you will ever meet here on this Earth.

I will never forget the day I saw Richard crying about the fact that he passed by a man sitting on a bench and did not witness to him because he was in a hurry. That haunted Richard, even though he had witnessed to thousands of people individually over the years. I have watched (and others state it as fact) how selflessly he devoted his time and energy to people with no regard for schedule but only regard for the individual's salvation. The fact that he believed he missed somebody broke his heart. That just shows how sensitive he was to the Holy Spirit of God. If you were walking somewhere with Richard you can rest assured, he would try to stop and talk to everybody along the way with the biggest smile in the world and sought to share the love of Jesus with them. What a life well lived and sacrificed for the Kingdom of God. God bless you my friend and thank you!

Then there's my friend **Douglas Cooper.** I've known Doug for five years. He suffered a traumatic brain injury when hit by a car. He lost his right leg below the knee and is a wheelchair. Doug's love for Christ and his knowledge of the Lord and his understanding and appreciation of God and life makes him a genius in my view. He has boiled down all the realities, issues, concerns, and things of the world into just one undeniable fact... And you see that in and through Doug every moment of his life... And that is his appreciation and love for Jesus and love for others. His ability to enjoy life and be joyful always, no matter the circumstances is an inspiration to me. He did not spend time bemoaning the cards he was dealt or the unfairness of his injury from the accident and the crippling results, instead, like Joni Erickson Tata, and many other courageous heroes and warriors of the Lord, he accepted the cards dealt to him joyfully and uses them to benefit the Kingdom of God. His sweet love and innocence and dedication to the Lord, along with his great sense of humor, is one of the most beautiful things I have ever seen.

I thank God that I got to spend these last five years with Doug and I look forward to many more. He and I show up to church early every Sunday morning and have some quality time together to joke, laugh, and share our love for the Lord. He is the ultimate jokester with a keen sense of humor, but it is never overshadowed by his love for the Lord. He is a friend and inspiration to me and so many others. Doug takes public transportation to get to church and other events, not letting his physical injuries interrupt his spiritual growth or His ability to minister for the Lord. His desire passion and sacrifice are immeasurable. Doug, you're my hero! Doug wrote a book called *Broken, But STILL Valuab*l*e*: *a guided adventure into the world of TBI* detailing his life before and after his traumatic brain injury. It is a great read.

Melissa Ann... Another friend of mine who has inspired me with her fierce and unquenchable determination to keep doing whatever she can each and every day to strengthen herself physically, spiritually, and emotionally and to impact the lives of others for the Kingdom of God, no matter the obstacles. She is an amazing inspiration. She wrote a terrific book you should read called *Hope, Love and Me: My Journey of Choices and Second Chances*.

Melissa partied her way through high school and after high school graduation right before she was going to start college, she flipped her truck in a drunk driving incident and has been paralyzed from the neck down and wheelchair-bound since. It's ten years later and I've watched God use her so mightily to inspire others. She gives lectures about the perils of drunk driving and partying, but more importantly about what God has done in her life. Her faith and determination to continue forward and her acceptance of God's call to use her this way, instead of the plan she had for her life, is truly one of the most amazing things I've ever seen. To see her not give up, to watch her fight to regain her physical strength, to see her desire to serve the Lord and have God use her circumstances for His glory is beautiful, heartwarming, and inspiring. It's her fight, her determination, her grip, the power of God within her, and the power of her own heart and soul that just blows me away. I think she realizes now that God has given her a platform that was not by her choice, but that she is to use for the Kingdom of God and His glory. She is doing that in an awesome way of personal ministry, online, in her books, and in the movie about her that I believe will be made.

Here are two other people whom I've never met personally but they have impacted my life greatly.
Evan Liversage. Evan has impacted my life and touched me in a greater way than some people that I have known for 50 years. Evan was an 8-year-old boy from St. George, Canada; he died in 2015. His worldwide fame came when the doctors told his family he was probably not going to make it to Christmas of that year... His family and the whole town (all 8,000 residents) decided to decorate the town and have a full Christmas celebration and parade so that Evan

would have Christmas in October. They did just that. 30,000 people came from far and wide and filled the town for Evan's Christmas parade. Evan had his Christmas early. His life and courage and the beautiful, loving response of the town and people around the globe are a continuing inspiration to the world and to me personally. It's been 5 years since Evan passed away and I can't wait to see the movie being made about his life. I am certain it will be a touching, far-reaching classic like the movie *It's A Wonderful Life*. Evan, we never met brother, yet you have moved me and touched me and inspired me since the day I heard about you. I've cried many tears of sadness and many tears of joy over you. I'm sure millions of other people feel the same. Your life mattered in the biggest of ways! Blessings to your family whose courage and faith alongside yours is truly inspirational!

Addison Sinclair. An eight-year-old girl here in Windermere, Florida who died of cancer Christmas 2020. She had been taking medicine and undergoing surgeries and treatment for cancer since she was three years old. I only learned about her a couple weeks before she died, when a 14-year-old friend of our family, Caleb Wolf played saxophone in downtown Winter Garden. Caleb does this every Christmas season, donating his earnings and tips to charity each year. This year I learned he was raising money for Addison. My heart broke as I learned about the touching story of the family's journey and Addison's life. Their faith, courage, and inspiration were a motivator and reminder to appreciate what we have, count our blessings, and not take for granted our lives, each other, and God's provision and gift of life. Thank you to the entire Sinclair family. We know we will see Addison in heaven again.

I have to admit there are times in my life when I get down on myself or others. God often uses people, like the heroes I've listed above, to remind me of the gratitude I am to have for life and not to focus on the things I do not have, and circumstances I cannot control. I (and you) need to trust God, to remember He is in control of all things. Anytime I start to feel sorry for myself, I think of Richard, Douglas, and Melissa and their courage, their circumstances, their refusal to give up. I think of how they gave everything for the Lord and how their love and faith grew stronger and stronger. I think of Evan and Addison and how God used them mightily to impact the world. I am reminded He wants to do the same to through all of us and all we need to do is cooperate, be willing, be grateful and be men and women of action for the Kingdom of God. That is the bottom line!

Their lives and inspiration always bring me back to the truth of God and I am refreshed, filled with joy and focused on the task at hand and so grateful for the life I have and the certainty of Heaven and the Holy Spirit within me. If you don't have any heroes in your life that you can look to inspire you, please feel free to borrow and use any or all of the amazing ones I've mentioned!

CHECK OUT

LIVE A LIFE THAT MATTERS FOR GOD

"From a clinical perspective, Live a Life That Matters for God has great value as a teaching and therapeutic tool for the soul. From a spiritual perspective it is a direct hit right to the heart of every Christian. This uplifting book will inspire you no matter what chapter you are reading. I love that you can pick up any chapter, anywhere, in any section in the book and be blessed immediately. Jack covers so many different topics that are relevant and critical to our growth as Christians, our happiness and our desire to walk closer with God. Jack's style is straight to the point and laser focused. Jack doesn't just tell you to do it, he shows you how!"

Julie Woodley,
MA, Division Chair American Assoc. of Christian Counselors

WHERE THE RUBBER MEETS THE ROAD WITH GOD

For every believer who wants to make sure they hear "Well done good and faithful servant." "A knock out punch for Jesus if there ever was one. Jack Alan Levine's book is the heavyweight champion of the world when it comes to Christians walking a life of faith with God. Read it and make certain you will wear the champion's crown of life for Christ."

Nate "Galaxy Warrior" Campbell,
3x Lightweight Champion Of The World

DON'T BLOW IT WITH GOD

In "Don't Blow It With God", Jack Levine reveals his road map to discovering God's blueprint for living the ultimate Christian life each and every day. Come along for the ride as God teaches Jack life-changing lessons that will help you in your life journey. Jack discovers how to live an abundant Christian life experiencing true joy, peace and happiness and along the way you will discover the formula and the insights about how you can too.

"Jack's unique style of communicating God's plan for an abundant life is a must read for all Christians. This book knocks it out of the park. If you've been striking out and want your life to be the perfect game for God then you need to read this book."

Chris Hammond, Major League Baseball pitcher

MY ADDICT YOUR ADDICT

This book is about addiction. Author Jack Levine has counseled thousands of people over the years who have gone through addiction, and knows what a torturous life it can be to be caught up in it. It's an awful thing.

He's experienced addiction in his own life and as a parent, as he watched his son struggle with addiction for years (it started when he was 18).

Whether you are in the throes of addiction yourself or seeing a loved one suffer through it, this book can help you. Jack has results and solutions for real-life situations. Each person's situation is different, but the root is the same for everybody. Through his own story, he can tell you what the choices are, the impacts of those choices, the results of those choices, and what sacrifices you'll have to make to get where you want to be.

SUCCESS BLAST

"This is it. A book that finally gives honest, real-world advice on what it takes to work hard, to fight for what you want, and succeed big. I'm already a well-read, successful executive and within the first few pages I simply HAD to start taking notes on all the powerful, creative ideas and inspiring stories that Jack Levine shares in these pages. This book will Blast you up to a whole new level!"

Aaron W. Kassler, Merrill Lynch Vice President & Senior Financial Advisor

JACK'S OTHER BOOKS...

DOWNLOADING GOD

"Downloading God is the file of information that today's generation needs to click on more than ever. Jack Levine's authentic and transparent self-disclosure rings through in his passionate devotion to his Lord and Savior Jesus Christ. His simple, straightforward, trademark writing style as in his previous books allows the reader to easily absorb, appropriate and apply the word and truth of God in a realistic, revolutionary and redemptive way. 'Downloading God' has short chapters all themed around a clever computer technology motif which makes the timeless truths of God both real and relevant to contemporary culture."

Dr. Jared Pingleton, VP American Association of Christian Counselors,
Clinical Psychologist, Credentialed Minister

TIME GONE

Each year we like to send a holiday letter to our friends and loved ones looking back at the past year and looking forward to the coming one. These letters are extremely personal but also extremely universal. Though written at holiday time, the observations I share are a true reflection of life all year long. In them I share my struggles, joys and thoughts, which like yours, change from year to year and I'm sure mirror many of the same things you go through.

I've left some personal things in here to give you a sense of who I am - a regular person like you with all the normal victories, defeats, happiness, sadness, joy and pain that we all share. Each letter contains reflections, lessons learned, wisdom and insight that God laid on my heart that particular year. I believe these will help you with your life and have great value to you. In these annual holiday letters I ask people to stop, take stock of where they were at, and consider how they were going to move forward. I hope that by sharing these letters with you it will cause you to do the same.

THE MOTIVATED LIFE

What powers your train? You know, some are powered by steam and some by diesel. Some are powered by electricity, and others are powered by battery. Some are even powered by solar energy. But, one thing's for sure. The train needs power to run, and so do you in your life.

So, what powers your train in life? Is it passion and purpose? Is it survival, money, or accomplishment? Is it fear? Perhaps fear of loss? Fear of missing out? It's very important to know what powers you, what motivates you, and what drives you forward each day. And, it's very important to have something that does all of these things. The more powerful your train, the faster and farther you can go and the quicker you can get there.

"It will encourage and accelerate you! Enriches, equips and inspires you to get the most out of every are of your life. I wholeheartedly recommend it."

Peter Lowe
President & Founder Peter Lowe International Get Motivated, Success Seminars

ADDICTION & RECOVERY HANDBOOK

An all-encompassing, never-before-seen compilation of addiction recovery opinions, ideas, and principles based on the real-life experience of addiction professionals and experts. The book details what has worked and what hasn't, providing all the information you need to make intelligent decisions regarding your personal struggle or a loved one's struggle with addiction and, more importantly, with recovery. When you look at the table of contents, start with the chapter that appeals most to you. Definitely read the whole book, but it does not matter the order in which you read the chapters. Addiction has haunted, destroyed, and ruined the futures, hopes, dreams, and lives of too many individuals and their families.

JackAlanLevine.com

www.ingramcontent.com/pod-product-compliance
Lightning Source LLC
Chambersburg PA
CBHW071910290426
44110CB00013B/1345